CW00865100

# Bucks, Beds and Bricks

## A Phorpres Childhood

Jean Blane Flannery

ISBN-10: 1466329653
ISBN-13: 978-1466329652

**For My Family**

**Past, Present and Future**
**With My Love**

This is first and foremost for my much loved grandchildren: Luke, Ryan, Bryce, Shannon, Loren and Caitlin.

Without them and their interested, enquiring minds this book would never have been written.

## Acknowledgements

My grateful thanks to: those who aided my memory, in particular my sister Carole; my parents, without whom there would be no story to tell; my wonderful children Carl, Winn and Kathryn, who have given me so much.

Many thanks also to those others of my family and friends who very generously searched out and shared their memories and photographs; to Bedford, Milton Keynes and Sheffield libraries for old photographs and maps; to Phorpres News and The Guardian newspaper for photographs.

Last but by no means least, my heartfelt thanks to John for all his continuing love, patience and care.

Errors are mine alone.

Jean Blane Flannery

December 2011

## Foreword

By way of some explanation, the Bucks in this title is Buckinghamshire, the Beds: Bedfordshire. They are the two English counties in which I lived as a child. And the Bricks? My father worked for the London Brick Company Ltd (LBC) all his adult life apart from serving in the British Army throughout WWII.

Phorpres (pronounced fourpress) was the trademark of the LBC, the Phorpres Man with his brick hod its logo. The term Phorpres derived from the fact that the bricks were pressed four times to mould them. Though why that spelling, I do not know.

With my life being moulded in the four homes of this account I might well be considered a Phorpres child. Born a few months after D-Day, before the end of WWII, my earliest memories are of the immediate post-war years.

I originally wrote this book for my family, mainly for curious grandchildren. It was never intended for a wider audience. But as others have also read and said they enjoyed it, here it is.

Just to add that some of the explanations here, and the 'translations,' are for the benefit of grandchildren growing up in the USA and New Zealand: a world away in distance as well as time from my own childhood. Spelling is mainly UK English.

Some of the names in this narrative have been changed.

## Blane and Wallis Family Relationships

Of the generations previous to mine only Jack, Kitty, Martin and Gwen are still alive in 2011

Year where shown is that of birth

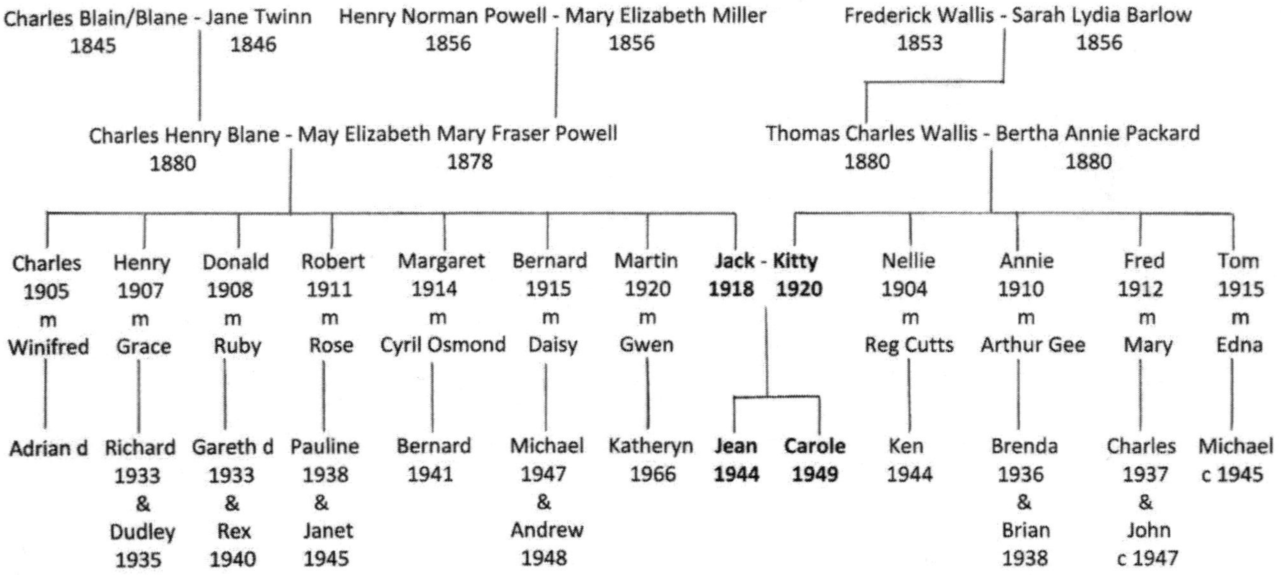

CONTENTS

Bucks, Beds and Bricks

# SETTING THE SCENE

Before I properly start the story of my childhood, let me just try to set the scene for you of what life was like in general. It's strange really, because as a child I couldn't dream that things would change so much or that anyone would ever *not* know how things were then. How could any part of my own life ever become the Olden Days? However it has. So although I only learned most of this later myself, here is what some things were like for ordinary people living in post-war England.

It was still a time of austerity, with rationing of nearly all goods and food not just continuing but extended. It was 1946 that actually saw the introduction of rationing for the basic foodstuffs such as bread and potatoes. Coal was also rationed, as were petrol (gasoline), clothing and furniture. Clothing and furniture carried the 'Utility' trademark, a remnant of the war years.

As late as December 1947 a buying permit was still needed to buy furniture and then priority was given to those such as servicemen returning and setting up homes, and newlyweds. The total allowance of coupons for furniture was 60 per household. Certain conditions applied before anyone could apply to buy furniture. If furniture was already in the house, or there was built-in furniture, then the allowance was reduced accordingly. The only available choices were from the illustrated copy of the Utility catalogue, used by all manufacturers.

To save fuel the firm chosen to supply the furniture had to be based within 15 miles of the delivery address. In some cases it was necessary to obtain a buying permit and priority docket to purchase curtaining and floor covering. Finally, stocks were so low that immediate delivery was not always possible.

The typical cost of a dining room suite (table, chairs and sideboard), two easy chairs and a dressing table was £68 and 38 units of coupons. Little was left from the allowance of 60 coupons for other furniture: wardrobe 12 units, bed 5 units, kitchen cabinet 8 units and so on. Every piece of furniture had a points value. The Board of Trade Utility Furniture Office in Southport controlled all of this.

Many goods were only available with coupons - even sweets (candy, lollies), which like butter were rationed to 2 ounces per person per week until 1953. Some rationing extended further, into 1954. Cost was also a deterrent to buying anything not necessary, when one considers that the **average wage** at this time was in the region of **£6 per week**. A police constable received a salary of £273 per year: £5/5/- (£5.25) per week.

For quite a number of years, running into the mid-late 1950s, purchase tax was imposed, similar to the present day VAT or sales tax but at the stratospheric rate of 33% on common everyday purchases. This rate was doubled to 66% for so-called luxuries such as refrigerators, radios (then known in the UK as wirelesses) and jewellery.

Nothing was available to excess as it was either rationed or one could simply not afford it. Beer increased in price and a bottle of whisky now cost £1/11/- (£1.55), a good quarter of an average week's pay. A ladies cardigan would cost £4/3/- (£4.15) and six coupons. Both knitting and sewing were far more than just hobbies!

This was in the days when a joint was what one roasted for Sunday dinner, a fag was stuck in the mouth and smoked, grass was mowed, coke was kept in the coal shed and used as fuel, making out meant that you managed on your wages each week, to be gay was to be light hearted and happy - and to be queer was to be simply strange or odd.

In *today's* money, nearly everything was extremely cheap then but not by the wages of the time. As I say, in 1947 the average wage was just £6 per week. Even by 1961, when I had started working, £15/10/- (£15.50) per week was the average weekly wage for men (no thought of equal pay). It puts the relative costs in perspective. Dad, returning to a fairly junior job in the wages section of the London Brick Company personnel department at Newton Longville near Bletchley after 6½ years in the army, earned less than the average wage in 1946. Money was always tight for Mum and Dad but they did not show that to us.

By the time Dad left the Newton Longville works in 1954 he was earning £10/10/- per week. He was given a pay rise of 10 shillings, bringing him up to £11, to move to Stewartby as Social and Sports Club Secretary. The rent for our first house in Whiteley Crescent (including rates, now council or house tax) was £1 per week. Our next house three years later, back in Bletchley, was older with just two bedrooms, and about the same rent. Because the house we then moved to in Stewartby was owned and subsidised by the brick company the rent there was still only just over £1 in 1954. So finances were a little bit easier, although of course other prices had gone up. When Hanson took over the London Brick Company in the 1980s, rents had gone up to just £9 per week, still very cheap. The days of subsidised rent then became a thing of the past as the houses were sold off.

Perhaps I had better explain a bit about the pre-decimal currency. It was generally referred to as LSD: nothing to do with the drug that came later! Strangely the L, written £, stood for pounds sterling, the S for shillings and the D for pence. Both the S and D were written in lower case when in actual use. This currency is in what is called the duodecimal system, with 12 pence in a shilling. There were 20 shillings in a pound. It sounds complicated now but we didn't think anything of it, knowing nothing else.

You can find out more about our old money (including how it was written and spoken), and pre-metric weights and measures, in the appendix. I am afraid that I still often think in those measures, even though I can readily covert most. And of course we do use a lot of the old ones on a practical, day-to-day level.

There are also maps of the areas where I lived and went to school in the appendix, to help you get a sense of the places I write about.

England, and certainly our part of it, was very mono-cultural. I don't think I knowingly came across anyone who was not basically of white Anglo-Saxon origin, other than the Italian ice cream men who came round with their van in Beighton, until we moved to Stewartby and had a Yugoslavian neighbour.

It's hard for me to imagine now but I was quite fascinated the first time I actually saw a black person in real life. It never occurred to me to link black people (the polite term then was Negro or Coloured, not Black) with golliwogs or the rhyme Ten Little Nigger Boys.

Real people just looked nothing like those images that to me were simply in the realm of story book or fairy tale characters. In fact it was not until several years after personally seeing a black person for the first time that I realised the caricature involved.

There were so many things we did not have that are taken completely for granted now. Some had just not been invented and some were simply out of the reach of ordinary people. There were no personal computers, cordless or mobile (cell) phones, game boys, personal music players, microwaves, dish washers etc. As for space travel: that really was the stuff of science fiction!

Cars did not have seat belts fitted as standard until 1987. There were no child and infant safety seats either. Babies might be placed in a carrycot on the back seat but an infant or young child would often be held in the arms, or sit on the knee, of a car passenger.

Pedal cyclists did not wear helmets and motorcycle helmets were not compulsory. Some motorcyclists still wore leather ones, like old style flying helmets, worn with a pair of goggles. Even by the time I was sixteen years old helmets were still worn with goggles, not visors. By then, although traffic had increased hugely from my early childhood, there were still fewer than half the numbers of cars on the road that there are today.

Among the odd little things that we did not have were nail clippers. We just used small nail scissors. There was no mousse or hair gel, only setting lotion for the women to comb through their hair before winding it around curlers or rollers (setting it). The men used Brylcreem on their hair and all the men I knew kept their hair short.

Some acceptable fashion customs were quite different too. For example, not many people other than gypsies even had pierced ears until about the time I started secondary education. I don't remember any other kind of body piercing. Very few people other than sailors or fairground workers had tattoos and all of those as far as I knew were men.

Vegetarianism was looked upon by most people almost as if it was some strange cult. There were no specific vegetarian foods for sale in the shops or restaurants. The popular image was of rather peculiar, sandal wearing folk, eating nut cutlets (even though we had no real idea what a nut cutlet might be).

Having been born towards the end of World War II I spent my childhood living in the Cold War. There was a continuing tense standoff between the Soviet Union, as it was then, and the West. Each side had nuclear weapons and the threat of nuclear war could feel very real.

On another sobering note, although we had no HIV or Aids, Swine or Bird Flu, or MRSA, medicine was nowhere near as far advanced as it is now. There were fewer treatments or procedures and things were often much cruder. We did not have keyhole surgery and there was no chance of an organ transplant, for example, let alone gene therapy.

Many drugs that we have now were also unthought-of. There were fewer vaccines, which meant that even childhood illnesses could be much more serious.

I was almost ten years old before the first polio vaccine was developed. Even then it did not reach England for another couple of years. Polio was a devastating disease, especially to children, and an epidemic was very frightening. Thank goodness 'Iron Lungs' and the devastating effects of polio are in the past.

Although there were now vaccines for diseases such as diphtheria, children were still at risk of serious complications and even death from others like measles, mumps and whooping cough. Sadly, with some children not having the MMR vaccine, this is again becoming the case.

When I had measles I had to stay in a darkened room for some days because the light hurt my eyes. Given that there was a possibility of serious eye problems, even blindness, as well as other complications and at worst death, it is no wonder that my parents were anxious.

Most labourers and Blue or White Collar workers rented their homes. Very few people had or drove cars. Dad could have learned to drive while he was in the army during the war. But cars cost around a year's wages at that time and Dad thought he would never be able to afford one. So he did not bother to learn to drive, either then or later, and in fact never did own a car. No ordinary working people went abroad for holidays (vacations). There were far fewer planes, those there were being much smaller than now, and no low cost flights or package holidays.

This will give you some idea of how expensive flying must have been when I was a child. Even by 1965, when I made my first flight, airfares were still terribly high.

When we moved to the USA I took Carl, then just three years old, on a charter flight (which was quite a bit cheaper than a scheduled flight) from London to Philadelphia, the only US destination available to us. It cost £500 one way then, the equivalent of about £7,500 today, in 2011! And we still had to travel the rest of the way to Glasgow Air Force Base in Montana.

There were no credit or debit cards and there was very little borrowing, although some goods could be bought on credit by Hire Purchase (HP) - or 'tick' as it was known colloquially. But this was rather frowned on. People usually saved until they had the money for what they wanted to buy. Many people did not even have bank accounts. Their wages were paid in cash and they made all their payments the same way. The rent collector came around weekly for his money, as did the insurance man.

I did not know anyone who had a home phone until after we moved to Stewartby and then only those in quite high positions in the brick company. If you needed to make a telephone call you had to use a public phone box: for example if you needed the doctor urgently. If you had a less urgent medical problem, you just went down to the surgery and it was first come, first seen.

I was six years old before I even saw a television set. Our family did not have one of our own until I was over thirteen. The pictures were all in black and white, no colour sets, and also the sets were mostly really bulky and with very small screens in the early years.

At first the UK had just one channel, the BBC. Then by the time we had our TV set, which stood on legs and had a rather smaller case and bit bigger screen, there were the BBC and the commercial channel ATV. That was it! On a weekday the programmes started in the afternoon and ended at 11pm, when the channels stopped broadcasting. At the weekend I know there were some morning programmes too, at least by the time I was ten years old – perhaps a bit earlier.

We didn't have any remote controls. Both televisions and wirelesses were powered by valves, which could burn out and need replacing. These sets took quite a while to warm up too, when you switched on.

We had a large wireless with a dial that lit up and a number of knobs. I don't know what all of them were for. There were two main stations, both BBC. One was called the Home Service and the other the Light Programme. We mostly listened to the Light Programme. I suppose the Home Service was more serious, more like Radio 4 is now.

Auntie Nellie and Uncle Reg had a wind up gramophone (record player) that played 78rpm records, the only kind we had. We had boxes of steel needles that needed frequent changing. As the mechanism wound down, the record would get slower and the sound lower and more distorted. Wind it up again and the sound got higher and faster as you did so: great fun for children!

None of the houses I knew had central heating. There was an open, coal fire in the living room (which went out at night) and sometimes in other rooms too, although those would seldom be lit. In the kitchen there was usually a boiler, which burned coke or anthracite (treated, harder and slower burning coal) that heated the water. These boilers were rather like a large, round, black, wood burning stove, with a solid door very low down for taking out the ashes and a lid on top, where the fuel was poured in from a hod. The slow-burning fire in these would stay in overnight.

The coal men delivered the fuel and emptied it from their sacks into the coal barn. Dad placed boards one above the other across the doorway to hold it in, as we always had a big load delivered in summer when it was sold at a discount. Gradually, as the coal stock went down, one board after another would be removed.

The chimney sweep came in summer too. That was a really messy job in those days. There was no vacuum sweeping. Everything possible would be moved out of the living room and all that could not be moved covered in old sheets to keep off the soot, before the sweep started. He would push his sweep's brush, attached to the first pole, into the chimney. Then he would add one pole after another as he pushed upwards, until his brush came out the top.

If we were at home when the sweep came, we children would go outside and let him know when we saw the brush poking out. He did have a sack at the bottom of the chimney to catch most of the soot. Dad kept that as fertilizer for the garden and allotment. Even so, when the sweep had gone there was a lot of cleaning up still to do. The freestanding boiler chimney did not get such a buildup of soot, as coke and anthracite burn more cleanly.

Some houses still had a range in the kitchen, a coal fire with an oven built in alongside it. A kettle might sit on an iron trivet above the fire, which could also heat water in a boiler on the other side. You quite often see them depicted in old films. The ranges were cleaned with lead blacking, which was rubbed in well with a cloth and then polished to a shine.

In the winter everywhere except our living room and kitchen would be really cold, almost like being in a garage or shed. Ice crystals would form patterns on the *inside* of the windows when it was frosty. There were even times when, in the bedroom, we could see our breath as we exhaled.

The outer walls of houses were built from two layers of brick, mortared together. There was no insulation, not even an air gap, between them. High up, one inner brick might be left missing from an outer wall of a room. The outer brick had a lot of little square holes through it for ventilation and was known as an airbrick.

This was fine in the summer but just added to the coldness in winter. So Dad would cut a piece of leftover linoleum (lino) to fit the gap and wedge it against the airbrick. This at least stopped the wind whistling into the room.

We had no fitted carpets, just lino on the floor, with rugs. There was a rug next to the bed and if your feet missed it on a winter morning, you knew it! Instead of duvets (unheard of, at least in our family) we had sheets and blankets with an eiderdown (thick quilt) on top.

Every night in winter we all had hot water bottles in our beds. The sheets were so cold until your feet got down to that. It was wonderful to feel its heat.

In the winter evenings I, and later my sister Carole too, undressed in the living room. In the mornings we hurried back down there to dress. Although the fire would not have been lit for very long, there was some residual heat in the room from the night before.

In the summer our living room fire would not be lit at all and our boiler only once a week, for baths and for washing clothes. The rest of the time water was boiled in a kettle on the stove for us to have a good wash over. The bathroom would be heated by an Aladdin brand paraffin stove in winter.

Later, when I was about thirteen years old, we had an electric wall heater in the bathroom. We also had an electric immersion heater fitted in the hot water tank. So we could have hot water all through the year, without the boiler *or* a kettle!

The first shower I saw was when I was ten years old. There were two cold-water showers in each set of changing rooms at Stewartby swimming pool, for rinsing off the chlorine.

There were no automatic washing machines and no dryers. The whites (all cotton in the post-war years) would be boiled in a special washing boiler, which by now was at least electric. To make the white clothes brighter, Mum also added what was called a blue bag to their wash water.

When I was very young all the clothes were rubbed on a scrubbing board with bar soap to get them clean. The clothes and linen were taken out of the hot water with long, wooden handled wash tongs and left until cool enough to handle. After washing, and again after rinsing, they were put through the two wooden rollers of a mangle, turned by hand, to wring them out. The boiler, put on first thing in the morning, filled the kitchen with steam.

Later Mum had an electric washing machine, a tub with a paddle to agitate the clothes and an electric mangle integral to it. But there was no automatic fill or empty and no spin action. When spin dryers came along, they took out more water than the mangle but you had to keep an eye on the outlet pipe in the sink!

Before I left home in the sixties Mum had a twin tub washer, with one tub to wash and one to rinse. You had to lift clothes from one tub to the other but at least they did get spun, although still no automatic fill and with a hose in the sink to empty water out.

Washing powder was used in the machines: no liquids, tablets or fabric conditioner. If the weather was too bad to get the clothes dry outside they were hung on a line across the kitchen, keeping it steamed up for hours.

Doing the washing, pegging it out and clearing away took up the whole of Monday morning. Then all the washing had to be taken in from the line later and folded. There were very few synthetics and no easy care fabrics so nearly everything needed ironing too. That was a job for Monday evening or Tuesday. Mum did have an electric iron but it had no thermostat and no steam, so ironing was quite a skilled job. With all this, it is little wonder that we did not change our clothes too frequently. Bedding was changed once a week but only the bottom sheet from each bed was washed. The top sheet became the bottom sheet, with a clean one over it. This was known to us as topping and tailing.

All male office workers wore white shirts and a tie, hence the term White Collar Workers. These white cotton shirts lasted longer, and were freshened up between washes, by having detachable collars. The collars and necks of the shirts had very small buttonholes in them. Little double headed collar buttons ('collar studs') passed through these holes to keep the collar in place. So the collar alone could be changed daily, rather than the whole shirt.

Those who could afford it might send washing to the laundry. It would be collected at the door and delivered back wrapped in brown paper tied with string. I only knew about this because although Auntie Nellie washed most of their clothes herself she did send the sheets, with Uncle Reg's butcher's overalls and aprons, to the Co-op (Co-operative Society) laundry once a week.

All housework took a lot of doing. In my earlier years every floor and any big rug had to be swept with a brush. Tile and lino floors were also scrubbed with a scrubbing brush. That was a hands and knees job. The small rugs were taken out and shaken every week.

Larger rugs were taken out less frequently, hung over the clothesline and beaten with a carpet beater to get out all the dust and grime. The carpet beaters we had were woven cane, shaped rather like a Celtic knot on the end of a handle, as you see in this picture. Later Mum had a manual carpet sweeper of the kind you can still buy today.

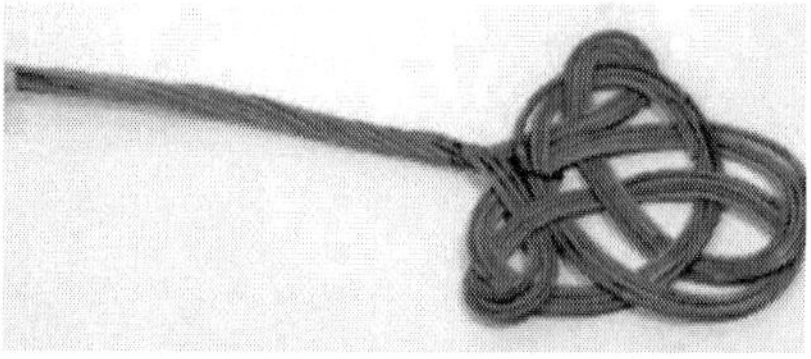

In the winter the living room needed a thorough clean every day. Ash and coal dust would have settled everywhere, however careful you were. The grate was emptied of ash first thing in the morning, after it had cooled down overnight. Then crumpled newspaper was placed on the grate, sticks layered on top, with a few pieces of coal placed on them. The paper was lit in several places, hopefully the fire caught and then more coal would be tipped on. If the wind was in the wrong direction, and the fire wouldn't catch, you'd hold a sheet of newspaper across it to funnel air through the kindling up into the chimney. But be careful! If the draught dragged in the paper and it caught fire you had to let go of it pretty smartly.

In December we wrote letters to Father Christmas, telling him what presents we would like. We held these just above and in front of the coals, let go of them and up the chimney they went. Since Father Christmas came down the chimney to deliver the presents, this made sense to us. Then as now though, Father Christmas didn't always bring what we asked for.

Every house had a front doorstep and most a back one too, which would be scrubbed every week, usually on the same day as the drains were cleaned, the grates over the drains being thoroughly scoured as well. We had metal dustbins and there were no bin liners. So the dustbin too needed a regular scouring. Even the draining boards by the sink were given a good scrub every week, being wooden.

While she was working Mum always had the wireless on, mainly music. Her favourite singer was Bing Crosby. I remember Housewives' Choice at 9.00am every weekday, with Workers' Playtime later in the morning. The latter came live from a work's canteen somewhere, supposedly in the mid-morning tea break, and was comedy and music. There was a weekly programme of requests called Family Favourites. On a Saturday morning we listened to Children's Choice, a programme of musical requests made by - you've got it - children.

Dad always worked within cycling distance of home. Every day he came back for his midday meal, which was our dinner. Carole and I of course came home for dinner too, until we went on the bus to Bedford to school.

We were rather spoiled in that Mum always woke us up with a cup of tea in the morning. She boiled the kettle on the stove and when we had a whistling kettle it really shrieked when the steam got going. All tea had to be made in the pot with loose leaves. After leaving it to brew, the tea was poured through a strainer laid across the top of the cup. This caught most of the leaves. But if you drank to the bottom of the cup, you still got a mouthful of the smallest ones. Ugh! That made you careful.

There were no tea bags or instant tea and both were also pretty nasty when they did first go on sale. But I've digressed enough!

After our early morning cup of tea we washed, dressed and had our breakfast. There wasn't much choice of cereal: none of the sugared, flavoured ones until Frosties and Sugar Puffs came along. There were cornflakes, puffed wheat, shredded wheat and Weetabix, with porridge in the winter. We had warm milk on our cereal then, although I wouldn't want that now. I used to like Weetabix as a snack, spread with jam.

We might have toast and marmalade, which I have always liked, after or instead of cereal. Sometimes it would be bacon *or* sausages *or* an egg (not often a combination), with toast and always a cup of tea. If we had a soft-boiled egg we broke the bottom of the shell afterwards, "So that the witches could not ride in it." The superstition was that witches went to sea in eggshells when there was a storm, sank the ships and drowned the poor sailors! We knew it wasn't true but enjoyed going along with the story.

When we weren't at school we usually had a cup of milky Camp coffee with chicory essence, and a biscuit, for 'elevenses' in the morning with Mum. Coffee had been very scarce in the war and chicory used as a substitute. Camp, in its distinctive bottle, has a sweetish flavour all its own and indescribable. Some people love it and it's still on sale now, although the label design has been slightly changed to show the two characters as equals.

Coffee and our evening milky drinks were made with equal quantities of milk and water, boiled up together in a pan. This small saucepan with a lip for pouring was in fact called a milk pan.

I don't know whether it was partly because sugar was rationed until I was eight years old, and we craved sweetness, but we all had two teaspoonfuls of sugar in our tea and coffee.

On the other hand, nearly everyone did take sugar in those days. Uncle Reg had *three* heaped teaspoons of sugar in his hot drinks! We always drank our tea and coffee from a cup and saucer, never a mug. Uncle would pour tea from his cup into his saucer and drink it from that, a practice known as saucering it. This was not considered to be quite polite but Uncle didn't care.

Included in our weekly sugar ration was 2oz of sweets per person. Mum always bought four separate paper bags of different loose sweets, which were kept in an old metal lunch tin. There weren't any left at the end of each week. I think I have probably never consistently eaten sweets in that way since.

For dinner we always had a main course and a dessert, known as pudding or afters. I don't know why 'pudding' because the steamed desserts were specifically known as pudding, as were milk puddings such as rice pudding and sago. We called the latter frog's eggs because it was just like a cloud of frogspawn in the milk, only without the black 'eye' in each 'egg.' Monday dinner was always leftover Sunday roast, often eaten with bubble and squeak (left over mashed potato and greens, mixed together and fried). Sometimes the meat was hand minced and turned into shepherd's pie, with leftover mashed potato topping. Pudding would be an easy one, being washday.

Our usual main course would be meat, with potatoes and a seasonal vegetable. Unless we had a beef stew or a casserole, Mum always poured homemade gravy on our dinner. Once a week on a Friday Mum made fresh fried fish and chips (no gravy on that either!). I am sure that Uncle Reg being a butcher helped with us always having good quality meat to eat.

I knew nothing at all of 'foreign' foods until I was well into my teens. The only pasta I ate as a child was macaroni, cooked as a milk pudding and known by us as pipe pudding. I didn't even eat it as macaroni cheese until I had school dinners at Bedford High School. Then came Vesta brand, freeze dried Chinese and Indian meals. They weren't really all that good but they were very different and seemed quite exotic to us.

We ate nothing grilled that I recall, other than toast, and in winter we often cooked that and crumpets on a toasting fork over the living room fire. We did not have a toaster, just the grill on the cooker. Meat was roasted, stewed, braised or fried. The frying was done in beef lard. In the earlier years of my life we didn't have any choice of cooking oils anyway.

Olive oil was used - but not for cooking. Highly processed, very far from virgin, olive oil was bought in small bottles from the chemist (pharmacy). It was used to treat earache! A few drops would be warmed and drizzled into the affected ear. It was quite soothing but I don't know if it did any good beyond that.

Healthy eating was never an issue. We simply ate what there was. In any case, nearly all our food was fresh and we had little in the way of snacks. We did eat more fried and fatty food than is now considered good for you but also a lot of fresh vegetables, with no real junk food.

We used up more energy too, not least keeping up our body temperature in the winter cold but also in walking nearly everywhere and, for us children, playing outside.

Mum wore her old clothes and old laddered stockings (a ladder is a run) in the mornings to do her housework. She always washed herself well at the kitchen sink after we'd had a cup of tea, and she had washed the dishes, following dinner. After her wash Mum changed into good clothes and stockings even if she was not going out. We had a cup of tea with Mum in the middle of the afternoon that was timed, once we had started school, for just after we arrived home.

Mum might do some knitting in the afternoon, or she'd maybe read her Woman's Weekly magazine. She also got some of her knitting patterns, which it still carries, from this magazine.

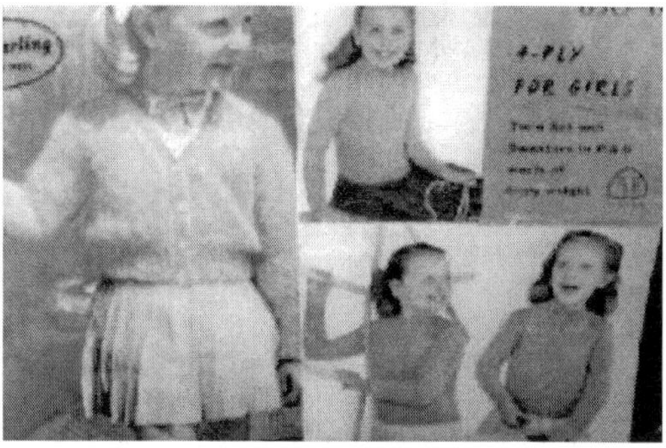

Knitting Patterns

All the magazines were made from very thin paper (like newspaper) for some years after the war. There were no colour pictures in them either. When we were really young, Mum used to read us the very short stories of The Robin Family that appeared in every issue of Woman's Weekly. Somewhat to my surprise, the magazine also still has those weekly stories.

Our dog Bess always lay at Mum's feet while she was sitting in her armchair in the afternoons. As did many dogs, Bess had at least four walks every day. One was before breakfast, the next two after dinner and tea, and the fourth later at night. It didn't trim her down at all though. Even though she just had her one meal a day and a plain biscuit at night she was always a fat little dog.

On the plus side, her black coat really shone. Mum said that was due to the saucer of tea she gave Bess every morning. Bess had the dregs of cocoa at night too.

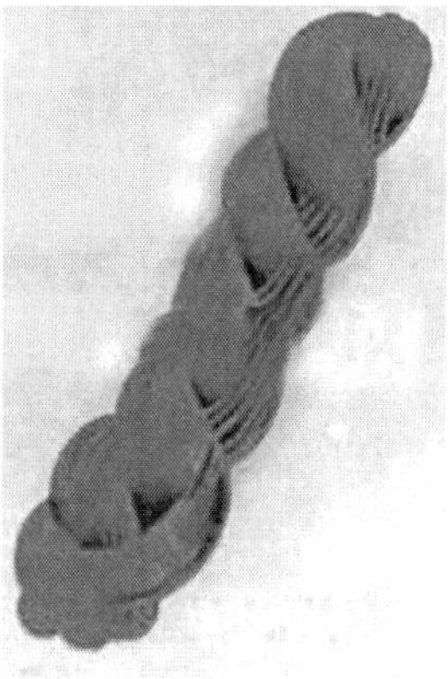

Mum knitted all the family warm sweaters and cardigans during these years. The wool came in skeins, long loops twisted round in sort of figures of eight, as in the picture here.

To use it, you first untwisted the skein. Then it had to be rewound. I quite often sat with my forearms straight out in front of me, the skein looped over them and pulled tight. Mum took an end and away she went, winding it from the skein into a ball. Then she could start knitting with it. But holding the skein for long did make my arms ache and they would begin to droop.

When we were very young, Mum made our dresses from simple patterns on an old hand worked

Singer sewing machine. In the early days she made all her own curtains too. Although still rationed after the war, you could get

more fabric for your coupons than you could pairs of ready-made curtains, even when you could find those to buy.

Everyone also darned socks. The area with the hole was stretched over a wooden 'mushroom' and wool of an approximate colour was woven back and forth across the hole with a large darning needle. Men's jackets had the elbows patched with pieces of leather when they became very worn, to make them last longer too. Make do and mend was a watchword.

Our old cotton sheets were also mended on the Singer machine. As the middle wore out before the sides, so a sheet was cut right down the centre and the two outer edges sewn together, to become the new middle. (Got that?) What had now become the worn outer edges were then hemmed. This was known as 'sides to middling.' That was real make do and mend!

When Dad came home from work just after 5 o'clock we had tea. This was usually bread and butter with jam, meat or fish paste from a jar or cheese, in the week. In the winter as I say, we sometimes had crumpets toasted on a toasting fork over the open fire or toast cooked in the same way. Whatever we ate first, it was followed by Mum's homemade cake. At bedtime we'd have a biscuit with Ovaltine, Horlicks or cocoa to drink. There was an 'Ovaltineys' club and at one time Carole and I had club mugs, with red plastic lids shaped like nightcaps to keep the drink warm.

Like most mothers then Mum did not work outside the home. The husband went out to work to earn the money to keep his family. The wife did all the work in the home and cared for the children. This was generally felt to be a fair division of labour in many households.

And it was nearly all 'husband and wife.' Hardly any unmarried couples lived together, generally thought of as 'living in sin.' There were also few single parent families, other than where a parent had been widowed. For one thing, for a woman to have a child out of wedlock was a real disgrace. For another, divorce was very difficult and expensive. There were not the same kinds of benefits available then as now either.

Dad, like most working men, had a vegetable allotment. This was a standard plot size of 10 pole, used here as a measure of area. For allotments this usually translated to an actual size of 5½ x 55 yards. Dad enjoyed his allotment, which was just as well since it was hard graft. It also gave us much needed fresh provisions. Money was always scarce and so was food in the shops, in the years after the war. A lot was still rationed then of course too.

Dad grew almost all of our vegetables, including potatoes. Some relatives and friends had fruit trees and would pass on excess produce to Mum. She preserved fruit for eating in winter and with fruit and vegetables made jams and chutneys, the latter rather along the lines of Branston type pickle or relishes. Mum also pickled onions and red cabbage. The fruit, onions and red cabbage were kept in big jars (Kilner jars): the fruit in syrup, the onions and red cabbage in seasoned vinegar.

One reason for preserving in this way was that home refrigerators and freezers were very uncommon. I didn't have either until going to live in the United States in 1965.

But now things have come full circle. More people are again making preserves of various kinds. Friends are giving me produce from which *I* am making pickle and chutney!

What houses did have then was a larder or pantry. This usually led off from the kitchen, in the coolest part of the house. In ordinary houses it was a very small walk-in room with shelves for storing bottles, jars, tins (cans) and packets.

Along one wall was a shelf that was a thick marble or concrete slab. It was for putting things on that needed keeping cold, the likes of butter, milk and cheese. Beneath it was a meat safe, a cupboard with a wire mesh door, both for keeping the meat cool and keeping flies out. In really hot weather the milk stood in a bucket of cold water to stop it souring. Although by the mid 1950s some frozen foods were available, such as fish fingers, they had to be eaten within a day or so as they could not be kept longer without a freezer.

The only real convenience foods we had regularly that I remember were gravy powder and stock cubes (Bisto and Oxo), Bird's custard, blancmange powders, jelly (Jell-O) cubes, biscuits (cookies) and crackers. Then there were the tinned foods such as sardines, cooked meat, peas, baked beans, soup and some fruits. Mum always made her own mint sauce and applesauce. We might occasionally have a shop bought cake but mostly Mum made these too. The only fast food outlets and takeaways were fish and chip shops. The choice there was either fish or fish cakes.

There were no convenience pet foods either. Once a week Uncle drove to Bedford to buy cheap meat especially for use as pet food. We reckoned it was horsemeat or the some such. He did have big walk-in refrigerators at the back of the butcher's shop he managed in Bletchley so all the meat kept fresh, although there were no refrigerated display areas. The meat was cut to order on wooden topped counters.

Mum used to boil the pet food meat for Bess and feed her a portion of it once a day, in the evening, with some of the stock and either corn flakes or shredded wheat mixed in. She certainly always seemed healthy enough on the diet.

The meat smelled lovely when it was boiling - and I have been known to steal a piece! It didn't do me any harm either, whatever it was. Dog biscuits were available and Uncle bought those for Fritz. They were something else that I would eat. The black ones were my favourites.

In the earlier years of my life nearly all types of dry foods were sold loose by weight. Throughout my childhood milk was delivered to the doorstep in pint bottles daily from Monday to Saturday. It was full cream milk, as there was no semi-skimmed or skimmed (that I ever saw). This milk was not homogenised as now but had a layer of cream on top. Mostly, the bottle would be shaken to mix the milk and cream. On a Sunday though we sometimes had 'top of the milk' on tinned fruit for tea. The baker's van came round daily too in the week, with freshly baked uncut loaves and rolls. We didn't have sliced, packaged bread.

At Bletchley, the milk came from the Co-op dairy and the bread from their bakery. Mum bought milk and bread checks at the Co-op shop. These were plastic tokens. She would leave milk tokens out with the empty bottles on the doorstep, for however many pints she wanted. The man who delivered the bread was paid with the bread tokens. If you weren't in, you could leave a bag containing your bread token hanging on the front door knob.

As I say, we had no sliced bread and the bread varieties were just white and wholemeal, the latter much less common than now, although we could buy different shaped loaves. We always had white bread for cutting, usually a crusty farmhouse loaf.

I liked the crusty cottage loaf Mum sometimes bought. This is one smaller round of dough on top of a large one. Even better were the little cottage loaf shaped rolls. Miniature wholemeal Hovis loaves were a treat too, split and buttered.

Meat and fish were bought fresh, as they would not keep for long without refrigeration. There was at least one fishmonger in every town as well as a butcher. In the villages a van selling fresh, raw fish (wet fish) often came around once a week on a Friday. The fish was mainly cod and both fresh and smoked haddock.

Vegetables and fruit were mostly seasonal, other than tinned of course. It was too expensive to fly in goods for the general market. Citrus fruits from the Mediterranean came in by boat, as did bananas from the Caribbean. We could buy grapes and sometimes saw fresh pineapples, peaches and apricots. They were all quite expensive though. I really don't remember any fresh vegetables being brought in.

For her main groceries Mum had an order book with carbon paper so that each order had its copy. After making her list, she took the book to the Co-op. She left it there and her order was made up, with the prices written next to each item and totalled. The shop kept the top copy and the order was then delivered on a set day each week with the returned order book. Mum could see how much she owed and pay the bill.

Speaking of paying bills reminds me of something else. Being paid in cash like most workers, Dad kept a small portion of his weekly pay for spending money. Mum had an old cash tin in which she put the rest. She divided it between the compartments, so much for rent, for groceries, the electric bill and so on.

Whenever you bought anything at the Co-op, which owned all kinds of shops and even department stores, you got a receipt that was like a little ticket. The total you had spent and your dividend number were hand-written on this. These tickets were in sheets, again in a carboned book so the Co-op had a copy too.

As the customers of the Co-op were its shareholders, every customer had one of these dividend numbers and each year the net profit was divided up between them. You received dividend money proportional to how much you had spent. This 'divi' came in very handy, especially coming up to Christmas time. There are still Co-ops around but nowhere near as many as 50 years ago, especially in the south of the country. And now it is swipe cards, rather than writing out tickets.

There were no supermarkets. The very first self-service shop in England, Sainsbury's (now a supermarket chain), opened in London in 1950 but these did not start to reach us for a few more years. In ordinary shops there might be some items on display that you could pick up and take to the counter but generally you asked for what you wanted and the shop assistant got it for you.

Shops closed for one afternoon each week, the same day for all the shops in each town, usually a Wednesday or Thursday. This was known as early closing or half-day closing day. With the staff working Saturdays, it gave them an extra half-day off.

Nearly all shops closed on Sunday although newsagents delivered the papers, as they did every other day (magazines and comics were also delivered), and opened for a few hours. It was the same with Bank Holidays and I don't remember any shop that was open on Good Friday, Easter Sunday, Christmas Day or Boxing Day. One quirky thing was that on a Sunday, although shops could sell food that was ready to eat, no shop was allowed to sell food that needed cooking.

The only shop I remember that was open on a Sunday when we lived in Bletchley was in Aylesbury Street, a sweet shop that also sold homemade vanilla ice cream. You had to take your own bowl to be filled! That ice cream was *really* creamy and delicious.

There was a very good postal (mail) service. Letters were all one price to send, no two-tier system, and nearly always arrived by the next day. We had two deliveries a day as well, one early in the morning (often before breakfast) and then another in the afternoon. What we didn't have, and that I wouldn't miss now, was all the junk mail coming through the letterbox.

Crime rates were quite low. Gun crime in England was extremely rare then. I am afraid we associated that kind of crime with America. I don't remember ever hearing anything about an illegal drug trade either, though I am sure some went on. But again, it was very uncommon. However suicide and abortion were both crimes - and those such as domestic violence and abuse tended to often go unreported and unpunished, even more so than now.

It's odd sometimes, the things you remember. I hated the toilet paper we had to use. It was in sheets, pulled out of a box rather than on a roll, although the box fitted into a wall holder. And it was so hard and stiff. The closest thing I can describe it to is being nearly like greaseproof paper (not quite as thick and shiny as waxed paper). You would pull out a sheet, about the same size as a sheet of soft toilet roll, crumple it and rub it between your hands to soften it. How it ever absorbed anything, I do not know.

At Stewartby Dad still used the old hard stuff for several years after the rest of us had taken to the now available soft toilet paper. So we had to keep two lots of paper on the toilet wall.

Throughout my early life we had no other kind of disposable wipes. For example, we had no paper tissues but used our cotton handkerchiefs, which Mum boil washed. Thinking of those hankies I remember how, when I was little and must have had a dirty face, Auntie - although never Mum - would spit on her hankie and wipe my face clean with it! I hated that, although it was quite a common practice.

Spills and mess were all cleaned up with cloths, which would be not just washed but boil washed regularly. The aforementioned greaseproof paper was the only wrap we had, no foil and no clingfilm. There were also no plastic bags, including carrier bags. You just took your own shopping bags or baskets with you.

We didn't have plastic bottles and I don't remember drinks in cans either. You paid a deposit when you bought drinks in glass bottles. This was returned when you took the bottles back. We children would sometimes take back bottles in return for keeping the few pence deposit.

It may seem strange now but all of this was quite normal for us then. Some people tend to look at the past through rose-tinted glasses, as you may have already discovered. Yes, some things were better when I was a child; some were worse than they are now. It would be wonderful if we could take the best of the past and add it to the best of the present, discarding the worst of each.

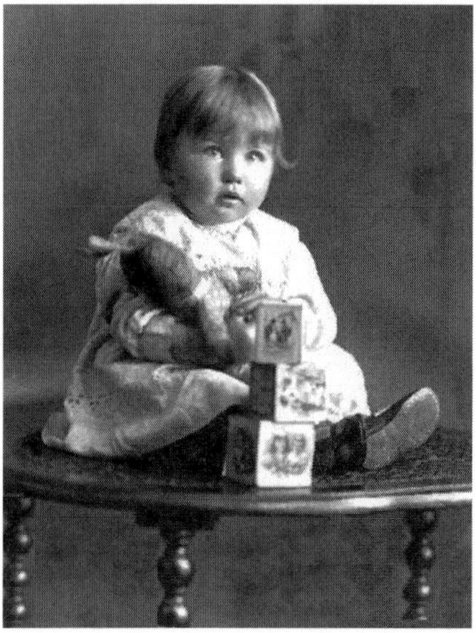

Little Kitty Wallis

Little Nellie Walls

# MY BEGINNING

Bletchley Station, facing Bletchley Park

Where to begin?

Let me first explain how it was that I came to be born at 12 Cambridge Street in Bletchley, which is now part of the new city of Milton Keynes.

In those days Bletchley had grown into a quiet, very pleasant, small market town. On the west it encroached on Fenny Stratford (Fenny), which had once been the separate larger village.

Fenny Stratford had its own little railway station on its northwestern edge, across the A5 Watling Street on the far side from Bletchley. At the east side of Bletchley as you reached the Buckingham Road was Bletchley railway station, with Bletchley Park just beyond. You can see it all on the map in the appendix.

Bletchley Park is well known now as Station X where the code breakers worked during the war, most famously on the Enigma and Lorenz codes. It is also noted for being where the world's first semi-programmable computer, Colossus, was invented. But during the war all that the locals knew, except for the few who worked in there, was that it was some kind of top-secret government institution.

Turning left out of the station approach leads into Bletchley itself. Coming under the railway bridge, on the right across the Bletchley Road, was an apron of hard standing behind the footpath. To the rear of that stood The Park Hotel, the Co-op butcher's shop, a pub and the working men's club where Uncle Reg played billiards one evening a week. There was a fish and chip shop a bit further along.

On the left hand side was a short row of funny little old corrugated iron ('tin') buildings that were actually the first shops that side of the road. Quite soon after passing those, but only on this side of the road, the pavement became a lovely, wide spacious area.

The tin shops as we called them
(Bletchley Station to rear)

The largest shop in Bletchley, a little further along into the town on the left, was the Co-op department store. There were a great many small shops in both Bletchley and Fenny Stratford but the Co-op was the closest to a chain store that there was. Nearly all the others were small, independent businesses.

The payment system in that big Co-op was fascinating. The shop assistant wrote a bill and took your money. Then the money and bill were placed in a lidded tub. The assistant pushed this tub up into a clear plastic vertical tube, which it just fitted. As the tub went into the tube, it shot up and then along under the ceiling to disappear we knew not where. Soon after, back came the tub with a receipt and any change. There was a grid of horizontal tubes under the ceiling and a vertical tube from each counter intersecting this grid, so you could often see several tubs at a time whizzing about to and fro. I could quite happily watch that while Mum shopped.

I know now that it was some kind of pneumatic system but when I was small it seemed almost like magic to me.

Bletchley Road around 1960, looking from the Co-op into town

The other shops just had old fashioned tills to ring up your payment. The sales assistant added up your purchases (mental arithmetic!) and entered the total, took your money, calculated what change you were due and handed it to you. If there was a power cut those tills weren't out of action. Yet today, with all our new technology, everything comes to a grinding halt without electricity - most frustrating!

Bletchley Cattle Market was behind the area where the Co-op butcher's shop stood. Beasts were traded on a Thursday and a general market held there on a Saturday.

My mother, Kitty Wallis, was born 19th February 1920 in Hackenthorpe, Derbyshire. By the time she was ten years old she had moved with her family a few miles to Beighton, then a small mining town, near Sheffield in Yorkshire. Her father had a clerical job at the local mine. He had a physical deformity, a humped back. This was caused when he was a baby and I have heard two stories as to how it happened.

One version had it that someone minding him let go of the pram (baby carriage) whilst out walking and it ran away downhill and tipped over, throwing him out. The other was that somebody who was playing with him, tossing him into the air, dropped him. Whatever the truth, Grandad Wallis wasn't fit enough to be a miner. However he was obviously smart enough for the clerical work or he would not have been employed.

Mum's mother baked pork pies for the local butcher. She was a lay nurse and the local 'hatcher and dispatcher' too. That is, she was an unqualified midwife who also laid out the dead, which involved washing and dressing them to make their appearance as presentable as possible. Whenever my grandmother had been to a laying out, the first thing Mum asked when her mother got home was whether she had washed her hands. My grandmother also had a lodger, Billy, throughout Mum's childhood. And she took in laundry. She must certainly have been a hard worker.

The youngest of five children by some years, Mum was never very healthy as a child. In fact the story goes that when her father first saw her after she was born he commented that it would be kinder to, "Put the poor little bugger out of her misery!" However she proved him wrong being now, in 2011, in her 92nd year.

My father Jack Blane was born in Bletchley, 14th August 1918, at 14 Brooklands Road where he lived until his marriage. He was the seventh of eight living children. His father was a train driver, driving steam trains out of Bletchley station, which was then a very large, busy main railway junction. His mother had been a schoolteacher. As was mandatory then, she left work when she married.

I didn't know Mum's parents. Her father died when she was sixteen years old and her mother when I was just two. So I really only knew my paternal grandparents. Dad's father died when I was eleven years old. Martin, Dad's younger brother, lived with my grandmother in the Brooklands Road house for a good many years, until Grandma finally needed sheltered accommodation. Eventually she moved to a nursing home in Newport Pagnell, where she died in 1971 at the age of ninety three.

Mum's eldest sister Nellie, who was some fifteen years her senior, married Reginald (Reg) Cutts in 1928 and moved with him to Bletchley where he managed the local Co-op butcher's shop near the railway station. (Mum is the small bridesmaid on the left, her sister Annie in matching outfit on the right here at Reg and Nellie's wedding.)

In those early days Uncle Reg really was a butcher. The animals ('beasts') were delivered live from local farms to the big shop yard, slaughtered and butchered (cut up) on the premises.

Although Mum was sickly as a child, when she holidayed in Bletchley away from the coal pits her health always improved. So when she left school at fourteen as was usual then, Mum's father and mother agreed that she could accept the offer of going to live in Bletchley with her sister and brother-in-law. This would be around Easter 1934.

Mum and Nellie were very close. Auntie Nellie and Uncle Reg had a special place in my life. Whilst not exactly like either second parents or grandparents but different to my other aunts and uncles, they always played a large part in my childhood. They were simply Auntie and Uncle. All my other aunts and uncles had their names added. This was just one of those things that was so normal to me I didn't even think about until I was much older.

12 Cambridge Street, Bletchley: 'Lyndhurst'

Lower left: Front (music) room
Upper left: Auntie and Uncle's bedroom
Lower right: Front porch and door
Upper right: Bathroom
Upper Side right: Landing window
Right: High gate and Garage

In the early 1930s Nellie and Reg had bought a new three bedroom detached house on Cambridge street. It even had a garage, which was unusual then.

Most ordinary folk owned neither their own home nor a car. I just did not realise when I was very young that Auntie and Uncle were certainly among the most affluent people I knew then. They were not really wealthy but never had to worry about finances. Uncle's older family members had all been reasonably well off and Uncle had inherited. He had a good job and Auntie taught the piano at home as well.

As you entered the front door of their house, the stairs led up on your right. The hallway went straight along to the kitchen door.

The kitchen was small and quite dark with just a little window at the side of the house, overlooking the small lawn behind the garage where there were two lovely lilac trees near the next door house's fence. Behind the kitchen, against the back wall of the house, was a one-storey brick extension. This contained a coal shed and an outside toilet. (There was also a toilet in the upstairs bathroom at the front of the house.)

The small kitchen table was under the window, with the door to the left and the cooker to the right of it - by the inside end wall of the kitchen. The sink was fitted to the back wall. The left hand sink draining board stayed in place but the right hand one could only be fitted when the kitchen door was closed because there was so little space between sink and door.

Opposite the table, on the wall between the kitchen and dining room, was a chimneybreast with an enclosed fire that had a back boiler behind it for heating water. In the alcove to the left of this was their dog Fritz's basket.

The pantry led off from the right side of the hallway, against the outside wall next to the kitchen and under the stairs. There was no room for another door in the kitchen and very little for cabinets. It's a good thing there was a pantry and that there were cupboards in the living room where crockery could be kept.

The doors to the other two rooms led off to the left of the hall. All the living was done, as was usual, in the back room. We might think of it as the dining room but it was living/diner then. For most people that was because heating two rooms would have cost too much. The kitchen fire warmed one wall there, too.

At Cambridge Street another reason we lived in the back was that Auntie's piano, for her teaching, was in the front room. This was where she gave her lessons: late afternoons after school, early evenings and Saturday mornings.

It is a shame the living was done that way round, as the front room had a bay window and was very light. The living room at the back only caught a bit of sunlight early in the morning. It never seemed to get terribly warm either, despite Auntie and Uncle having room sized carpets covering the floors in their house. Auntie did not feel the cold, so there was usually just quite a small fire going in the living room. And of course, it had to pretty chilly for the fire to be lit at all.

Upstairs, the small bedroom door faced the top of the stairs. Next to this was Mum's bedroom, behind Auntie and Uncle's room. Like their bedroom, the bathroom was at the front. It was above the front end of the hallway and bottom of the staircase.

For when there was no kitchen fire lit, the bathroom and kitchen each had a geyser to heat water. This was a kind of little boiler, fitted to the wall, which only fired up and heated the water when you manually turned it on. A long horizontal tap (faucet) could be swiveled to where you wanted the water.

The outside toilet was quite primitive, no heating of course and not even a hand wash basin. The interior walls were simply white washed brick. As you might imagine, that toilet didn't get used too often.

Much later, beyond the time of this story, when the kitchen was remodelled the outside door to the toilet was blocked up, an inside doorway knocked through and a heater fitted.

View from Mum's and 'my' back bedroom window, with tennis courts and Central Gardens to rear

The house had a lovely big, long garden. The end of the garden backed on to the tennis courts of the municipal park, the Central Gardens. This ran from Bletchley Road to Western Road (see map), with an entrance on each.

There was a big shed to the left of the path, just behind the house. The garden had lawns, flower beds and a rockery, a fishpond under the back window, a large vegetable garden and fruit trees. I loved it. Uncle grew the vegetables and Auntie the flowers. Gladioli were one favourite, all different colours and ramrod straight. Auntie particularly loved carnations though, big blooms of all colours heady with the scent of cloves

Looking toward the front gate

Garage barely visible on left, corrugated iron shed on the right

Upper left window, small bedroom

Upper right, just in view, Mum's (later my) bedroom

(The honeysuckle arch had gone by the time I took this picture in the late 1950s.)

A mass of evergreen honeysuckle trailed over a heavy wooden square arch, across the path near the shed. In the summer it was covered in blooms and the scent drifted in through the open kitchen door. We used to pick the flowers and suck the nectar from the ends. The honeysuckle was from a root that Mum and Dad dug up in the woods when they were courting and gave to

Auntie. Dad took a cutting to Stewartby when we moved there and I now have a plant from it in my own garden.

I know it is not my imagination that a lot of flowers then had more scent than they do today. Growers bred out scent in favour of beauty, yet I never did understand why we couldn't have both. And now in response to customer demand growers are breeding the scent back in!

There is an old rose bush in a front garden along the street where I live now. As you walk past when it is in bloom the scent almost overpowers you. It really transports me back in time. I have a scented rose bought a few years ago but the blossoms still don't have that intensity.

Part of Central Gardens: tennis courts to left, Western Road to rear

Mum and Dad's Wedding
Bridesmaids: Aunt Edna and Auntie Mary, with my cousin Brenda

My parents started going out together when Mum was sixteen years old and they married 9th October 1940 at St Martin's Church in Vicarage Road, Fenny Stratford. Dad was in the army and having returned back to England from Dunkirk earlier that year, he was able to take some leave for his wedding.

Dad spent that Christmas at home and was stationed in England until December 1941, when he was sent to North Africa. He was away for over two years. Mum still lived with Auntie and Uncle.

Dad had a leave, his first time back in England since December 1941, in January 1944. He embarked for France on D-Day and I was born that October. I was born in the Cambridge Street house itself, in the larger of the back bedrooms that was Mum's and where I also slept when I visited, as I did regularly in later years. Mum was a bit disappointed because when she went into labour she hoped that I would be born that day, as it was my parents' wedding anniversary. However, I did not oblige! I waited until just after midnight, so 10th October is my birthday.

Mum chose my name. She said that she just wanted a name she liked that nobody else in the family had. However even if unknowingly, she did choose a name that connected me with Dad. Jack is a derivative of John and the Scottish girl's name Jean is the feminine form of John. I'm also told that everyone who saw me as a baby said I looked like Dad. Mum told them she ordered me like that to avoid doubt about paternity, with Dad being away.

There was a houseful in Cambridge Street as Auntie and Uncle had two evacuee sisters also staying with them, sharing the smaller back bedroom. They were Joan and Marjorie (Marj), from Chiswick, London. They were there from, I believe, 1940 until 1945. Their parents used to visit and even years later kept in touch, being Uncle John and Auntie Ruth to us. I do still speak with Joan occasionally now and she says that those years were the best of her childhood. She loved living at Bletchley with Auntie and Uncle.

Things must have been very crowded in the house though, with Joan and Marj sharing the small bedroom and all of us living in the one room downstairs.

Auntie and me, Marj, Joan and Uncle

The house always smelled strongly of cigarette smoke. I didn't really notice it as it was just something I was used to. Nobody knew about the health hazards of smoking then and Uncle must have smoked about sixty Senior Service cigarettes a day. These were shorter than today's cigarettes but very strong and untipped. Dad smoked first a pipe and then 'roll ups,' hand rolled cigarettes, but nothing like as much as Uncle.

Uncle could not read music but he could play some tunes by ear. As one background to my childhood I can remember him accompanying himself as he sang the comic songs Abdul Abulbul Amir and O'Rafferty's Pig. We loved those and as we got older sang along with him. There were other old, humorous songs that we enjoyed too.

Some months before I was born Uncle bought a German Shepherd puppy, Fritz. The name German Shepherd wasn't used, mind you, due to wartime connotations. During these years the breed was known as Alsatian. Obviously Uncle didn't care, giving him a name like Fritz! Auntie had been rather frightened to have an Alsatian as one had attacked their previous dog, a Cocker Spaniel. However, she too soon came to love Fritz.

For me, he was simply always part of my childhood. Some of the earliest photos show him sitting with me all of his own accord. I think that for him, I was *his* puppy.

Watching over

Uncle trained Fritz well and he was a very obedient dog. The only thing that strained his patience was if he saw a cat when he was out on the lead. But he had a lovely temperament.

Now I am getting a bit ahead of myself. So to go back: for the first months of my life I was apparently a fractious baby. I think it is hardly surprising as my mother was terribly anxious.

Dad was somewhere in Europe, moving into Germany in the last stages of the war. Added to that Mum felt rather inhibited living with Auntie and Uncle, feeling that she must always be thinking of them. She says that there were times when she threatened to throw me out of her bedroom window into the fishpond below, feeling at her very wits' end.

Auntie could not have children (and there was no real fertility treatment then). Mum felt that she must let her sister have as much of *me* as she could. So, for example, Mum would offer to do any jobs needed and let Auntie be the one to take me out in my pram for a walk.

Meeting his new daughter
Dad on leave March 1945

It would seem that Mum and I both started to feel better around Easter the following year. Dad had a short home leave from 6th March, after being at Nijmegen in the battle for the Rhine.

Then Mum took me for a first visit to her mother in Beighton. Grandma Wallis was apparently well known for her soothing Jolly Drops. Mum put my quieter mood down to these. Goodness knows what was in them. Various drugs that you don't even see today, such as laudanum, were readily available and still in use at that time. Personally, I think Dad's home leave did the trick!

Also, the war was drawing to an end. VE Day was declared not long afterward so there was great relief and rejoicing. Even though Dad was still in Germany for some months more, Mum could now see a future and an eventual end to the shared living.

At the end of the war, whilst Dad was in Germany, he was hospitalised. This was not due to enemy action. He had bronchitis very badly. In hospital he occupied himself by making me some soft toys. I remember a navy blue felt elephant, with seams blanket-stitched in orange. The cream coloured tusks were so thin that looking back I don't know how he managed to stuff them. He also made me an orange duck.

(Forwarding several decades Dad took up soft toy making again in retirement, still all hand sewn. Over a period of nearly twenty years, until his sight failed, he made hundreds of stuffed animals and raised a great deal of money for charity with them.)

Who is Uncle training?

Dad returned to England for good on 'demob' leave in December 1945 and spent his first Christmas at home since 1940. When he was discharged in February 1946 he came back to live with us all in Cambridge Street, while my parents waited for a house that would finally be their own.

There was a real housing shortage after the war and a big programme of council house (social housing) building was started in the late 1940s by the government of the day. This was to give ordinary working folk decent, affordable housing. These houses were much sought after. Unfortunately, since the estates all had to be built from scratch the wait for a house could be quite lengthy. This building programme did however mean that the brick industry was in a very healthy state.

Dad went back to working in his old job for the London Brick Company at Newton Longville, a few miles outside Bletchley on the Buckingham side. He cycled to work every day, as did Uncle to his shop near the station. Despite Dad's ride being longer, he still came home for dinner.

Weekend relaxation in the garden

Uncle would leave for work very early in the morning to prepare things in the shop for the day ahead. He came home for his breakfast and then opened up the shop at 9 o'clock. Like most shops in those years, the butcher's closed for an hour at dinnertime in the middle of the day.

For his dinner Uncle followed an old Yorkshire custom by almost always having a first course of a plate sized Yorkshire Pudding with gravy, and with English mustard on the side. (It had to be Taylor's, which I myself still prefer to this day!) He started his dinner with that because he liked it but the practice originated in Yorkshire, many years earlier, as a cheap way of filling your stomach when meat for the main course was very expensive for working families.

The only time Uncle changed this routine was when Auntie had made a Spotted Dick, steamed suet pudding with raisins, for afters. Then Uncle did not have his Yorkshire Pudding starter. Instead he had a lump of Spotted Dick with his main course, (including gravy) instead. I was quite fascinated by this but did not fancy it myself. I liked my Spotted Dick with Bird's Custard, thank you very much.

To go back again: Mum took me on a number of visits to Beighton to see Grandma Wallis. Here is a picture of the two of them, with me being held by my cousin Brenda as of course we saw other family members too. I think this picture may have been taken on our last visit before Grandma died.

My earliest memories will be from when I was about two years old. One is of sitting in the Cambridge Street kitchen between the table and the open door, with the sunshine pouring in, dipping raw rhubarb sticks in sugar and eating them. The other is of choking on a boiled sweet, being turned upside down and hit on the back by Auntie until it came out!

Although I do not remember this, apparently I really loved butter. If the butter dish had been left out within my reach I dipped my fingers in to scoop out the butter and just eat it on its own. This gave Mum the horrors as, not being able to stand butter herself, she even hated wiping my fingers and mouth.

On the other hand Auntie apparently used to suck the butter off my fingers with every evidence of enjoyment, finding it great fun, something that Mum couldn't even bear to watch her doing. It's strange the way that something seeming quite innocuous to one person can affect another so strongly.

Dad is in his 'demob' suit.

In the winter of 1946-47, when I was two, I wore a matching wool coat and leggings for going out in the cold. Apparently I did not like having my leggings on and would fight Mum, going rigid and screaming. She would eventually get so frustrated that she would slap my legs to make me behave. Then she felt dreadful, with me in tears and Auntie wringing her hands.

On a happier note, Mum used to cycle quite a lot. She would go to look round the shops in Leighton Buzzard and Newport Pagnell. I went along too, strapped into a rear child seat. Although I don't remember that either I wish that I did. Mum always cycled to Newport Pagnell in the spring, to buy a bunch of the first daffodils for Auntie.

Once when she had me on board, Mum's bicycle tyre had a puncture as she cycled through a village on the way home from Newport Pagnell. She was really worried, with no way of contacting anyone in Bletchley. However a Good Samaritan saw her plight and saved the day by mending the puncture for her.

I had a friend next door, at number 14 Cambridge Street, whose name was Carole. She was a bit younger than me. We played together in the back gardens. Her grandfather lived with the family and kept chickens in a run at the end of their garden. They were fascinating to a young child, though looking back they were quite scrawny, smelly and noisy. I'm told the grandfather would sometimes shout at them, "Shut up you bare-arsed buggers!"

When I was two years old, in the summer of 1947, Mum and Dad took me to the Isle of Wight for a holiday. We stayed for a week in a boarding house (see Early Holidays), with a landlord who was rather unpleasant - but in those days you didn't argue! This landlord took the ration books, as was normal, so that he could feed us for the week. But apparently the evening meal was always just a basic salad with a bit of meat, cheese or fish. There was never a cooked meal: and Dad has never liked salad. The other thing the landlord insisted on was that I should be in bed before the evening meal. So by 6.30pm every evening, that was the day over for me.

I continued to sleep in a cot (crib) in my parents' room until the next big event in my life. Auntie and Uncle adopted Ken. I was just three years old and he was six months older. He came from a London orphanage and was a poor little scrap at first. He had my cot, which had been moved into Auntie and Uncle's room, and I now slept in a bed in the small back bedroom.

Cupboards were built into the alcoves on either side of the chimneybreast in the living room. An armchair sat alongside each cupboard. I barricaded my toys between one cupboard and armchair to keep them from Ken. So of course, that was trouble. I was not amused with Ken, never having had to share before. It did, I know, cause some friction in the household.

Looking back I am sure (and Mum agrees) that, if Dad had not come back from the war, we would have stayed at Cambridge Street and Auntie and Uncle would not have adopted Ken. In fact before the adoption, Mum felt so beholden and so sorry for her childless sister that she even considered leaving me to be raised by Auntie and Uncle. Mum knew that she could have another child, where they could have none.

She agonised over this as she also felt that I could have a better material quality of life with Auntie and Uncle. She knew of course that they very much loved me and that I loved them. But she just couldn't bring herself to give me up. Poor Mum, struggling with what felt to her a huge dilemma.

As I replied when she eventually told me of this (long after I grew up), much though I loved Auntie and Uncle and my home in Cambridge Street, she is my Mum and I am glad that she did not leave me there. Mind, I do think that Dad might have had something to say about it as well!

Anyway it was not long before not only did Auntie and Uncle come to love Ken, but Mum and Dad grew very fond of him too. He became to me just part of the way things were, one other in the main circle of people in my life. It simply didn't occur to me to imagine things without him. This though for me was after things settled down following more big changes.

Auntie and Ken

# CHANGES COME APACE

Despite Ken's arrival I know that I did not want to leave Auntie, Uncle and my home. I didn't know why we had to move. But I am also sure that my parents were more than relieved when they were finally allocated a council house, number 1 Whiteley Crescent on a brand new housing estate at Far Bletchley, beyond Old Bletchley between Bletchley and Newton Longville. A lot closer to where Dad worked it was a three bedroom, semi-detached house on the left-hand corner entering the crescent.

Mum was thrilled with her first home and a brand new house, too. One unusual feature she really liked was that the living room fireplace was in the middle of the house, against the dining room wall, so no heat was wasted. The only problem, as with our later house in Stewartby, was that the window frames were of painted iron and collected condensation in the winter. But that wasn't serious enough to worry Mum.

In all our houses, with no double-glazing and doors not fitting tightly, the draughts whipped through in the winter. So two big brass hooks were fitted at the top on the inside of each exterior door and the living room door. In the winter a pole was placed across these, from which hung a heavy curtain. A 'sausage' or 'snake,' a draught excluder made from a stuffed tube of material, was also laid at the base of the door.

With being on the corner our garden was triangular in shape, the base toward the house. It was still big enough for Dad to grow some vegetables in, as well as having his allotment. All the fences were quite low and made of open wooden railings, so you could see and talk to any neighbour who was close enough. The fronts were open and grassed. We moved in around Easter 1948, when I was 3½ years old. So that was the next big event for me.

Furnishing the house can't have been easy. Not only did Mum and Dad not have much money but it was still not easy to get new furniture, which remained also mostly utility furniture. They even needed coupons for the lino floor covering. We had two big utility armchairs, which lasted for many years, in the living room. They were square with wide arms, covered in a dark green fake leather, with similar coloured fabric seats.

The dining room suite, which again lasted many years, was also utility furniture, though their nicer bedroom suite wasn't. This consisted of one large and one small wardrobe and a dressing table, which they had until moving into their care home in 2010. Most of the rest of the furniture was given to them or bought second hand.

There was no fitted kitchen. The main furniture item in most kitchens was a freestanding kitchen cabinet, some six feet high. The top part was a storage cupboard with a shelf. Below this a drop front door, which served as a work surface, hid another storage area. And under this again were drawers and a bottom cupboard with another shelf.

Bedroom curtains were lined with blackout material. Everyone used this during WWII for all their curtains. A nationwide blackout was declared very early on in the war, to help prevent enemy aircraft from accurately pinpointing targets. Don't forget: there was not even radar at that time, let alone GPS, for navigation. I really liked the blackout curtains. For many years I slept much better if my room was totally dark.

In the summer of 1948 we had a really lovely week's holiday in Great Yarmouth. Mum was by now pregnant again and that was the last proper family holiday Mum and Dad could afford for another ten years, until I was thirteen years old.

With Mum and Dad on Great Yarmouth Beach

We did go to stay with relatives in the years between. I was lucky in that I also, as you will see later, went on holidays with Auntie, Uncle and Ken.

Two more big changes, additions to the household, soon followed. My sister Carole was born in February 1949. Poor Mum! Carole was born a day late too, not for Mum's anniversary but for her birthday. Carole was born 20th February, on a snowy Sunday. Although she wished her birthday had been the earlier one Carole, unlike Mum, was glad that she didn't have to share it. Auntie and Ken had come to us for Mum's birthday tea on the Saturday. I expect they came in the afternoon when Uncle was still working in the shop. We did usually all get together for birthday and other celebrations.

Mum had made a sponge cake that morning for tea, even though she was not feeling quite right. She was an excellent sponge cake maker but says that this one was "As flat as a fart!"

Even though Mum could not eat much and had a terrible backache, she didn't tell Auntie how she was feeling. Carole was born at home in the early hours of the Sunday morning. When I woke up Dad brought Carole into my bedroom to show me our new baby. I knew that Dr Luffkin came and thought that she had brought the baby in her bag.

Auntie told Mum off later, saying that she would have taken me away back to Cambridge Street to stay with them if she had only known just how Mum was feeling. Then I would have been out of the way of all that was going on, one less worry.

Front door, Whiteley Crescent
Mum and I with new baby Carole

The baby's name was my choice for her, Carole after my friend next door in Cambridge Street. I suppose I wanted her to be a friend like that to play with - but of course she was just a little baby, so rather disappointing to me. But Mum was happy that she now had a baby that she could feel was completely hers.

With no worries about Dad either, apparently both Mum and Carole were much calmer and more relaxed than she and I had been. So it was very different for Mum to when I was born, when she had all her anxieties and feelings of guilt.

When Carole was born Mum gave me her own cherished doll. It had a china head and a soft body. Soon after, I fell down the stairs with it. Mum heard me crying so loudly that she thought I must be badly injured. But I wasn't really hurt. I was just shocked and very upset because the doll's head was smashed when I fell. Mum, on the other hand, was quite relieved that it wasn't *my* head.

When I was given a new doll, she was plastic with blonde nylon hair. Auntie used to crochet and made some lovely dolls' clothes. One dolls' dress was crocheted from what felt like silk. It was blue with frills around the skirt that were edged in a golden colour.

Out for a walk, early spring 1950

The new doll of course lasted me a very great deal longer than did Mum's treasure. I can still recall dressing her in her various outfits well after we moved house again. I very proudly took her out for walks as you see, Mum with Carole alongside.

For my fifth birthday Mum and Dad got me the second hand doll's pram. It was a smaller version of the lovely big prams of that time. The middle section of the mattress base lifted out, with quite a big space for storage underneath.

We went out walking most fine days, Mum with Carole, I with my doll's pram as in the picture. The front of Carole's pram could drop down to make a sort of really big first pushchair (stroller).

Carole and Bess

At somewhere around the time of Carole's birth our Dad brought home a really sweet little black and white puppy, our dog Bess.

Mum had not wanted a dog. However the dog of a workmate of Dad's had died. He ordered another and in the meantime was given a puppy. So here came Bess, brought home in Dad's pocket. And guess what? Mum was too soft hearted to turn her away and grew to really love her.

Bess and Fritz got along well too. I don't remember there ever being any kind of trouble between them.

When we went on holiday Auntie and Uncle had Bess to stay with them. Mum and Dad did the same with Fritz when Auntie and Uncle went away. It was an arrangement that worked very well for everyone, including the dogs.

I soon came to enjoy living in Whiteley Crescent, which was the last road in Far Bletchley. Across the road from us on the Newton Longville side was a clay embankment where the Oxford to Bletchley railway line ran. This became the Bletchley to Cambridge line (via Bedford) in the other direction from Bletchley. The complete stretch was nicknamed the Oxbridge line.

The train to Oxford passing Whiteley Crescent

Beyond the railway line was the brick company knothole, the pit where a machine called a Navvy dug out the brick clay - Oxford clay as it was known, the type found throughout the whole area.

There weren't many other houses around, although a new housing estate was being built across the Newton Road from us. Until a parade of a few shops was opened there our nearest store was Chandler's, a small grocer on the Buckingham Road on the way to Bletchley. The shop had a little fridge freezer. After I started school, in the warmer weather I would sometimes beg a penny from Mum at dinnertime. Then in the afternoon after school we children would go into this shop and buy penny ice blocks. To make these the grocer froze orange squash in ice trays, with a little wooden ice cream spoon in each compartment. They were a great treat to us. We did sometimes get an ice cream at home when the ice cream van came round in the summer, too.

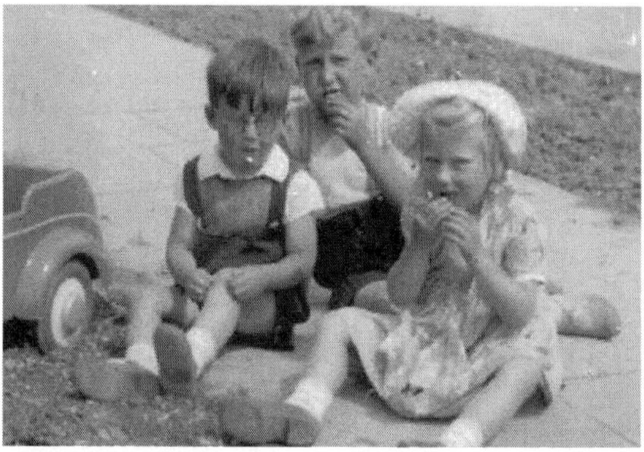

I made friends: Robert (with the glasses) who lived next door, in the first house on the corner of Newton Road, being one. He was known as Wobert, because of his very real lisp, poor boy.

Sandra who was a bit older than me, and lived a few houses further down the Crescent, was my best friend. She was rather short for her age, stocky, and spoke in quite a gruff voice. I didn't realise at the time, although I knew she often had to go to the hospital, that this was because she had a growth hormone deficiency.

We all used to wander about and play together. Our parents didn't worry about where we were or see any dangers in our being out on our own. Often we went along the Crescent, across the very quiet road and under the railway bridge. Down a little lane was the brick company sports ground, surrounded and sheltered by high hedges. We sometimes played over there. But more often, we scrambled up the clay bank to where we played and looked over the knothole and the Navvy digging out the clay.

Very little grew up there on the clay. There was some scrubby coarse grass and there were a few varieties of wild flowers, mainly low growing ones such as Bird's Eye and Lady's Slipper. The former had very small, brilliant blue flowers. For some reason we knew Lady's Slipper as Eggs and Bacon. Maybe it was because some of the little yellow flowers had red streaks through them. Mum and Dad didn't know we went up on the clay banks. We all knew that we certainly wouldn't have been given permission as my parents have also since confirmed, in no uncertain terms.

This picture shows the Navvy as it was being assembled at the base of the new knothole, which had been dug out to that level with smaller machines. You can see the steps the men cut by hand to get in and out of the pit.

Another play area was in the hollow centres of thick hedgerows across the Newton Road. This was a favourite in the evening, as parents could not find us when they called us in. We didn't leave it too long before going home though as we didn't want to be in real trouble. At other times we just played in the Crescent or at one another's houses.

Grandad had retired from his train driving and I loved it when he came to visit, as did Carole when she was a bit older. "Grandad, have you got your reading glasses?" I am sure he helped me learn to read. I had a weekly comic, Tiny Tots. Later Carole had the companion comic Chicks' Own.

One method we used for learning to read was phonics, sep,ar,at,ing words into syllables - like that. I still have an old early reading book, the Blackie's Second Infant Reader. I don't know when it was published but an imprint says the paper and binding conform to war economy standard. The paper in the book, its front pages pictured here, is in reality quite yellow in colour. But although it's true that the paper is old, it was never really white and it is also very thick.

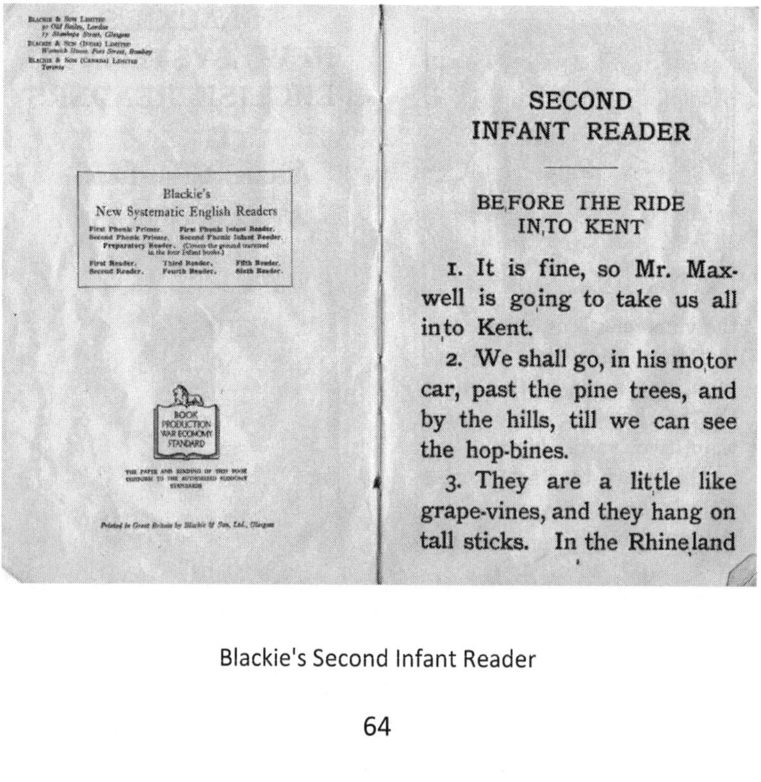
Blackie's
New Systematic English Readers

First Phonic Primer. First Phonic Infant Reader.
Second Phonic Primer. Second Phonic Infant Reader.
Preparatory Reader. (Covers the ground traversed in the four Infant books.)
First Reader. Third Reader. Fifth Reader.
Second Reader. Fourth Reader. Sixth Reader.

BOOK PRODUCTION WAR ECONOMY STANDARD

Printed in Great Britain by Blackie & Son, Ltd., Glasgow

SECOND
INFANT READER

BE,FORE THE RIDE
IN,TO KENT

1. It is fine, so Mr. Max-well is go,ing to take us all in,to Kent.
2. We shall go, in his mo,tor car, past the pine trees, and by the hills, till we can see the hop-bines.
3. They are a lit,tle like grape-vines, and they hang on tall sticks. In the Rhine,land

Blackie's Second Infant Reader

For some years as a child, rather like Mum I was quite 'sickly.' I had bouts of tonsillitis until I had my tonsils out and in the winter months particularly, bronchitis as well. I remember Dr Luffkin coming and my having to take penicillin medicine, still pretty new then. I hated it. It was thick, pink and supposedly raspberry tasting - ugh! I used to try to hide under the piano stool when I heard the doctor arrive.

I also remember being in bed when I was ill and having picture and colouring books. Once when I wasn't well I sat in bed for stretches of time with Mum's pastry board tilted on my knees. I had been given a little plastic, jointed Muffin the Mule (a children's TV puppet character), which would walk down a slope.

The air needed humidifying when I had bronchitis. The round Aladdin stove for heating the bathroom was about two feet high and stood on the floor. There were round ventilation holes in the top. When I was ill this was placed in my bedroom with a saucepan of boiling water on it to provide steam.

I remember Dad coming in during the night and taking the saucepan to top up with water. I would lie in bed looking at the ceiling, where the light shining through the holes made a pattern. Having the heater in there, the bedroom was also nice and warm.

The bouts of bronchitis were something that lingered until I was about ten years old. I also frequently wet the bed for some years, I don't know why.

My bed wetting must have been difficult for Mum, especially with no modern washing machine, but I was never scolded or punished although I did feel ashamed of it. As with the bronchitis, before I finished junior school I just eventually grew out of that too.

I'd had most of the childhood illnesses by the time I was ten years old, with there being no vaccinations against the common childhood diseases.

A more unusual illness I had at the age of four was scarlet fever. By then it was a less serious disease for children than it had been years previously. I don't remember feeling particularly ill but Carole was just a baby and it could have been dangerous for her if she had caught it. So I went into hospital in Northampton, for I think about two weeks. Although family could not visit in the ward, due to the risk of infection, they did come to the hospital and bring treats. We could see one another through a little window. That hospital stay was like a holiday, playing on the ward. I couldn't bring out any toys or books I had there though, again due to the risk of infection. When I was discharged Auntie and Uncle came in the car to take me home. I cried when I got home because I didn't want to go. Poor Mum, it did upset her.

I got my come-uppance when I was five though. I went back into hospital to have my tonsils out and was really looking forward to it. What a shock! Firstly, they put a sickly sweet smelling anaesthetic mask over my face. Then, when I woke up after the operation, how my throat hurt. It was just no fun at all. I was only in for one night that time - and couldn't wait to get home.

That operation must have been in one of my first school holidays. The big change of starting school was something I had found very hard to wait for. My friend Sandra went and I desperately wanted to go with her. Now, back then there was no state ('public' in US terms) pre-school or kindergarten. Formal state education in England began at five years old but you didn't start until the term after your fifth birthday, unlike now.

I so much wanted to go though, that Dad persuaded the school to let me start *on* my birthday, in the middle of term.

Church Green Road

We had no choice in which school we went to. Each one had its own catchment area and so all children just went to the school nearest to them.

Our little two-room school was on Church Green Road behind the Buckingham Road in Old Bletchley, between Far Bletchley and Bletchley itself. Old Bletchley had been the original Bletchley village.

The school was called Church Green Road Church of England School, a bit of a mouthful. But everyone just called it Church Green School.

We children walked to school on our own. We went down Newton Road, across the Buckingham Road at the crossroads by the Shoulder of Mutton pub, and a short way along another little road. Then we turned right into Church Green Road, which led slightly uphill to the school.

Shoulder of Mutton pub and crossroads, with Newton Road to the left

Once a week on a Thursday morning we had a church service. We all walked in a 'crocodile,' two by two, to St Mary's Church. It was not far along Church Green Road, going toward Bletchley. In the nice weather we also went on nature walks, looking for plant and animal life. Special finds were taken back to school to be placed on the Nature Table at one side of the classroom.

In the spring we picked young hawthorn leaves to eat on the way to school, calling them Bread and Cheese, although I don't know why that name as they didn't taste like it. In summer we broke off Cow Parsley (Queen Anne's Lace) stems to use as peashooters, with the missiles being the seeds of the same plant. In late summer we picked and ate blackberries. Wild roses (dog roses) grew in every hedgerow, giving a display of brilliant red rosehips in the autumn. That time of year also brought bright orange Chinese Lanterns, which we would pick and carry.

On foggy autumn mornings we broke off thin, springy twigs and held them with the ends together. Then we used them to gather the glistening spiders' webs and called them our mirrors. On really cold, frosty winter mornings we would slide on the ice until it was like glass. When it snowed, it was as exciting for us as it is for children now and we had fun throwing snowballs as we went to and from school.

Children from the ages of five to eleven were taught in the two rooms of the school. Each room had an old, black, freestanding coke-burning stove near the front (actually quite close to the teacher's desk!) to provide heat for the winter. One room was for the 'infants' of five to seven years old, the other for junior school age, eight to eleven. We sat, two to a desk, at old-fashioned (and old) wooden desks with bench seats attached. Being old wood, the desk surfaces were quite uneven, making writing sometimes a bit wonky. They all had holes for inkwells but we did not progress beyond pencils in the infant class.

All necessary supplies for the pupils in state schools were provided. Parents were not asked, either, to make donations to the school for extra equipment. And we had no school outings or trips, other than those to church and the nature walks.

At morning break each child had a free third-pint bottle of milk, with a paper straw. The bottle tops were cardboard, with a perforated centre to push out and make a hole for the straw. We used these tops, two placed together, to wind Mum's leftover wool round and through, to make pompoms. To finish off the pompoms, you cut through all the wool between the two bottle tops. Then you tied another piece of wool tightly around the middle, pulled off the bottle tops and fluffed out the pompoms.

With the bottles sitting outside in crates, when the weather was really cold the milk would expand and push the tops up above the rims of the bottles. The teachers brought in the crates to sit by the stoves, where we could watch the tops slowly sink down. I really liked the milk with flakes of ice in it.

I think, boys and girls alike, everyone must have had cold knees in that weather. We young girls all wore short skirts or dresses, although we did wear knee socks in winter. The boys, until they started secondary education, wore short trousers that ended just above the knee, again with knee socks. It's a good thing we all had nice warm winter coats.

As I mentioned earlier I, like Dad, went home for my dinner every day. Many people at that time did so, work and school generally being within easy travelling distance.

Chandler's shop on the Buckingham Road

At dinner time especially my friend Sandra and I would often take a different route home from school. We walked along a footpath straight out on to the Buckingham Road, near Chandler's grocery shop, and crossed over the road at that point. This took us into Holne Chase Spinney (a little wood), where we would play.

There was a pond in the spinney that always seemed to have planks of wood across it, probably put there by the older children, and we would lose all sense of time as we played there.

Dad arrived home from work just after 12.30pm for his dinner, too often to be met by Mum with the news that I hadn't got home yet - again. So off he came on his bike to find me. Mum hated it, knowing I was in trouble. They tried all kinds of punishment until they found one that did work.

One day, Dad left me to get home in my own time. This turned out to be about when I was due to set off back to school. I was sent to my room for the afternoon and had to take a letter in next day, explaining my absence. I didn't know that Dad had already been up to the school. I hated missing the afternoon and felt mortified to have to hand over the letter. That really cured me.

I had a big adventure with Carole whilst we lived at Whiteley Crescent. I knew my way to Cambridge Street as we still used to visit regularly, sometimes on the bus and sometimes walking.

One afternoon I was looking after Carole in her pushchair (no longer the big pram one) while I was out playing in the crescent. I decided to take her for a walk to visit Auntie. So off I set.

We moved back to Bletchley when I was 7½ years old and I should think that this was the previous summer. It was certainly before my 7th birthday.

None of us knows how long the walk took me but fortunately Auntie was at home when I got there. She was horrified to see me on my own with Carole and brought us straight back. Mum was very surprised to see *her,* as she had not yet realised that Carole and I were away from the area. She just thought we were still out playing nearby.

This picture in our garden, with Carole in a doll's pram, must have been taken around that time. (I don't know how the smudge on my face in the picture happened.)

When we lived at Whiteley Crescent Mum would go to visit Auntie one weekday afternoon a week. They went round the shops in Bletchley together. It was a rush to catch the bus as before I started school we always had to have Listen with Mother, a programme for children on the wireless at 1.45pm, on for me to hear. I think the bus must have been at our stop on Newton Road shortly after 2.00pm, the time the programme ended. When I was at school and Carole old enough to listen to it she was just the same.

Mum and Carole in the garden

On Sunday mornings I went to Sunday School at a little Baptist chapel on Newton Road. I think this must have been because Mr Richardson, the father of my friend Carole in Cambridge Street, was the local Baptist minister.

I saw my first television at the house of a friend on Newton Road. It was the story of The Little Mermaid, which affected me quite strongly. I can still shudder at the thought of her feeling as though she was walking on knives when on dry land!

One Saturday every summer the Newton Longville brickworks (like the others belonging to the London Brick Company) held a Sports Day. This was on the sports ground under the railway bridge, where we used to play. I don't remember too much detail about the day but I know it felt very exciting to me. There were a lot of people there, all kinds of races, games, tugs-of-war, various stalls as well as ice cream and refreshments to buy. In my mind, as I think back, Sports Day was always sunny and hot.

Also in the summer, my cousin Brenda came down to us from Beighton for a holiday. Brenda was the daughter of Mum's other sister, my Aunt Annie. Later on in my childhood I reciprocated these visits.

Brenda and I have always got on very well together, despite our age difference of almost nine years. Even now, although we are not in contact very often, when we are it is as if we spoke to one another only yesterday.

All through my childhood we got together with Auntie, Uncle and Ken for everybody's birthdays and for Christmas. Auntie and Uncle also started taking me on holiday to Southsea with them and Ken and I shall tell you more about that later.

The only presents I gave that stick in my mind are my birthday presents to Uncle. I had no trouble at all in choosing these. He loved big Jaffa oranges, which were relatively expensive then. He peeled them and then dipped the segments in sugar to eat.

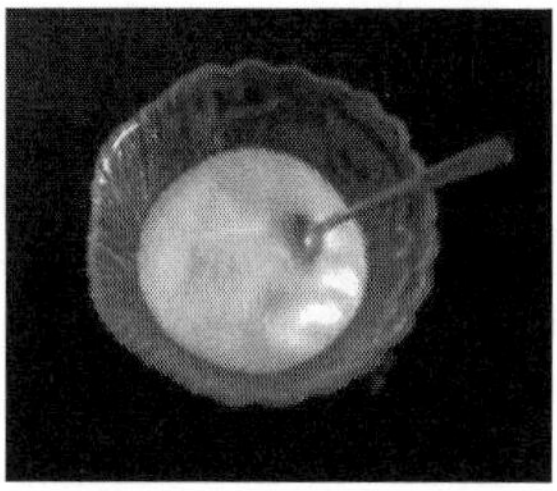

With his sweet tooth Uncle also loved Clarnico creams, a kind of sugar fondant that came in assorted fruit flavours. They were really tooth rottingly sweet. So every birthday I gave Uncle either a Jaffa orange or a small box of the Clarnico sweets, much like those in the picture. I did that for some years, until I was older and had more than just my pocket money to spend.

Thinking of tooth rotting reminds me of something else. Mum would occasionally open a tin of condensed milk - creamy, thick, sticky, *very* sweet, which was a real treat spread on buttered white bread. We loved to eat a spoonful of it neat, too. Now I'm afraid even the idea rather sets my teeth on edge!

# CHRISTMAS PAST

I think it is easier to speak of our Christmases as a whole rather than try to run through them year by year. So here is what they were like for me as a child.

The first intimation of Christmas every year came towards the end of November, when Mum made the Christmas puddings. As she mixed them we all had to have a stir and make a wish. Then the kitchen was filled with steam as they cooked for hours. In my early years they were steamed in the washing boiler. Some were given away to relatives and the rest kept. The pudding eaten on Christmas Day was always one made the year before. It would seem that like a good wine they matured with keeping.

While we lived in the Bletchley area we alternated spending Christmas Day between our house and Cambridge Street. We usually went to Grandma and Grandad's for tea on Boxing Day. Of course there were no buses running over Christmas and Boxing Day, so when we lived in Whiteley Crescent it was quite a walk there and back. Carole rode in her pram and then later a smaller pushchair. One year I had a big red tricycle for Christmas and I rode down on that

We always had a real Christmas tree, over six feet tall. We could hardly wait for the week before Christmas, when Dad brought it home. Nobody put up their tree early, which I think helped to keep Christmas very special. Dad filled an old metal bucket with earth to hold our tree firmly. After it had been positioned in one of the chimneybreast alcoves, Mum wrapped the bucket in red or green crepe paper with a contrasting band around the middle.

In later years the tree stood in a green painted concrete block, rather like a cut off pyramid hollowed in the middle.

I just don't know whether it was anything to do with the heat from the fire, or is more nostalgia, but in my memory I carry a strong sense of the wonderful scent of those trees.

Dad and cigar by the tree. See the fairy on top.
Cards and lights hang round the picture rail

Our first tree decorations were quite basic, some made of plaster. I kept a plaster moon, which must date from 1948. We had a fairy on top of the tree and tinsel around it. The string of lights had pastel coloured plastic shades, with scenes from Walt Disney's Cinderella. They were bell shaped and quite large compared to the usual tree lights nowadays, brighter too and with fewer to a string. The whole effect always seemed quite magical to me.

Crêpe paper streamers criss-crossed from the corners of the ceiling and we had fold-out paper bells and balls dangling, too. We children made paper chains from strips of coloured gummed paper, which were also strung across the ceiling. String was pinned to the picture rail, which all houses had around the living room walls. Our Christmas cards were hung over this string. After we had we lived in Stewartby for a few years, Christmas lights too started to be strung along the picture rail.

Before Christmas, as younger children, we made Christmas presents of calendars for aunts and uncles. We would stick a picture cut from a birthday card or out of a magazine on to a piece of stiff card. Then we would attach a little calendar, bought from the stationer's, to the bottom of this with ribbon or tape.

Sometimes we would sprinkle and glue glitter on the pictures. We were very proud of these calendars. Bath salts were another present we made for aunts. For these we poured soda crystals into a nice jar, added some scent and liquid food colouring, and gave it all a good shake when the lid was on.

Presents weren't placed round the tree or seen at all before Christmas Day. On Christmas morning I woke up to a stocking and pillowcase full of presents at the foot of my bed. The stocking smelled of tangerine and of a lemon shaped, strongly lemon scented soap - lovely! I emptied the stocking there and then but we opened all the bigger presents together.

Father Christmas, dressed in a long red fur-trimmed robe with a fur-trimmed hood, brought all our presents in the night. When I was able to read, and noticed labels on the presents from various relatives, I did ask about this. The answer was that Father Christmas had so many presents to deliver that people sent him money for their nieces and nephews, grandchildren etc, to help him out. It seemed to make sense and anyway, I suspect that we didn't really want to delve too deeply into the mystery.

I don't know how we managed all the food we ate at Christmas. After opening the presents on Christmas morning we had a fried breakfast. We might have a mince pie, jam tart or sausage roll mid-morning with our coffee. Dinner was turkey *and* pork (leftovers eaten cold on Boxing Day) with all the trimmings, followed by Christmas Pudding with rum sauce. I didn't much care for Christmas Pudding but always had a small piece. Mum put old, real silver sixpences in the pudding mix. If you found one in your piece of pudding, Mum swapped it for a modern sixpence.

Mum and Dad set the table for Christmas tea

Then for our tea we would have ham sandwiches together with sausage rolls, trifle, mince pies, jam tarts and the rich Christmas fruit cake! There would be snacks in the evening too. All the cakes, puddings and pastries were homemade by Mum, right down to the mincemeat in the pies and the jam in the tarts.

Auntie Nellie bought what must have been one of the first artificial Christmas trees, to stand on a table in Cambridge Street. It didn't look anything like a real tree. I suppose it stood about two feet tall. The trunk was a green wooden pole. The branches stuck out, rather sparsely, at right angles. They looked like dark green bottlebrushes, each tipped with a red wooden berry.

As Uncle was the one with a car, after we moved to Stewartby he, Auntie and Ken then came to us every year, usually on Christmas Eve and staying over until Boxing Day. I remember that Uncle always brought a great big box of Black Magic dark chocolates with them. He brought cigars for him and Dad too. The smell of the cigar smoke was another real Christmas aroma. Uncle also, of course, provided the meat for Christmas dinner.

On Christmas Eve we all played cards, silly games like Cheat - and how Uncle could! There was a lot of laughter and more food, with sausage rolls, crisps and nuts later in the evening. We children might even be allowed a glass of very weak port and lemon (English lemonade) to drink as well as lemonade on its own.

There were always tins of fancy biscuits as well as boxes of chocolates, tangerines and bowls of nuts that needed shelling with the nutcrackers.

Walnuts were easy to crack open, hazelnuts and almonds less so. But hardest of all and most difficult to open were the Brazil nuts. They were very good to eat though.

We didn't have huge amounts of presents - a big one from Mum and Dad and then presents from grandparents, from Auntie and Uncle and some of the other relations, plus our stockings - but it seemed a lot to us.

None of the presents would have been really expensive, with money less than plentiful. But that did not matter. They were such fun to open and the only real disappointments were when someone would send me a set of handkerchiefs. They may have been embroidered and pretty but they're not what a child is hoping to get at Christmas! Still, that was minor. I really looked forward to Christmases and remember them with great pleasure.

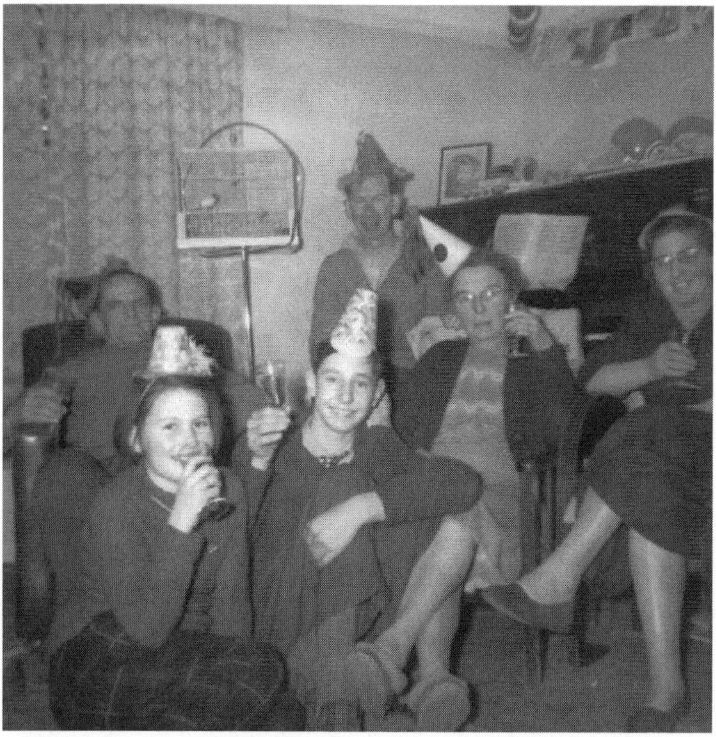

Christmas at Stewartby 1959

Back: Uncle, Dad, Auntie, Mum
Front: Ken and Carole

Time to leave Christmas now and move on again with my story.

# BACK TO BLETCHLEY

Mum really worried about Uncle and Auntie. Uncle suffered with stomach ulcers and was taken into hospital several times for surgery, which was the only real treatment then; although I do remember there were Rennies' indigestion tablets, which Uncle sucked, all about the house in Cambridge Street. I know his diet did not help him. Uncle always said that the fat was the best part of the meat - and ate it with gusto. Nearly every day too, as Mum remembers right from her first visits to Bletchley, they had a supper at about 10 o'clock at night: homemade deep fried chips (thick French fries), cooked in lard of course, with either egg or steak, also fried. This was in addition to the three other meals.

Even though we only lived a few miles apart, Mum felt so far away in the event of emergency. Without telephones there was no way of making quick contact and no way of getting to them fast either, without a car. So Mum and Dad looked for a council house exchange back to Bletchley. One with just two bedrooms (although large ones) came up in Western Road. This road was a continuation of Cambridge Street. In those days, you could walk down Cambridge Street from Bletchley Road until, as you came to a sharp right hand bend in the road a hundred yards or so beyond Auntie and Uncle, it became Western Road, running gradually uphill to Victoria Road in Fenny. The map will show you.

The house was a mid-terrace, number 106, some distance up on the left hand side. Dad went to see it before we moved but Mum did not. She was so disappointed when we moved in, after living in the new house in Whiteley Crescent. This was an older house, double fronted. The front door led into just a small square hall at the foot of the stairs. To either side was a downstairs room, the bedrooms above.

We used the right hand room as a living-dining room, so only needed the one fire. This room ran from front to back of the house, with a window at each end. Along a short passage through a door in the left hand wall to the rear of this room, past the back door, was the kitchen. The bathtub was in the kitchen! It had a tabletop that was lifted and fastened back to the wall for our weekly baths and hair washes. The toilet lay beyond the kitchen. The left hand downstairs room was smaller with the kitchen behind it so had only the one, front window.

There was a very small front flower garden. The back door led on to a paved back yard, with beyond that a footpath that ran along behind all the houses, and beyond that again the back garden proper. This was bigger than the garden at Whiteley Crescent but of course Dad still kept his allotment as well. Behind the garden was an area of overgrown waste ground, a child's delight.

A short track, a little distance down from us, led back to this waste ground. As you entered the area there was a big pond to the left, an old gravel pit with overhanging trees where we would climb and play. We climbed into the trees, right out over the water, but I don't remember anyone ever falling in. Either side of the track were beds of stinging nettles. These were not so good! This area was such a contrast to the Central Gardens.

The Western Road gate to the Gardens was on the opposite side of the road to us, further down towards Cambridge Street. We liked the Central Gardens but they were not a real play area, as the waste ground was. They were instead beautifully manicured with lawns, flowerbeds, bowling greens, a bandstand and shelter and of course the tennis courts.

Central Gardens looking toward Bletchley Road entrance
Tennis courts to right

We moved before the end of the school summer term in 1952. For the last few weeks of school I caught the bus (on my own) from Bletchley Road to the Eight Bells pub on the Buckingham Road. I crossed the road carefully then walked up Church Green Road, in the opposite direction from previously, to the school. I didn't have to cross the main road for the bus home though.

Then came the summer holidays. Although Mum and Dad knew people in the area they had to get to know their new neighbours and we children had to make our friends. Carole Richardson no longer lived in Cambridge Street but I got to know other children. My best friend there was Liz (Elizabeth) James. She was the middle one of three sisters. They lived nearly opposite to us. I loved going to play at their house. Mrs James was very easy going, didn't care what we did, not house proud at all. In fact the house was rather shambolic. But I thought it was wonderful.

Becky the older sister would put makeup on our faces and paint our nails, using her own cosmetics. Best of all though was after their bitch had a litter of puppies. She'd had a big wooden kennel built for her, for whelping and nursing the puppies until they were old enough to go to their new homes. Then she was a housedog again and we had the kennel (which still smelled very much of dog!) to play in. Carole remembers it well too.

The only thing I didn't like there was Mrs James' tea. Whenever she made us a cup it was extremely weak, milky and very sweet. I didn't drink really strong tea at home and had a fair amount of milk, plus two spoonfuls of sugar. So hers must have been quite exceptional.

Many years later I found out that Mum, although she never once said then, hated it when we had been to Liz's house. Apparently we smelled quite strongly and she checked us for nits, too! Mind you, she never found any. I suppose really the family was a bit rough and ready but that wasn't an issue for me. They were so warm and friendly.

Thinking of the dog kennel reminds me that our Bess had her only litter while we were in Western Road. She too had a kennel in the back yard for a while then. She had five puppies but only two were kept, for which homes had been promised. We were just told that the other three had died but I suspect they were put down because nobody wanted them. The two left were lovely, and Carole and I would have liked to keep them, but at about twelve weeks old they went to their new homes.

As well as Liz, I made friends with other children on Western Road. However there had to be one fly in the ointment. There was a boy named Andrew I remember, a little older than me, who was quite a bully and made my life a bit of a misery for a while. Dad encouraged me to fight my own battles and showed me how to make a fist. As with most bullies, Andrew was a coward and once I stood up to him and hit back, he left me alone.

I also spent quite a lot of time at Cambridge Street, where I played with Ken and his two friends, Teddy and Terry. One of our activities was climbing the fruit trees in the garden, sitting in the branches and eating apples in season.

Ken had a little two-man pup tent that would be put up on the lawn behind the house in summer, for us to play in. Sometimes Ken and I had our tea in the tent. I remember squashed banana and strawberry jam sandwiches! I also remember that whatever sandwiches Auntie made, she never buttered the bread right to the edge. I often think of her when buttering my own now.

Sometime we took messages to Uncle at the shop. (Remember, we had no phones.) Each time I walked in I recoiled from the raw meat smell, then quickly became accustomed to it. I loved to watch sausages being made, finding the process quite fascinating.

We played out and about in the area too. Parallel to Cambridge Street between Bletchley Road and St Martin's Street, on the opposite side to number 12, were some streets of terraced houses. Their gardens did not back directly on to one another. Rather, there were wide alleyways between each set of gardens, giving access from the rear. These 'backs' were great places to play. We all still roamed about quite freely.

With various friends I would sometimes go the 'Rec,' the Recreation Ground behind the school on Bletchley Road. This was a very large grassy park area with trees all around. It had an enormous sand pit as well as a play area with a big slide and other equipment to ride on. I really liked playing on the giant Witches Hat swing and the highest slide.

When I was seven years old I started having piano lessons from Auntie. Each lesson lasted for half an hour. I also practiced just about every day on the piano at home, in the spare downstairs room to the left of the front door. It was really cold in winter but very pleasant in the summer. Sometimes on a warm day I found a butterfly in the room. I would catch it and keep it in a covered glass inkwell in an inkstand that stood on the piano. I released it when I had finished my practice. It does seem a bit odd and I don't really remember why I did it.

I learned to ride a bicycle around this time. Mum and Dad bought me a little second-hand one and Dad taught me to ride. My first solo ventures (no training wheels), with Dad letting go of the saddle, were along the track to the waste ground. I didn't think this was such a good idea when I fell off my bike into the stinging nettles. Bare legs and arms didn't much like that!

Dock grew amongst the nettles and dock leaves rubbed on nettle stings ease the pain and the rash. One summer Liz and I decided to make a lotion for nettle rash. We pounded dock leaves and left them to soak in old jam jars full of water, before removing them to leave just the liquid. I think it did work but of course it did not keep and we soon abandoned that good idea. We made rose water from rose petals too, I'm afraid with the same result.

Apart from climbing and exploring, our outdoor games included various let's pretend ones, such as Cowboys and Indians, and those that were seasonal. Somehow you all just found that you were playing marbles, jacks, hopscotch or skipping, for example. The game of conkers was of course dictated by the coming of autumn and the ripening of the horse chestnuts.

We played cat's cradle, string or wool round our fingers, indoors and out. We would also get two empty tin cans, as I recall usually cocoa ones for some reason. With a hole punched in the bottom of each by Dad, we threaded a long piece of string through, knotting each end on the inside of the tins. When we stretched the string taut, we could speak through the tins and hear one another, our version of a telephone or walkie-talkie.

Our indoor activities included board games, such as Ludo, and jigsaw puzzles. Dad hammered little nails into empty wooden cotton reels for us to do French knitting, using oddments of Mum's knitting wool. Lengths of French knitting were coiled round and sewn together to make tablemats, sometimes as gifts for relatives. We also made plaster of Paris figures in red rubber moulds and painted them. When I was a bit older, at Stewartby, I put together kits of plastic figures and painted those too - a knight in armour, a Red Indian squaw and a chief with a long feather headdress are the ones that I especially remember.

On summer evenings I would read in bed. My bed was near the front window and I'd lean through the curtains, resting my book and my elbows on the windowsill to read. Carole was already asleep in her bed and I was supposed to be going to sleep of course, once I went upstairs. But even back then I loved to read. I would only stop when, having lifted my tired eyes from the page, I couldn’t make out the print when I lowered them again. Then I felt quite cross but did lie down to go to sleep.

A great annual summer treat was the arrival of the funfair, which was set up on the cattle market. I think I went every year from when we moved to Western Road until I was sixteen years old. For a young child it was terribly exciting with the rides, the stalls and sideshows, the lights, the noise and the crowds.

Dad often won a coconut at the coconut shy. When we got it home he made holes through the ‘eyes’ and poured out the coconut milk, which we drank. Dad then split the shell open with a hammer and we ate the flesh over several days.

Surprisingly, goldfish won at the fair (by hooking a bobbing duck) and carried triumphantly home in a plastic bag of water, survived. For some time we had two that lived in a glass barrel holding about a gallon of water. I don’t know where Dad found that but it even had a cork bung near the bottom. The goldfish seemed fine in there with strands of weed and a daily sprinkle of fish food.

A bonus for me in the summer was that I did not have bronchitis. When I did, in the winter, the trusty Aladdin stove came out again. It is here that I most remember it.

Even before we moved to Western Road Mum, Carole and I would go with Auntie and Ken to Bow Brickhill woods for picnics in the summer. We took the train from Fenny station.

Looking back, I don't know why it was always Fenny and never Bletchley station. Perhaps it was simply that it was cheaper, being only one stop away from Bow Brickhill where Bletchley was two.

Old Picture of Fenny Stratford Station

To the right is the footpath up to Fenny High Street, the Watling Street (old A5). In the distance are Brickhill Woods.

If you can make them out, the lighter patches are houses straggling up the hill, with the church tower above them.

We got off the train at Bow Brickhill Halt. It was called a Halt because there was no proper raised platform, just wooden boards lifted slightly above the ground. The old steam trains let down steam operated steps from the guard's van for the passengers to board. Prams, pushchairs, bicycles etc, had to be lifted up and down.

The steam hissed and steps rattled as they came down and then went back up again. It was quite a performance. You certainly didn't bother trying to speak during the operation.

Bow Brickhill Halt

From the Halt we had what seemed like a very long walk. It felt quite a way just into Bow Brickhill itself and the woods lay up the road beyond the main village.

Eventually the road forked, the right hand road becoming very narrow and running steeply uphill to the woods. Carole could ride in the pushchair, lucky thing!

Ken and I of course trudged up the hill with Mum and Auntie. We were very glad when we came into the coolness of the woods. The sunlight only reached down into the 'rides' and clearings.

The woods themselves had a lovely piney smell and seemed almost magical to us in their green dimness. Allowed to explore with no restrictions Ken and I always enjoyed our visits, even with the long walks at either end.

Looking down from the top of the road

We took sandwiches and perhaps biscuits, cakes or fruit, together with diluted orange squash and a thermos flask of tea. The woods were great fun, some areas quite dark and exciting.

Ken and I found one tree we called a wishing well tree. It had a hollow in the bark where rainwater gathered. We always went to find that each time we picnicked. There was also a little wooden house, seeming to us to be deep into the woods, reminiscent of the witch's house in Hansel and Gretel. I suppose it was the woodsman's cottage.

I don't know how often we had these picnics but in my memory the weather was always sunny and hot for them, lovely but making the walk very tiring. I am sure that we were worn out by the time we reached home. But that didn't spoil the enjoyment and I think Mum and Auntie did really well to take us so often.

Looking along a ride, into a clearing at the far end

Mum was happy to be living in Bletchley again, whatever she felt about the house in Western Road. She was close by Auntie and Uncle and the shops were all within easy walking distance.

One evening a week Dad and Uncle would baby sit their respective children while Mum and Auntie went to the cinema, the 'pictures' as it was known colloquially.

In those days every town would have at least one cinema. There were two in Bletchley. The Studio on Bletchley Road, not far from Cambridge Street, was the more upmarket of the two. The County was on Fenny Stratford High Street, a stretch of the Roman Watling Street - the old A5 trunk road.

View toward town from the school end of Bletchley Road. The Studio cinema is the big white building further back on the right, with the Central Gardens entrance and Cambridge Street lying beyond.

The County was where I saw my first film. I'm not sure what age I was but I must have been quite young. The film was the cartoon version of Alice in Wonderland. Sadly for both Mum and me, when the Cheshire cat disappeared and all that was left was a big toothy grin I was just so scared by it that poor Mum had to take me out. It was a bit of disaster really.

The County cinema also put on a Saturday morning matinée for the children. Saturday morning pictures, as we called it, cost 6d. It was good value for money. First there was a cartoon. Then we had a serial, either a cowboy or else something like Flash Gordon. They were wonderful. Each week we were left with a nail biting cliff-hanger, not seeing how the hero could possibly escape. The following week, as the serial continued, you discovered that he had not really been in such dire straits after all!

An interval followed the serial. Then we had a full-length feature film. Sometimes the cinema would become very noisy with excited, rowdy children. The projectionist would stop the film, the lights would go up and the manager would come to the front. He'd threaten us with stopping the whole film show unless we quieted down and behaved. That usually sorted it for any particular Saturday.

Uncle or Auntie would take Fritz for walks to the old gravel pits on the other side of the Watling Street. Sometimes I, or Ken and I, would go with them. We turned right out of the house toward Western Road. But instead of continuing round the curve in the road, we crossed to go straight down North Street and then on to a cycle track/footpath alongside the railway embankment.

All along the path at the foot of the embankment was a 3-strand wire fence. When you banged the wire Fritz, let off his lead, raced up and down barking and looking for intruders coming through. Nobody ever did of course but we all enjoyed it.

Fritz's collar was made from heavy metal chain links and just slipped over his head like a necklace. His lead was plaited leather. (I sometimes played at being a queen using Fritz's collar, wearing it rather precariously on my head as a crown.)

We passed under the railway bridge and crossed the Watling Street to get to an expanse of open ground that was almost like a big park, where there were several large old gravel pits that had become filled with water and so were now lakes. Fritz ran around enjoying himself, sometimes going for a swim. He would also hunt for moles. Auntie hated it when he caught one. He would need a thorough de-fleaing when he got home!

As you can see, I also went to the gravel pits when I was very much younger but that was with Auntie or Auntie and Mum. Here I am sitting with Auntie on a pile of logs, with a gravel pit and trees behind.

In springtime, from my earliest years living at Cambridge Street, Uncle sometimes brought back moorhens' eggs for breakfast omelettes from his walks with Fritz to the gravel pits. He always left some eggs in each nest. Even so, you couldn't do it in this day and age. But back then it didn't seem to make any difference to the moorhen numbers. And the omelettes were very tasty!

As well as the gravel pits, there was another lake on the Buckingham Road side of the station. We went along the Water Eaton Road, under a small railway bridge to where a little unmade track led off to the left alongside the railway embankment. To the right of the track was some wild, rough ground. In that was the lake, another disused gravel pit I think but for some reason called the New Found Out. Bulrushes grew thickly along the edges and when they were in season we would go to pick them. Mum and Auntie grouped them, a rich brown colour and velvety smooth, in tall vases. Aside from the bulrushes it was just a really good area to play.

Once each year I had my piano exam. The examiner from the Victoria College of Music came to Auntie's house on a Saturday. He examined her pupils and those of at least one other teacher in Bletchley who belonged to the Victoria College of Music. The exam consisted of an oral theory section as well as a practical.

This was quite an exciting time for me. The night before the exam I had my hair washed. Then Mum would put a few rows of the old metal curlers along the bottom of it and a metal 'butterfly' in the top. The next morning I had fluffy curls and a big wave in my hair. Wearing my best dress, I felt very smart and confident. Auntie did the same for me for another year or two after we moved from Bletchley to Stewartby. I always did quite well in the exams, too.

In the autumn we looked forward to Bonfire Night (Guy Fawkes' Day) on 5$^{th}$ November. We never really thought much about poor old Guy Fawkes. We did know the broad history: that he had been involved in a plot to blow up the Houses of Parliament a long time ago. Because that was treason, he was executed. And so we continued to burn a guy, to celebrate the foiling of the Gunpowder Plot.

Well before the day itself children made so-called guys, old clothes that were usually stuffed with newspaper or rags, with a mask for the face. Some, mostly boys, then sat them in carts. These they pushed along to people's houses or walked round the streets with, calling out, "Penny for the guy!" Any money they collected would go toward buying their fireworks. They often did quite well with their money raising if the guy looked good.

There were no organised fireworks displays when I was young, at least not locally. Auntie and Uncle would buy fireworks and so would Mum and Dad. Uncle made a bonfire of his collected garden rubbish, probably ours as well, and various other materials. We all gathered at Cambridge Street and when it was dark Uncle lit the bonfire at the bottom of the garden, the guy perched on top to burn away. We waved sparklers about and had a great display of the other fireworks, set off by Dad and Uncle.

Rockets were stuck in milk bottles to be set off and Catherine Wheels pinned to the door of the shed. Other, static fireworks such as Golden Rain, were let off on the garden path, well away from us. We did have a few Penny Bangers, which were not very strong and were thrown as far as we could manage, to go off with their loud noise. We also had Jumping Jacks that you don't see now. You lit the fuse, dropped the firework on the ground and it jumped about randomly, with a 'crack' at every jump. We had to really watch where they went and sometimes jump out of the way ourselves but thought them great fun.

We ate our tea before it was time for the fireworks. But there were then extra goodies to enjoy. Mum made Parkin, a kind of sticky gingerbread and Bonfire Toffee, a black treacle (molasses) toffee that was very brittle but as it melted in your mouth, just stuck everywhere. We loved them both! The smell of wood smoke now can readily transport me back to all those memories.

From autumn and all through the winter we children were dosed every morning with a spoonful of malt and cod liver oil, to ward off colds. This was a thick, sticky mixture. Fortunately the malt, which had quite a pleasant taste, overshadowed the cod liver oil. I don't know how much it helped with the colds though.

This picture is looking from Bletchley Road toward the station. The big bridge (the flyover) was built in my mid teens, to replace the ordinary little railway bridge that previously spanned the road. However that is the only real change at this time from probably before I was born.

The Park Hotel is the farthest building back on the left, with Uncle's Co-op butcher's shop next to it. Then, moving toward to front of the picture, come a pub and the workingmen's club before getting to the fish and chip shop near the end of that row. The tin shops are back right. The big Co-op is out of the picture, behind where the photographer was standing, also on the right.

It all looks very quiet. Today there is no longer a through road leading towards Buckingham. Instead a dual carriageway cuts through Bletchley, separating Cambridge Street and Western Road, before merging with the Buckingham Road just this side of the station. Houses were demolished to make way for it, there is no Central Gardens now and it is sad to see the town despoiled for the sake of moving traffic more readily.

# EARLY HOLIDAY MEMORIES

As I mentioned previously, Auntie and Uncle took me with them on holiday in the summer. We would go to stay for a week in a small boarding house at Southsea.

Ken heads for the beach

With no self-catering, boarding houses were where most families would stay for their holiday. They were fairly cheap and were often just ordinary large houses in which bedrooms would be let to holidaymakers in the summer.

All the booking and arrangements would usually be made by post, although sometimes by now over the telephone.

Boarding house landladies were a standing joke, depicted as strict dragons. There were rules to be observed. After breakfast, where there would be little choice of food, you would have to leave the boarding house for the day by a set time. That would certainly be no later than 10.00am. Then no matter the weather, you were often not allowed to return until early evening. You had an evening meal at the boarding house, with usually two choices on the menu: take it or leave it!

Our landlady at Southsea though was a kindly, elderly widow, whom we children knew as Auntie May. We even exchanged cards at Christmas for many years.

Uncle drove us down to Southsea. It was a long drive and we always stopped for a picnic on the way. There were no motorways and no service areas to stop at for a drink or a meal. When we knew we were getting close to the coast, Ken and I would vie to be the first to catch a glimpse of the sea.

I had an accident once when we stopped for our picnic on the way there. I went into a more wooded area to answer a call of nature, as there were no public toilets to stop at anywhere along the road. When I came back to the car Auntie exclaimed and I looked down. The inside of my left ankle, just over the anklebone, was bleeding heavily. I had cut it to the bone on broken glass, without even knowing. The cut was doctored up and on we went.

That year I was not allowed to walk across the beach. Uncle carried me into the sea and back to our blanket. Most of the beach at Southsea was pebbled but there was enough sand to get in an open wound. Although I had a sticking plaster (Band-Aid) on the cut, it came off each time I went paddling. I think the seawater must have helped the cut to heal but I still have the scar.

Another year my back got dreadfully sunburned. I remember lying prone on my bed in the boarding house in real pain. Auntie put cloths soaked in cold tea on my back. I don't know how healing that was but it was very soothing.

In the evenings all the fancy lights came on. They were strung over the promenade (prom), between lampposts, and sparkled around and amongst the plants and water features in the gardens that ran alongside the prom. All shone and twinkled, brightly coloured in the dark. Some made patterns and pictures, many of these even appearing to move, seeming quite magical.

One quirky memory I have is of walking along the prom in the later evening (well it felt late to me!) sucking Horlicks tablets. I presume they were just pressed from the powder with which the drink is made. They are an abiding memory of Southsea.

1954 with holiday friends: Ken far left, me far right
Uncle smiling on at the rear

I also remember going to Portsmouth to see Nelson's flagship, the Victory. We went all round it and I was very impressed. My strongest memory though is of the plaque on the deck that commemorated where Nelson fell, fatally wounded. We knew it was serious that Nelson had been killed at the Battle of Trafalgar but, being children, Ken and I also thought it funny that this raised plaque might make other people trip and fall. So we ourselves pretended to trip and it was, "Jean fell here" and, "Ken fell here," with much laughter. I know, very juvenile - but then, we were!

With Mum, Dad and Carole, I went on holiday to stay with relatives, most often to Aunt Annie and her husband Uncle

Arthur. They had two children, my cousin Brenda whom I have mentioned before and Brian, a few years younger than Brenda.

They still lived in Beighton, where Mum grew up. My Uncle Fred, Mum's older brother, lived there too with his wife Auntie Mary and their two sons, Charles and John. Brenda lives there to this day with her husband Keith.

Brian and Brenda about 1951

In Swallownest, one of the nearby villages and within walking distance, lived my Mum's other brother Uncle Tom, with his wife Auntie Edna and their son Michael. Uncle Tom owned a shop in which he sold hardware and home decorating supplies.

Just getting to Beighton was an adventure. First we took the train from Bletchley (later from Stewartby) to Bedford. When Carole was very young her pram went on the train too. At Bedford we came into the little St John's station, on the south side of the town. There was no through line then to the main station, Midland Road, on the north side. With a connection to catch Dad would dash across Bedford through little side streets that are now non-existent, pushing Carole in her pram. Mum and I, with the luggage, rode across in a taxi. That part of the journey was a bit easier when Carole no longer needed either pram or pushchair.

Even this train though did not go directly to Sheffield, the nearest main station to Beighton, and we had to change again en route. That could be a bit fraught. The journey took much longer then than now and there were no refreshments sold on the train. Mum packed up food and drinks to keep us going. Toward the end of the journey we were all looking out of the window to catch sight of the crooked spire of the church in Chesterfield.

Then we knew we were nearly there and it would just be a case of getting to Beighton from Sheffield station. I knew when we were getting close too, when I could smell the collieries (coalmines), which seemed to be everywhere around.

It is a smell I have savoured ever since. It did mean though that all the buildings had a blackened look to them.

Brookhouse Colliery, just outside Beighton

From Sheffield, when Carole was still in her pram, we would take yet another train to the little station at the bottom end of Beighton.

In later years we took a bus from the bus station (which was next to the Sheffield train station) to the top of the town. And I do mean top and bottom! Beighton was built on a real hill.

Aunt Annie and Uncle Arthur lived at the top end of Manvers Road, with some shops nearby and a few others round the town. A walk down Manvers Road led to the bottom end of the High Street where the main shops and cinema were. From there the High Street ran to the right, uphill.

Bottom end of Beighton High Street.

I loved staying there. Although like Uncle Fred my Uncle Arthur was a coal miner, he owned a newsagent's shop as well.

He and Aunt Annie lived in a three bedroom detached house. The shop was the front room, with a separate outside door to the main house. At the back of the shop was a door into the living room. This door had a curtain across it. So they could leave the door between their living area and shop open to hear when the shop doorbell rang as a customer came in, yet still be private.

The smell of newsprint is another that brings back happy memories. Imagine how wonderful, to be able to read a copy of all the comics (comic books) as they came in! The shop sold sweets too, more joy.

It always seemed to be Mum's relatives we stayed with, rather than Dad's. But then most of his family did live locally to us, other than his brother Henry who lived in Felixstowe and Don on the Isle of Wight.

A later picture of the Wallis siblings and spouses
Back: Fred, Arthur, Tom, Dad
Front: Nellie, Annie, Mum, Edna, Mary

I do remember having a holiday at Anstye Cross, a village near Haywards Heath in Sussex. Dad had been billeted with Uncle Eddie and Auntie Jo (courtesy titles as they were not really relatives), when he was in the army. Dad and Mum had been down there to stay together too, after their marriage. Uncle Eddie and Auntie Jo had one son, somewhat older than me, named David.

Uncle Eddie was the village policeman. He never made higher rank than Constable but he did not want to leave the job he loved. The family lived in a police house and there was a cell adjacent to this. On the rare occasions when a prisoner was briefly kept there Auntie Jo cooked for him. (I don't think they ever had a woman in the cell.) She always cooked the same good meal as she did for her own family saying, "He's some mother's son."

A model wireless that was a money box stood in the bedroom Carole and I shared in the house there. Somehow David and I managed to convince Carole, who was very young, that it was a real wireless. We made static noises and did the voices as we 'switched it on.' Naturally, we thought that a great joke.

Mum and Dad at Anstye Cross with young David

Uncle Eddie and Auntie Jo came to stay with us too and I remember David coming to Western Road. Relatives from Beighton came down sometimes, to stay with us at Stewartby after we moved there, and with Auntie and Uncle at Bletchley.

With David outside the front door at Western Road, as Mum peeps out

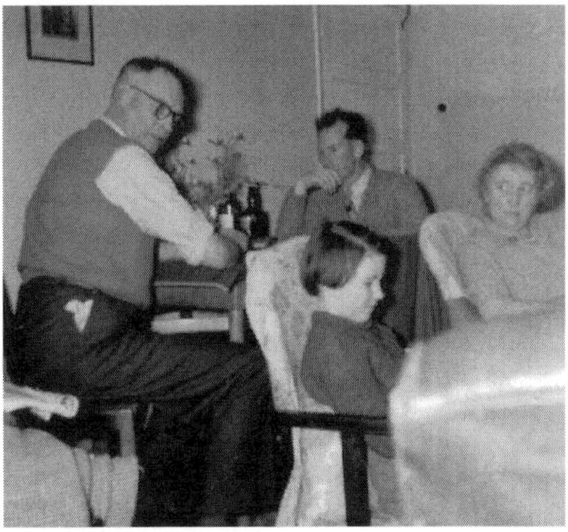

Uncle Eddie and Dad, with Auntie Jo and Carole, Stewartby

Uncle Arthur and
Aunt Annie

Uncle Fred and
Auntie Mary

# Return to Life in Western Road

So there was summer and there were holidays. Then there was school. Bletchley Road School was a very different kettle of fish to the Church Green Road one. To me, after a little school with just two classrooms, it seemed huge. It covered right from infant all the way through the senior years. I didn't much care for it at all. And I was really put off maths. I didn't like the teacher and I just simply did not understand what he was trying to teach us.

Carole started school and had one term in the infant class while we lived in Western Road. The infant school here was separated from the junior school playground by a tall, metal-barred fence. Every playtime Carole would be at the fence looking for me. She hated the school. But more than anything she hated the infant school toilets. They were in an outbuilding and apparently they were filthy and smelly. Carole absolutely refused to use them. It was a good thing we went home at dinnertime.

We always walked to school up Western Road, away from Cambridge Street. We turned right on to Victoria Road, which was technically in Fenny Stratford. That sloped down to the far end of Bletchley Road, coming out some way to the left of, and on the opposite side of the road to, the school.

There was a sweet shop on Victoria Road and we would sometimes be given a penny to spend there after sweet rationing ended in February 1953. The shop sold all sorts of little sweets that were four for a penny so this was like a treasure house, the variety and the first time we could buy our own. How to choose? It was just so difficult but so enjoyable, too.

Bletchley Road School is on the right. The white building at the far end standing between Victoria Road and Vicarage Road, facing Bletchley Road, housed the council offices.

Just off Victoria Road was a clinic housed in what seemed to me like a big shed. I had been diagnosed as having flat feet and had to go to this clinic once a week for exercises. The exercises were all right but not the scratchy coconut matting used to cover the floor. I still remember the feel. I had to balance and walk on the outsides of my feet. Then, I had to draw my toes back without bending them, keeping them straight. It took me ages to master that - but I can still do it now. I also had to wear 'sensible' shoes and closed sandals, with the soles built up in a certain way.

I think it was the school nurse who discovered my flat feet. We went to the clinic next to the school to be checked but at most schools the school nurse came round regularly, I'm not sure if it was twice or three times a year. She checked height and weight, basic hearing and eyesight, and feet, at least once a year - and hair for nits whenever she saw you. Fortunately nits were something that neither Carole nor I ever had as children.

All pupils at state schools also had free treatment from a school dentist. In Bletchley the school used a dental surgery in the clinic. A group of us would troop down and wait our turn to be examined. It was all a bit crude. They didn't bother filling first teeth and extractions were done at speed under a general anaesthetic.

Aylesbury Street

Baptist Church on the near right, just out of this picture

We nearly always went to Sunday School both morning and afternoon on a Sunday. We walked down to the Spurgeon Memorial Baptist Church on Aylesbury Street in Fenny (Mr Richardson's main church). We generally enjoyed it because the teachers made it fun.

We had cards that were always ink stamped with a star for attendance and there were prizes every year, both for little exams we took and for the attendance. Over this time I won some storybooks, now long gone, and a small Bible that I still have on my bookshelf.

Dad and Uncle were keen anglers and both before and after the war went out fishing most Sundays in the season. I remember that best from when we moved back again to Bletchley.

Dad usually cycled, with his fishing basket and rod over his shoulder. The nearby river and Grand Union Canal were popular places to fish. But sometimes he went farther afield, perhaps on a bus with the brick company fishing team. This picture shows him on the left in front of the bus on one of these trips. He entered many competitions and won a number of trophies over the years.

Even though I never heard Mum complain I know that she really hated Dad being away fishing for the whole day on Sunday.

Mum, Carole and I still had our own dinner at mid-day. Dad's was plated up and covered with a saucepan lid. When he came home Mum sat the plate, covered with the lid, on top of a saucepan of simmering water to heat up his dinner. The food never tasted quite as good though as when it was fresh and gravy always seemed to dry up a bit, despite the lid being over the food. I remember it well from when I had my own dinners served up like that at tea-time in later years.

If there was no competition then Dad would just go out fishing for the morning, often with Uncle as you see them in the picture.

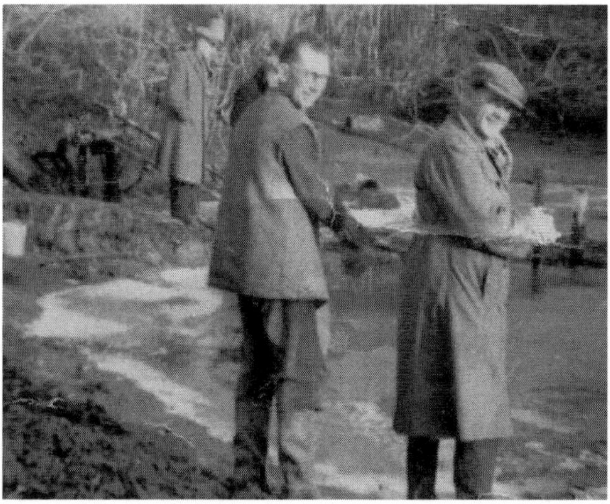

Dad and Uncle fishing, with Dad in his old leather army jerkin

Some Sundays out of fishing season (or when there was no competition) we all went for an afternoon ride in Uncle's car. In the spring we went primrosing and bluebelling. You are not allowed to do that now, as they are both protected flowers. At that time there never seemed to be any shortage from year to year.

Mum would pack up some bunches of primroses in moist moss and send them off to relatives as a treat. We always picked the bluebells very carefully, breaking off the stems rather than pulling them right out of the ground, which we were told would kill the plant. We gathered armfuls.

Mothering Sunday came in the spring too, halfway through Lent. Mother's Day, Father's Day and all the other 'Days' just did not exist for us. Mothering Sunday was an old tradition. Children used to leave school at a very young age and often worked and lived away from home. They were given this one day off between Christmas and Easter to visit their families and on the way picked wild flowers to take as gifts for their mothers. We used to do the same and later buy bunches of daffodils or little pot plants. It was not a very commercial event at all when I was a young child.

Palm Sunday, just before Easter, we picked pussy willow. It was a long time before I realised that real palm was something completely different.

On Maundy Thursday Mum made her Hot Cross Buns in the big mixing bowl she also used for Christmas Puddings. We children of course joined in although I suppose we were really more hindrance than help. But Mum was very good humoured about it and we all enjoyed a bun fresh from the oven, although they were really made for eating the next day. She made some for Auntie, Uncle and Ken and I think perhaps too for Grandma and Grandad.

After Mum's homemade Hot Cross Buns heated up for breakfast on Good Friday, we looked forward to our eggs on Easter Sunday. These were fairly simple but the scent and taste of Easter egg chocolate was always somehow better than any other.

On Monday evenings I went to Girls' Life Brigade Cadets at the church in Fenny. That was fun as well. In the winter it would be quite dark when we children walked home and I often had to walk part of the way on my own. But, in a small town especially, parents did not worry then about such things as they do now. I never did have any problems and just never thought that I had anything to fear. I've also always quite liked dark nights with the street lights on and glimpses into lighted rooms, even more so at Christmas with the festive lights and Christmas trees in windows.

While we were living at Western Road the Duke of Edinburgh came to open a new playing field on the Simpson road. There were a lot of local children ready to greet him and cheer when he came. I stood and waited with the Cadets. The trouble was, a boil had just come up on the back of one of my knees! The Duke was two hours late getting to us and I was in agony by the time the occasion was over. I had to walk home - no mobiles to use to ask for help and no phone at home anyway.

When I got to Victoria Road I was able to stop for a rest. Dad's sister Auntie Margaret was working in the Co-op there at the time and found a chair for me to sit on. I eventually managed to get home and when Dad came in from work he took me on the crossbar of his bike down to the evening surgery. The doctor lanced the boil. That day is a really painful memory, as you might imagine.

I recall another painful experience when Auntie was at our house one evening. I had said my goodnights and left the living room to go upstairs. As I started to climb the stairs I inadvertently had my hand in the edge of the doorjamb. Auntie closed the door. It trapped my fingers and I screamed! Auntie was so taken aback she actually pushed a bit harder on the door before reopening it. So it was quite a while later before I finally got to bed that night.

Another bad memory, in a different way, is of a traffic accident on Western Road. As I have said, there was actually very little traffic on the roads then and so traffic accidents were rare, even more so in a residential area. However Western Road was a nice long stretch and a young motorcyclist decided to speed down it one day. Unfortunately, he hit a little girl. I don't know if she ran into the road or if she was already there as he came around the slight bend. However it happened, he did hit her and she was badly injured. He almost scalped her. An ambulance came to take her to hospital. All the emergency vehicles then had bells, not sirens. We did not see or hear many but the bells made a fast, very loud, high-pitched clanging sound. Seeing an ambulance was bad luck if you didn't keep touching your collar until you saw a dog!

To return to my story, the little girl was in hospital for a long time and there were real fears for her life at first but thank goodness she did eventually recover. However even after leaving hospital she had bandages round her head for what seemed like ages. Then afterwards it took a long time for her hair to grow back.

On a happier note, one really big national event during our time at Western Road was the Coronation of Queen Elizabeth II, on the 2nd June 1953. Auntie and Uncle bought their first television in time for that. We did watch the Coronation ceremony itself on the little black and white screen. It was quite an occasion.

Here we are: me, Carole and Ken

There was a fancy dress contest in the town. Mum made the costumes from crêpe paper for Ken, Carole and me. I was 'Red, White and Blue' (with a crown). Carole was 'Hip, Hip, Hurray!' and Ken was 'Royal Herald.' I felt very miffed that Ken went on to actually win the competition in an outfit made by *my* mother.

We all shivered in our costumes, as the day was very cold for June - and it rained too. But it was still a truly special day for us to remember. All the children were given souvenir Coronation mugs and plates.

See my crown!

There were town as well as individual celebrations, with a party for the children in one of the local church halls. We had a celebratory tea with sandwiches, jelly and cake. Flags and bunting were to be seen everywhere.

One of my birthday presents that year was a big, round Coronation jigsaw puzzle. In the middle was a picture of the Coronation itself. Around the edges were scenes from the Queen's life. Although difficult it was a really good one to do.

Television then was nearly all live, which could make things quite interesting at times. There were often technical faults and then we would have clips of film until the problem was resolved. These clips were quite boring really. The one I remember best is the Potter's Wheel. It was just somebody making a clay pot to a musical accompaniment. You only saw the wheel, pot and hands. It could go on for some minutes, which felt like a very long time.

Horizontal and vertical hold would often 'go' on the television. The picture would roll up the screen or flicker diagonally. This meant twiddling knobs at the side of the television to bring back a steady, undistorted picture. It was all a far cry from today. Still, it did not affect us directly then, as we did not have a television in our house. We did not have a record player either (never mind tapes, CDs or PS3s), just the wireless for a few more years yet.

There was another exciting event before we left Western Road. 30$^{th}$ June 1954 saw a total eclipse of the sun. In England, although it was not quite total here, it was still a big event and very impressive. We were at school that day and all of us children were taken outside to see it. We were given pieces of smoked glass to look through, to protect our eyes. Given the dire warnings nowadays it's a wonder we are not all blind!

I think it was in this term too that I had my TB patch test. The nurse scratched a small area of skin on my upper back and placed several drops of serum there. This area was covered with a sticking plaster and I was not allowed to get my back wet for the few days that it took to get a result.

My skin itched a bit but I don't know if that was from the serum or the plaster. Whatever the reason, my test result was positive. As I did not actually have the disease this meant that I must have been in contact with TB and made antibodies, so I did not have to have the vaccination. As I expect you can guess, that pleased me more than a little.

It may have been at around this time that I really upset Mum. I asked who was the oldest, Auntie or her? As soon as I had spoken I realized that it was a mistake. Mum, in a hurt voice, asked, "Do I *look* older than Auntie?" I knew the right answer there wasn't, "Yes!" so I quickly replied, “No, no, I just didn’t know.” I mean, to me as a child they were simply two grownups, otherwise ageless.

Auntie and Mum in spring 1945, with Joan, Marj and me

# ROUND AND ABOUT

We often walked to Brooklands Road to visit Grandma and Grandad. And sometimes I walked round there on my own. Dad's youngest brother Martin, known to us as Uncle Mate, still lived with them too. In fact he lived at home for many more years, until he married later in life. As he worked, being an insurance agent for the Co-op, he was not there in the daytime during the week so we saw less of him than of our grandparents. When we did see him, he sometimes played his piano-accordion for us.

Grandad and Grandma

The three bedroom terraced house on Brooklands Road was similar to the house in Lincoln where I live now. Grandma and Grandad rented the house and I think they had lived in it right from new. A bathroom with a toilet had been added behind the small kitchen though, rather than upstairs as in my own home.

Their front room was the parlour, only used for special visitors. All their living, even when rearing eight children, was done as usual at the back, in what was intended to be used as the dining room. Like us at Western Road, they had a little paved yard at the rear and then the path running along behind all the houses. Beyond the path was a long garden with Grandad's greenhouse.

Grandad and his greenhouse

Grandad grew vegetables and fruit in the garden, as well as having his allotment. He was also known for his very large, shaggy headed chrysanthemums. He had given Mum a great big bunch of them when I was born.

Every year after that he gave her a big bunch on her and Dad's wedding anniversary. Grandad also grew beautiful Hellebores (Christmas Roses). Mum and Dad took a root of that to Stewartby and I in turn brought one to Lincoln.

At the far end of the Brooklands Road garden was a hen house with a run. Nesting boxes were built into the back wall of the hen house. Grandad let us children feel inside to see if we could find any freshly laid eggs. It was wonderful when we did. We were often given one to take home, when we'd have a very fresh boiled egg for tea. Sometimes however, disappointingly, all we felt was the china egg that was put there to encourage the hens to lay.

When a hen was past laying it was killed for food. It would be too old and tough to roast or fry so would be boiled instead. Even this stewed chicken wasn't on the menu very often, as Grandad didn't have that many and they kept laying for quite some time.

Chickens were rather a luxury food in fact. There was no battery farming or any kind of intensive rearing so they were quite expensive, only eaten on special occasions other than when they had finished laying. Roast chicken was a real treat. With hens laying on their natural cycle eggs were scarce in winter, so they were sometimes preserved in isinglass.

I also remember eating tongue, which I quite liked, as a cold meat (cold cuts). I had never thought of where it came from or why it had that name anymore than I thought it of, for example, ham. But then one day I happened to see a whole, unskinned ox tongue being cooked in a big saucepan by Auntie. I am afraid that put me off eating it for good!

Auntie's cooked cabbage was rather off-putting too. She boiled it for ages with a pinch of bicarbonate of soda to keep it green, until it was virtually mush. Even though Mum cooked all our vegetables until soft, this went way beyond everything else. Then of course the kitchen smelled of it for hours afterwards.

Auntie Margaret, Uncle Cyril and their son Bernard moved around in the Bletchley area. But for a few years they lived next door to Grandma and Grandad. So then we would visit them too.

Once, Uncle Cyril was planning to paint outside. Poor Carole, we played another joke on her. Remember, she was not more than five years old. Bernard and I, with Uncle Cyril's connivance, persuaded her that he was using striped paint! In so many words we said that the paint in the pot was in multi-coloured vertical stripes. When you dipped a brush in the paint it would come out stripy. I don't know how we could sound so convincing and still keep straight faces.

As you know, Auntie Margaret worked for a while in the Co-op grocery shop on Victoria Road in Fenny Stratford. I can see it now if I close my eyes and bring it to mind.

But it wasn't the Co-op that I went to on a Saturday morning, before the children's matinée at the County Cinema. Mum sent me to a little bakery to buy crusty white bed rolls. I don't know why we only had them on a Saturday. I suppose they were just a treat, as they would cost more than cutting slices from a loaf for bread and butter or sandwiches.

Those rolls were lovely. As you bit into them the thin, crispy crust shattered, with shards that you could pick up with a moistened finger after eating the roll. The interior was soft, light and fluffy.

Uncle Bob and Auntie Rose lived in Bletchley too, with my cousins Pauline and Janet. They lived on a side road close to the market and we went to visit them occasionally. Uncle Bob was a manager at the Co-op and he and Auntie Rose owned their house, which I remember as also having a lovely big garden.

Water Eaton was another village that had been encroached on by Bletchley. It was a short walk from the bottom end of Brooklands Road to where Uncle Bern and Auntie Daisy lived with my cousins Andrew and Michael. We walked through some allotments and over a little stream to their home. I remember several big family gatherings there for special occasions.

The last of Dad's siblings to still live around Bletchley was his eldest brother Charles (Charlie). He ran a hostel in Great Brickhill for railway workers. In those days it was not uncommon for companies to provide hostel accommodation for single men who were working away from their hometowns. Accommodation was also provided for Uncle Charles, who lived there with Auntie Winifred and their son Adrian. Adrian was quite a lot older than me and I don't remember seeing much of him when I was a child.

The Blane Family
Back: Henry, Dad, Charlie, Don, Bob, Bern
Front: Margaret, Grandad, Grandma, Martin
(And of course Pat the dog had to get into the picture too!)

So six of Grandma and Grandad's eight children lived locally. Uncle Henry, his wife Auntie Grace and their sons Dudley and Richard, lived in Felixstowe. We very seldom saw them. And you also already know that Uncle Don and his family had moved to the Isle of Wight. But later they emigrated to Vancouver in Canada. Uncle Don's younger son Rex still lives in Mission, British Columbia, with his wife Kathryn.

Both Dad and Mum's families worked hard. One thing Dad did was to teach himself to touch type and he became quite fast and accurate.

The typewriters were all manual. Mistakes had to be erased, and the paper reinserted to just the right place, to make corrections. So you can see that accuracy was even more important then than it is now. I know. I learned to type on one of these!

Dad also went to night school to learn woodwork. He made a little bookcase for the living room and a lovely sewing table, that included a tray with compartments lined in green felt, for Mum. Until Mum and Dad moved together into a care home in Bedford in 2010, those two items stood in the hallway of their retirement bungalow in Stewartby. They still remain in the family.

Auntie Nellie had gained her qualifications as a piano teacher from the Victoria College of Music. As still a fairly young woman she went on to become a Fellow of the college, when this picture of her was taken. She always wore her gown and hood on examination days. But I never saw her in the mortarboard!

Florence Ellen (Nellie) Cutts
Fellow of the Victoria College of Music

# THE FINAL HOUSE MOVE

It just never occurred to me that we would ever leave Bletchley, where I felt comfortable and at home. It was really only school that I wasn't so happy with there and that was mainly maths, where I know that I didn't do as well I could have. I have realised since that, although I am no genius, the maths teacher I had at Bletchley Road School was not very good at his job. But that was the only fly in my ointment. However, this era of my childhood came to an end in August 1954 with what felt to me a huge move.

Apart from holidays, outings with Uncle and Auntie and the occasional shopping trip, the Bletchley area was my world. Even going to the shops in Bedford, some twenty miles away, felt like a real expedition.

Then Dad had the offer of a job as Social and Sports Club Secretary at Stewartby, a village a few miles from Bedford on the Bletchley side. It was a promotion and would bring a nice house with it. The job involved more than running the brick company social club in Stewartby. Dad would be responsible for organising all the activities associated with it, overseeing the upkeep of the sports facilities and ensuring the smooth running of the various sports clubs. He would also have overall responsibility for clubs at the other company brickworks round and about.

Uncle was by now was not having the same trouble with his ulcers and after Mum had seen and liked the house on offer in Stewartby, they did not feel they could afford for Dad to turn the job down. A few years earlier he had turned down a promotion move to the Bristol area, 100 miles or so from Bletchley, because Mum couldn't bear to live so far away from her sister and all she knew. He really felt that if he turned down this Stewartby move he would be stuck where he was for the rest of his working life.

I became quite excited when Dad told me that we were moving to a village. Sadly my ideas were of a storybook type village in the middle of countryside and woods. I remember asking Dad if there were fields there. Somewhat bemused he told me that yes, there were. He did not know my thoughts and after we had moved I was so disappointed. There *were* fields all right but they were nearly all fenced and in agricultural use, whereas I was thinking of that idyllic countryside. I did once try to take a shortcut across a field and got caught up in the barbed wire fence. I panicked and struggled and of course tore my clothes before freeing myself. Then I was in trouble. That wasn't something I ever tried again.

Moving to Stewartby really was a very big change. 1954 was the year of my last holiday in Southsea too. My summer holidays after that were very different, as you will see.

The Stewart family founded the London Brick Company and the brickworks at Stewartby, which had grown into the biggest in the world by the time we were there. There were so many brick kiln chimneys, more than thirty when we moved to Stewartby. They made a real landmark, especially as two of the central chimneys had, respectively, LBC (for London Brick Company) and STEWARTBY written down them in large white letters. Even though the chimneys were so tall when there was no wind and atmospheric conditions were right the smoke sank to the ground, shrouding the bottom of the village. It didn't affect us so badly where we lived but even so the smell of sulphur was awful.

The brick company owned a lot of land around the area. It meant that when one knothole was exhausted they could start digging out another. The laboratory in Stewartby tested the quality of everything, from the clay right through to the finished article; bricks, roofing tiles, hollow blocks and field drainpipes. Exterior facing bricks, unlike plain interior ones, were made in different colours and textures. Very hard 'Rustic' bricks, a pleasant red in colour and rough textured, were used to build the village houses. Miniature brick ashtrays were hollow and divided into three compartments, with green felt on the base. They were made in all the facing varieties as promotional novelty items. We always had a few of those in the house.

The brick company also owned farms on its land. From these it tested the grass and the cows' milk for pollutants from the brickwork's chimneys.

The Stewarts built a so-called model village on the site of the tiny hamlet of Wootton Pillinge, providing homes for the brickyard workers. The first phase of 210 houses, started in 1926, was completed by the beginning of WWII. It was excellent company housing for workers in those days.

The construction was of high quality, of course using the brickwork's own products. Mains water and electricity were brought in to the village, although oddly enough not gas. Every house had an indoor toilet and bathroom (not universal then) and a garden.

The village footpaths were made from pieces of broken clay tile, in its various shades of mellow deep red, set in cement. The look was very unusual and pleasing to the eye. When simply walking you hardly noticed the slight unevenness of the surface, although it was different when pushing a pram or riding a bike.

Stewartby initially comprised one long street running up the village, deviating at intervals to wind around in four 'Closes.' In these closes the houses were arranged around the road, which bordered a central grassy area. There was no other road exit from them, except for Montgomery Close. From the back of that you could take a road left down to the 'New Houses,' a small estate built behind the main road some years later.

The largest house in the village, where the works manager Mr Forbes and his family lived, was near the club. This was quite separate from the other village houses. The brickworks, club, village hall and Co-op shop (incorporating the post office) were all at the bottom end of the village. Then houses ran along both sides of Stewartby Way, on the flat ground from the brickworks end, as far as a lane just before the school. After that the road started to run uphill.

From this point the ordinary houses were only built on the left side of the road, opposite the school, up to the main London - Bedford railway line. This was known to us all as the Bedpan Line because from Bedford it ran into St Pancras station in London.

Running uphill from the school opposite these houses, in the curve of a road called The Crescent, was a big grassy area. Just four large, detached houses stood behind this on The Crescent, not far from the school, when I was a child. They were designated for the head teacher of the school, the Scottish Free Church minister, the head of the laboratories and the head of production at the brickworks.

The ground levelled out again at the roundabout by the top end of The Crescent. There was a wide grassy area between footpath and main road through the village, on both sides at the bottom end. Here some large old trees grew, together with younger lime trees planted by the company. Then on the left, where the footpath and grassy area continued, just a row of lime trees marched all the way up the village.

It was after World War II that the main road through the village was named Stewartby Way and the closes called Churchill, Alexander, Montgomery and Wavell as tributes to those particular wartime leaders. The senior school became what was known as a Secondary Modern School. Its entrance was on The Crescent, whereas the building housing the infant and junior schools, although next to it, was actually set back just behind a small grassed area facing Stewartby Way.

The Sir Malcolm Stewart Homes, the retirement bungalow complex at the top end of the crescent and opposite the houses on Stewartby Way between the roundabout and railway line, where my parents lived until 2010, had yet to be built. We lived on the corner of Wavell Close and Stewartby Way. Across the main road was Carter's Farm where we sometimes bought duck eggs, which make cakes rise wonderfully. Between the farm and the railway embankment were a number of allotments and then a footpath where blackberry brambles and dog roses grew.

The houses on the corners of Alexander and Wavell Close were next largest in size to those on The Crescent and were semi-detached, whereas most in the village were terraced. One of the corner houses on Alexander Close was the village police house.

Stewartby had its own village constable (bobby). What was our brick shed, opposite the back door, was his office at that house.

Across a side road from the sports ground was Stewartby United Church. A doctor from the GP practice in Kempston came to hold a surgery in a hut next to the church twice a week. There was also a regular mother and baby clinic held there. The other small estate of houses, the so-called New Houses, had been built behind here, running up the hill.

On the far side of the road that ran from behind Montgomery Close down to the New Houses was a rough, grassy area that was a riot of flowers in the summer. Wild white marguerites, or ox-eye daisies, grew in great abundance. We called them dog daisies and the area was known as the Dog Daisy Field. It looked lovely but the vegetation was thick and long and the ground too uneven to do much playing on.

The village was designed to be self-contained, with the Co-op grocery shop come post office, company owned and heavily subsidised workingmen's club with its sports ground, village hall, church and the infant, junior and senior schools. The village hall had a beehive carved in relief above the big entrance doors. I think this was to symbolise Stewartby as a hive of industry.

Stewartby even had a swimming pool in the days long before they were at all common in this country. It was outdoor and unheated but nonetheless a full size, properly maintained pool, with a springboard and a diving board. There was also a little paddling pool for very young children. The pool and changing rooms were surrounded by a high brick wall.

Above the female changing rooms, on the opposite side of the pool to the entrance, was a walled flat concrete roof. A flight of concrete steps led up to this. Once there you could either just sit or lie down, and relax, or look over the low wall to see what was going on in the pool and its surround. There were also benches against each long wall in front of the changing rooms, the male changing rooms being alongside the entrance.

For some reason the pool was sited at the end of a path that led down beside the laboratory. Like the club it was heavily subsidised by the brick company and all the school children, whichever village they lived in, had free lessons there.

All of the maintenance in the village, apart from interior house decorating, private gardens and allotments, was taken care of by the brick company. The trees, bushes, shrubs, grassy areas and rose beds always looked well kept.

Mr Fletcher was the head groundsman. We would see him riding his mower around the village in the summer and he would always smile and wave, or speak to us if he had finished cutting a stretch of grass and stopped the mower.

The groundsmen planted out the roundabout and took care of the rose beds in the village. They also cut the thick mass of privet bush outside our house and the other corner houses on Wavell and Alexander Closes, as well as pruning trees.

The whole village looked really lovely. All the houses were kept in excellent condition too, with any problems taken care of by maintenance men employed by the brick company. It really was in many ways a truly 'model' village.

I am afraid this view of the roundabout, coming up the village with Carter's Farm to the right, is not very clear. I think they used blue rather than white flowers on this side. However in the middle you can see the Phorpres Man, the London Brick Company logo. To the left of the logo is written LBC and to the right the year, in this picture 1959. Notice the lamp in the middle. It used to swing violently in its holder in a strong wind.

View facing down the village to the brickworks

The London Brick Company, although it was a limited (public) company, was basically run by the Stewart family who must have owned a majority shareholding. The Stewart family was very paternalistic. Some folk nowadays might consider them patronising but the Stewarts were genuinely concerned for the wellbeing of their employees and families. They even considered the schooling needs of the children in surrounding villages. Sir Malcolm Stewart set up a trust fund in his will to provide free sheltered housing for company pensioners and widows.

That is not to say that the founding London Brick Company Stewart, Sir Halley, was not controlling. For example, being very Calvinistic he would not allow washing to be hung out on a line on a Sunday. To break this rule meant eviction! But overall, employees and their families got a good deal from the company. And by the time we moved there the no hanging out washing on a Sunday rule had died along with Sir Halley, some years previously.

One thing that was not so good at that time was the company pension scheme. The ordinary workers had literally just shillings a week from that when they retired and it was not index linked.

Wavell Close about 1959. Footpath front right leads to 199

When we first moved, it all felt very strange. Dad was allocated our semi-detached house on the corner of Wavell Close, number 199, between the roundabout and the railway line at the top of the village, due to his position as Club Secretary.

In this picture the Co-op is beyond the big trees on the right, with the only village phone box alongside it.

You can just see a corner of the club roof, the club standing behind the Co-op to the right of the picture. Some of the many brickworks chimneys are in the background, behind a few of the lime trees that had been planted by the brick company.

And here is a picture of the front of the Co-op then. It hasn't altered all that much, though now it is a private newsagent and general store.

Although our house was one of the larger houses in the village, the way the village layout was designed meant that on that corner we only had a very small back garden.

Our front door and dining room faced the square (the village name for a close) but the living room window faced on to the front, Stewartby Way. This could lead to some confusion with the actual house frontage being on Wavell Close but, "The front" when spoken, always referring to Stewartby Way. The privet bushes to the front and - front! - were of course cut and maintained by the brick company gardeners.

199 Wavell Close

Lower left, toilet
Lower right, dining room
Upper left, landing
Upper right, my bedroom

Back gate to the left of the house

(I can see the bushes are ready for cutting!)

The original houses in the village, four closes and Stewartby Way, were numbered straight through. So the house adjoining ours, with its front door and hall next to our living room, was number 200 Stewartby Way where we were number 199 Wavell Close.

I suppose that before the new estate of houses was built behind Stewartby Way all anyone would need to find where you lived was the house number.

199 Wavell Close and 200 Stewartby Way

In this picture the windows on the left front are Mum and Dad's bedroom and our living room. The others on the front belong to 200. To the right of 200 is their shed, attached to the house. A covered passage linked that to the shed of 201. This passage led to their two garden gates.

In the terraced houses a passage ran between the lower floors of each pair to their garden gates. So there was extra space upstairs over the passage in one of each of those pairs of houses.

We did have a bathroom upstairs in this house but our only toilet, with its little window facing the square, was downstairs to the left of the front door alongside the staircase. We had a big open front hall but really, it was rather a waste of the space. The stairs went up from the hall, behind the toilet. Near the top was a half landing with a back window. There you turned left and the last few stairs led to the landing along the side of the house facing the square. Then another turn to the left led you along between the upstairs rooms.

The big living room fronting Stewartby Way was south facing and very light. The fireplace was on the wall against number 200. Mum always felt rather aggrieved that our living room open fireplace and chimney were against our next door neighbours' wall. This meant that we provided heat for their hallway and one of their bedrooms, rather than for another area of our own house.

Our fireplace was a big one, built of brick and tile. The mantelshelf and hearth were made from red tiles that Mum polished each and every week with Cardinal Red polish. I think she must have cursed those tiles, too. On the left of this picture you can just see the bookcase Dad made, with the big old wireless on top. Can you spot the model Indian squaw I made, standing on the left of the mantelshelf?

Apart from eating breakfast, and sometimes dinner, in the kitchen, all our living was done in this room in the winter. The two big armchairs stood either side of the fireplace. You can see Uncle sitting in one in the Christmas picture, as well as the piano that also stood in the living room for a few years. Along with the living room furniture we had the dining table and chairs in there next to the piano in the winter. The trouble with the dining room was that it did not even have a fireplace. There was just a little two bar electric fire on one outside wall. So it was difficult and expensive to heat in cold weather.

The kitchen, behind the living room, wasn't a bad size. However it was more or less north facing, the window set in the back wall with the sink below. Even though there was a boiler in an alcove that adjoined the living room the kitchen wasn't very warm in the really cold weather, although nice and cool in the summer heat. The kitchen cabinet stood against the wall that jutted out beyond 200, just past the alcove (heating next door again!) and by the cooker. We also had a quite large table and chairs in the middle of the room. A big old cabinet about three feet high, with two drawers and then a double cupboard under, stood against the wall adjoining the living room. One thing Mum didn't like was that, with no gas laid on, the cooker was electric. She has always preferred cooking with gas to electricity. I am still the same.

The kitchen had a walk-in larder to the left as you entered from the hall. Beyond that was the back door. This faced the door of the coal barn, across a little porch area. The coal barn was rather strangely situated. Although its door was outside the house itself, the barn actually ran under the stairs. The door of a good-sized brick shed was across from the porch, facing the house, and the area between it and the house was roofed over.

My bedroom was a big one and felt wonderful: all that room just for me. It was on the corner of Wavell Close and Stewartby Way, above the dining room. As I discovered, the drawback was that it was the coldest bedroom. The living room chimneybreast ran up behind the wall in Mum and Dad's bedroom. They even had a two bar electric fire on that wall, too.

Carole's smaller bedroom was above the kitchen so there was some heat from the boiler in winter. The room was L shaped: the short leg, behind the end wall of the upstairs hallway, ran above the back of the kitchen and the boiler alcove. There was a curtain across that to separate it from the long leg of the room, which ran along over the main part of the kitchen that extended beyond 200's back house wall. So that side of the bedroom was not protected from the elements. The window was at the far end of this long leg, opposite the bedroom door. The bathroom was to the left of Carole's bedroom, the bathroom door opposite mine.

Stewartby is so exposed that the wind really whips around the houses, howling bitingly in the winter cold as we discovered. Wind or not, on really cold mornings there would still be traceries of frost on the inside of the bedroom windows. As we moved in August, all that was to come. What we did have in late summer were wonderful lightning displays. We were at the edge of the Ouse Valley, with the ground beyond Stewartby rising towards Ampthill. Thunderstorms seemed to play around the edge of the valley. It felt really exciting watching bolts of sheet lightning, from Mum and Dad's bedroom window especially, and hearing great cracks of thunder.

In the winter we had sheets, several blankets and an eiderdown (thick quilt) on each bed. The cotton sheets felt really cold. Even when we had flannelette sheets, they felt cold initially. But a couple of hours before bedtime Mum took the filled hot water bottles upstairs, putting one under the covers at the foot of each bed to warm it.

As well as rubber ones we had old-fashioned 'stone' hot water bottles, as they were called. They were actually made from thick pottery and could be filled with really boiling water. One of Dad's old socks was pulled up over the filled hot water bottle as touching it would have burned our feet. But sliding down between the cold sheets, it was wonderful when your feet hit the hot water bottle. If you woke up in the middle of the night you could pull off the sock and the bottle would still be warm.

Mum and Dad had a bolster on their bed. It was not common to have four pillows on a double bed. Instead you had two pillows on top of the bolster, which was like one long pillow going right across the bed. It was a bit of a job getting the cover on and off.

My bed and washstand

With just lino covering the floor it didn't pay to miss the rug at the bedside when you got out of bed on a chilly winter's morning!

Also at the side of the bed, as bedside tables, Carole and I each had an old cane bottomed chair. She and I did not have wardrobes in our bedrooms.

None of us had a lot of clothes and all our dresses hung in Mum's wardrobe. In my room I had a washstand cupboard with a marble top as well as the chair. My books went both in and on top of the cupboard. Various odds and ends also went inside and ornaments on top. When I had the washstand next to my bed it became my bedside table, with a lamp and alarm clock on it as in the picture.

We soon got to know our neighbours at 200. There was just a chain link fence between us but the addition of a privet hedge between their garden and 201. Our house made up another side of our garden. The brick shed, extending to a short, high brick garden wall, bounded Wavell Close. Our solid wooden gate completely filled an opening in the wall between the house and shed.

A chain link back fence ran alongside the garden path leading down the side of 198 Wavell Close. Since that path was hardly used, the garden and back of the house felt very private.

Mrs Holden, a widow, lived at 200 with her son Richard, around my age, and two daughters. Jenny was about Carole's age and Lana a few years younger.

Carole soon became good friends with Jenny and they played a lot together, Lana joining in when they would let her. Also living there was Croz, a Yugoslavian lodger. I never did know his real name but he was a very gentle, kind man, who was actually Lana's father although none of us children realised this for years. Croz had fled Yugoslavia when the communists moved in, remaining a staunch royalist. He never went back to visit his home country, fearing for his life had he done so.

Aren't Carole, Jenny and Lana doing a good job of clipping the grass? This shows more than half the length of our garden! 198 is at the back. The garden of 200 is just a little further to the right and our shed to the left, both just out of the picture.

There were quite a few East European refugees working for the brick company. In fact there was a hostel for them at Kempston Hardwick, an old Ministry of Defence depot just a few miles away toward Bedford, on the Ampthill Road. Mr and Mrs Scott ran that, an elderly couple who lived on site and with whom Mum and Dad were friendly. We liked going to visit them as they had a lovely Old English Sheepdog. And with no children or grandchildren of their own, they also made much of us.

It was the blank side wall of 198, with the garden path leading to the rear of the house running alongside it, which faced the bottom of our little garden. Miss Ellis lived there by herself. She was an older woman who worked in the offices at the brick works. We did not see much of her although she was always pleasant. As children we were fascinated by her hairstyle. Her hair was grey and obviously quite long. She wore it in two plaits (braids), which were wound round in flat coils and pinned one over each ear. We called them earphones.

Miss Ellis also collected cats! She had some of her own but put fish and food scraps out in her back garden every day for the 'strays.' So of course all the cats from round and about came to enjoy the largesse. One or two may have been genuine strays but mostly they were simply neighbourhood cats that knew when they were on to a good thing.

Aunt Polly joins a snowball fight

Further down the square lived an elderly woman known to all the village children as Aunt Polly. She lived alone, had no children of her own and made much of all of us. We all liked her. She also went shopping for the 'old folk,' some of whom were certainly younger than her. Aunt Polly had an ancient 'sit up and beg' bicycle with a basket on the front. She rode this bike down to the Co-op to buy and deliver whatever items had been requested.

I was fond of Aunt Polly and she must have been fond of me, too. When she left her house in later years to move into a Trust retirement bungalow she gave me this ornament, which I still cherish.

Dad had an allotment, where he grew our vegetables, just across the road from Wavell Close. He certainly had no room to grow them in our garden. Mind you, Mum did have a patch of mint that she grew in an old metal bucket with the bottom knocked out, sunk into the earth.

Mint just spreads like wildfire given half a chance and without containment would have taken over what bit of garden we had.

Some of the vegetables fresh from the allotment were lovely. On a Sunday when Dad brought in a bucket of freshly picked peas we would help to shell them for dinner - those we didn't eat as we were doing the job. The small young carrots were lovely too.

Both peas and carrots are really sweet tasting when first harvested. Within hours the sweetness begins to fade as the sugars turn to starch. So bought ones taste nothing like those from Dad's allotment.

Freshly dug new potatoes, cooked with a sprig of Mum's mint, were also delicious and I liked the runner beans too. Broccoli was all right. What I didn't care much for then, like most children I think, was cabbage (although I ate it). But it was really good that Dad had the allotment. Even though he did have to give it up after he started having serious problems with his back, it was a shame when that land and Carter's Farm were taken to build the Sir Malcolm Stewart Homes, the Trust bungalows.

As for the village itself, it was so small and with only the one shop. For a few years of my childhood there was another little shop somebody opened at the back of Montgomery Close. It couldn't really compete with the Co-op though, especially since the Co-op had the post office as well.

There was a little playground at the edge of the sports field and we played on the grandstand behind the club. But it wasn't like the waste ground or Rec at Bletchley.

I know that although Mum really liked the house she did not like living in the village. She missed both Bletchley and Auntie. Once a week she would go into Bedford to look round the shops and buy what she could not get in Stewartby. There were a lot more goods available now and self-service had even started reaching some shops in our area.

In the village, as well as the Co-op store there were the vans that came round daily with milk and bread. A small mobile grocery van came round once a week too as well as a butcher, greengrocer, wet fish van and a fish and chip van on a Friday evening. So basic food was no problem there.

Once a week the baker brought sticky buns in his van along with the bread. These buns were slightly sweet, round currant rolls, with a sugar syrup glaze on top. Being like all the bread freshly baked that morning, they were sometimes still warm when they arrived. In the school holidays Carole and I would each have one buttered for our elevenses: delicious!

Uncle and Auntie visited us every Monday afternoon. That was when Uncle drove to Bedford to pick up the pets' meat. So he delivered a supply for Bess and they stayed for an afternoon cup of tea at the same time. Ken came with them in the school holidays.

Mum also took the train back to Bletchley once a week on a Thursday, to spend the day there. The train left from Stewartby Halt on the Bedford to Bletchley line, at the bottom of the village. There were several halts along the line, serving small villages, as well as some ordinary stations serving larger towns. Just beyond the railway line, on the left side of the road, was a huge knothole, with an overhead conveyor carrying the clay across the road to the brickworks. That knothole is now a lake, used for international as well as national and local sailing events.

The road ran past the halt across the railway line, which had manually operated crossing gates. Mr Webb the crossing keeper lived in a railway house on the Stewartby side of the halt. He had a little hut by the nearest platform, where the train going into Bletchley stopped. In the hut were the signal levers, which he had to move after he had heard the bell clang to tell him a train was coming and he had closed the gates to traffic. Then when the train had passed he changed the signals to stop any unexpected approaching trains, before opening the gates to traffic again.

Also in the hut were a coke stove, a chair and a wooden bench. In the winter Mr Webb would let us sit on the bench to thaw out and warm up a bit while we waited for the train.

When Mum went to Bletchley she always left a complete beef stew in a saucepan, slowly cooking for our dinner. Carole and I weren't fond of Thursday dinner times, when Mum wasn't there, but she was always home in time for tea. (Of course we went with her in holiday times until we were older.) But I think those weekly trips are why, for a long time, I didn't really like beef stew.

Do you remember I said I took piano lessons from Auntie? Well, after we moved to Stewartby I rode back to Bletchley on the train every Friday after school and most school holiday Fridays too, returning on Saturday afternoon - although in the holidays I would sometimes spend longer there when at home.

I knew the railway line very well and most of the guards, who were regulars on the line and lived in Bletchley. With Grandad having been a train driver, and our family well known in Bletchley, Mum and Dad knew them and they were familiar faces, all older men and quite fatherly to me. Most of the drivers knew us too.

I usually rode in the guard's van, chatting to whichever guard was on duty that day. The train journey took about half an hour from Stewartby to Bletchley and far less time to Bedford as there was only one other halt on the way. Sometimes I used Bletchley station on my visits and sometimes Fenny Stratford.

Fenny station, once you reached it, was better in the winter for coming home. Bletchley was big with a number of draughty platforms. There was a waiting room at Fenny with an open fire.

So the passengers would wait in there. Then when we heard that the signals had changed to say the train had left Bletchley station we crossed the track to the only other platform, for Bedford.

At Fenny Station, heading for Bedford.

I would get to Bletchley in time for tea on a Friday and then the rest of evening was free. Ken had moved into the small back bedroom when we left Cambridge Street so when I went to stay I had the big double back bedroom all to myself.

There was a wardrobe in one chimneybreast alcove in the bedroom, in which were various old, unused items. One was a fox-fur stole, or tippet. It was a real fox pelt, complete with head and glass eyes. You wore it around your shoulders, held in place at the front with a hidden hook and eye. I found it fascinating and used to dress up in it.

Although I liked to sleep in a darkened room, Ken was the opposite. He had his bedroom door slightly ajar and the landing light left on. Auntie still fried up egg or steak and chips in the late evening, well after our bedtime. If I had not got off to sleep I would smell the frying and creep out on to the landing. There I sat for a while at the top of the stairs, my mouth watering, without the courage to go down. I knew I was supposed to be asleep. Years later, I was laughing over this as I told Auntie. "Oh, my dear" she said, "You should have come down. Of course you could have had some chips." Sadly it was too late then.

Like Mum, Auntie brought me a cup of tea in bed in the morning. By now we took cod liver oil capsules, rather than the malt and cod liver oil mixture. I always had one of those capsules with my early morning tea. One Saturday morning at Bletchley I had a horrid experience. As I went to swallow the capsule I somehow bit into it. The cod liver oil flooded my mouth, tasting absolutely foul. I don't know how long it took to get rid of that taste.

Auntie gave me my half hour music lesson on Saturday morning. Then apart of course from my meals I mainly had the rest of the day free, other than Ken and me washing and drying the dishes. We nearly always argued over that as we both wanted to wash. When Ken dried he picked up the wet cutlery, wrapped it in a tea towel, and just shook it about before emptying it into the drawer. I might have thought that was no way to go about things but I wasn't going to offer to do it myself!

For the first few years of my going to Bletchley from Stewartby Ken and I often watched TV shows like The Lone Ranger after my piano lesson on Saturday morning. One episode really sticks in my mind. The Lone Ranger was sinking in quicksand and Tonto was using Silver to pull him out. As the Lone Ranger was dragged out with a rope, the surface of the 'quicksand' parted. It looked like duckweed on a pond, to me!

I would often visit Grandma and Grandad too, before catching the train home in the late afternoon. Sometimes I ran little errands for them to the local shops. One thing I remember is that they each liked a daily fifteen-minute radio soap. Grandma's was the daytime Mrs Dale's Diary, now defunct. Grandad's, in the evening, was The Archers. That's still going strong after over sixty years. I also occasionally saw other relatives on these weekends.

One Saturday afternoon I was chatting with the driver before getting on to the train. He asked if I would like to ride in the engine, 'on the footplate' as it was called. Well, what else could I say? So at Ridgemont station I got out of the guard's van and went forward to the engine. I rode with the driver and fireman for two stations to Millbrook, the stop before Stewartby. It was a wonderful experience in a steam train.

The fire threw out so much heat and there was that indescribable smell, as well as the feel of it and looking up the railway line round the side of the cab. I had to go back to the guard's van at Millbrook though, as that was a proper station not a halt, and the driver wouldn't let me jump down from the cab at Stewartby.

Perhaps if there had been trains on a Sunday I might often have tried to stay at Bletchley until then, although I did quite like Sunday mornings at home. I often stayed in bed until late, sleeping and then reading. The smell of the Sunday roast permeated the house. We always had our coffee mid-morning with Mum. When she basted the roast, at about the same time, we had 'dip.' Mum cut thick slices from a crusty white loaf and dipped them in the meat fat and juices for us to eat - naughty but very nice.

After cooking roast pork or beef Mum poured off and kept the rest of the fat and juices. These, though not those from lamb or poultry, made lovely 'dripping.' Mum did not eat butter or margarine so this was what she mostly spread on her bread, sprinkled with salt. We sometimes had it on toast for tea. In winter we might have that with celery. We poured a little pile of salt on to our plates, then took a stick of celery and kept dipping it into the salt as we ate it with our 'dripping toast.'

To return to Sunday, we always had the wireless on at dinnertime. Two Way Family Favourites was a programme of requests to and from armed forces members overseas. Then it was Billy Cotton's Bandshow, a big band sound.

Also on a Sunday, we always had something different for tea. I liked it when it was ham or corned beef but not when we had tinned red salmon containing little soft bones. With the meat or fish, we sometimes had salad: lettuce, cucumber and tomato, perhaps radishes, or 'cucumber and onion.' This was cucumber and onion thinly sliced, placed in a bowl of malt vinegar for a few hours before serving. After we often had tinned fruit, either peaches or fruit cocktail - or perhaps jelly. We usually had cream from the top of the milk or Carnation evaporated milk with this.

The ice cream van came round in the late afternoon in summer. Then Mum would sometimes buy a block of vanilla ice cream, wrap it in newspaper and leave it on the stone slab in the pantry until we had tea. It might be a bit soft by then but was nonetheless a treat with the fruit or jelly. We still had cake afterwards, too.

Although birthdays were really special they were celebrated in a rather low-key kind of way compared to today. We would have a party at the house for family and a few friends, with no hired in entertainment and no party bags either. Well, we'd never heard of them! There wasn't anywhere much we could have gone to away from home to hold a party, especially without a car. In any case, it was just not a consideration. We played party games and had sandwiches, perhaps sausage rolls, crisps, jelly, fairy cakes and of course a home-made birthday cake. One year Mum had a rare culinary disaster. She made Carole a birthday cake with cherries in and it was really stodgy. However all was not totally lost. Next morning she steamed it in a pudding basin and it was lovely with custard, for our pudding after dinner.

Crisps (potato chips) then were all just plain and unsalted. They came in individual cellophane bags (no large or multi packs). In each bag was a little twist of dark blue waxed paper, containing salt. You fished that out of the bag, untwisted it, sprinkled the salt in your bag and shook it. Now you had your salted crisps.

Sometimes the salt would be damp and come out in a clump. Sometimes there was no salt at all. And sometimes, if you weren't paying too much attention, you would sprinkle on your salt and then later bite into a 'crisp' that was pure salt – an extra twist being in the bag!

Another time marked out as different was when Auntie May came to stay each year. Not the Auntie May of Southsea, this was the widow of Uncle's older brother. She seemed quite old to me. Tall and kindly she wore glasses with very think lenses. Carole was a bit wary of her but I think that was perhaps because of her height, accent and how her glasses distorted her eyes. She met us from school when she came to stay and she taught us old-fashioned children's songs.

Auntie May

Auntie May's great hobby was pegging homemade rugs. She drew a pattern on a piece of coarse sacking, then pegged in cut up pieces of old clothing or fabric. Much of the latter was factory surplus. She sewed on a sack backing when the rug was finished.

These rugs looked really good and for many years we had a large one in front of the living room hearth and smaller ones at our bedsides. She made one for the bathroom in peach and green coloured nylon fabric that was also surplus from the factory.

Even after we had our first big carpet in the living room, given to Mum and Dad by Auntie when she bought a new bedroom carpet, we still had one of Auntie May's rugs in front of the hearth. They were all hard wearing and lasted for a very long time.

When Auntie May was with us she helped to shell the peas. The trouble was, her eyesight really was quite poor. She couldn't see where there was a maggot hole in a pea, never mind the little maggot itself, and I am sure that Mum surreptitiously rechecked when the job was finished. I suppose that pests are the down side to fresh, home grown produce. But I think it is a small price to pay.

Mum and Dad relax by the fire with Bess
See Auntie May's rug and the sewing table Dad made

As you will see from the map it was quite a distance from our house to the station, although the school was much nearer to it.

Buses ran infrequently from the stop at the bottom of the village, which was near the laboratory and across from the village hall and the club - on a little side road that looped round through this end of the village and came out on to the A421. One exit was on the Bedford side of the village, one toward Bletchley. Uncle took the A421 to Bedford on his Monday shopping trips to buy the pets' meat and whenever the Bletchley family visited us after our move to Stewartby.

The other bus stop was at Stewartby Turn. This was some way beyond the top end of the village, at the junction with the Ampthill Road. The buses there ran every hour. There was an old wooden bus shelter on the Stewartby side of the road, where the buses stopped on their way into Bedford. Unfortunately, with that shelter being quite enclosed it was used by tramps and was, to say the least, not very salubrious.

It felt like a long walk to that stop, even though we lived at the top end of the village and it wasn't actually as far away as the other. The footpath ended just beyond the railway bridge. There were ditches and low hedges either side of the road and there was no street lighting. There was also no shelter from the wind but the fortunate thing was that traffic was very light.

1950s LBC lorry

The only times we had any heavy traffic were when the loaded red London Brick Company lorries left the works early in the morning and returned empty at the end of the day. We had to get used to hearing them in the very early morning. After changing down for the roundabout, they were upping gear as they passed our house from about 5.30am! They returned at around teatime, 5.00pm.

Even the workmen coming and going did not add a lot to the traffic. Many of the ones who did not live in the village cycled and some came on special buses, especially those from the hostel. There were a few buses coming and going to the school as well but there was no school run in cars (other than some teachers).

We did also have to get used to the noise of the trains on the main Bedford to London line. There were just eleven houses and a narrow footpath between our house and the railway embankment. However it was not long before we hardly noticed the sound of either trains or lorries, although visitors certainly did. And in the garden you might have to stop speaking for a short while as an express train passed.

We did notice the noise when workmen were on the track at night. Although few trains ran then, when a workman saw the signal change down the line he sounded a klaxon, to warn the others that one of those few was coming. That could wake us up.

As well as my final week's holiday at Southsea, in the summer of 1954 I had the first of another kind, very different. Aunt Annie had asked Mum and Dad if I could go up to Beighton for a holiday there. I went on the train, on my own from Bedford, and she met me at Sheffield station. We took the bus to Beighton. She and Uncle Arthur made much of me, although he could appear a bit curmudgeonly at times. I slept in my cousin Brian's bedroom over the front hallway and I don't know where he slept. Perhaps he stayed with friends although I did see him about the house.

There were no real pop idols at this time, not in the way that there are now, and no TV stars. It was films and film stars that fascinated everyone. As well as the shop comics I would avidly read Brenda's film annuals, with all the year's stories and articles about the stars. None of it then was critical or dishing the dirt. It was all Hollywood glamour.

But there was also some sadness in Beighton that year. Brenda's fiancé had died in a car accident a few months earlier. An old friend spent a lot of time with her doing things that summer and one of these was making elderflower wine. We all went out picking the elderflower heads and did have some fun making the sparkling wine.

I often visited Uncle Fred and Auntie Mary, who lived a few streets away, where I always had a warm welcome. The family virtually lived in their big kitchen, which was cluttered but warm and friendly. Auntie Mary still had an old fashioned black range in there. Once a week she made bread baps (big soft rolls), baked in the range oven, which were delicious. A thin little bird of a woman, Auntie Mary was always on the go.

As well as pasteurised milk, the milkman delivered sterilised. This was what Auntie Mary ordered regularly. It came in a bottle similar in shape to a wine bottle, with a cap like that on a beer bottle. So it was easy to tell which was which as the ordinary milk bottle shape hasn't changed much at all.

This sterilised milk was rather like tinned evaporated milk. It was nice in coffee and for baking but I thought that it made tea taste really peculiar.

Uncle Fred was a jovial man and good with children. There was a poem about 'Uncle Fred' in one of my books that always reminded me of him. A trick he used to do for us, both at home and when he and Auntie Mary occasionally came to stay with our family, was to take out his full set of false teeth. Then, holding them in one hand, he would make them ‘talk.’

164 Manvers Road, where Aunt Annie and Uncle Arthur lived, was set back from the road at the rear of a small forecourt. A few yards away to the right as you looked at the front, and separated from the house by a low wall, was a fish and chip shop. To the right of that again was a workingmen’s club. To the left, a short row of terraced houses ran up to the end of the street. On the opposite side of the street, long rows of terraces stretched right down Manvers Road to the High Street.

Looking up Manvers Road. 164 is off up to the right in the far distance, just about out of view.

I loved the fish cakes from the fish and chip shop. These consisted of a slice of fish between two slices of potato, the whole dipped in batter and deep-fried. We had nothing like that back at home.

Mum made ordinary fish cakes, patties of flaked fish mixed with seasoned mashed potato, coated in breadcrumbs and then fried. These, sold by the fish and chip shops at home too, are what in the Sheffield area they rather disparagingly knew as fish rissoles.

I also drank Dandelion and Burdock or Ice Cream Soda, bottled pops (sodas). I don't know what they were actually flavoured with really but to me they were quite exotic. We hardly ever had fizzy drinks at home anyway, and if we did it was mostly lemonade (English style, like 7Up) or sometimes cherryade.

I played in the street with the local children and one thing we did was to collect bottle tops from outside the workingmen's club. They were the kind you use a bottle opener to prise off and had cork inserts that we removed. Then we pressed the bottle tops into the front of our dresses or shirts and pushed the inserts into them from the back to hold them on and make badges. We collected bottles to return to the nearby Matthews' off-licence for a few pence, too.

Matthews' Off Licence and Shop

We all played outside until well into the evening.

However even though later than at home I still had a bedtime to keep, which felt rather unfair. Being at the front of the house, when I lay in bed I could hear the local children out playing for what seemed like ages after I had gone upstairs.

It took me a very long time to go to sleep and I think I might just as well have still been outside playing with the others! Then I might have been really tired when I went to bed.

It felt like a different world and was very strange all over again when I went back home at the end of my Beighton holiday. I even had a bit of a South Yorkshire accent for a while, as I did each time I went to stay there.

# LAST JUNIOR YEARS

We started school soon after this holiday. The infant and junior schools, for the village children, were in one small building with just four classrooms. Behind that and up a step to separate it (no fences needed) was the secondary school. The Stewarts built a large enough secondary school to accommodate children from the surrounding villages, so that they did not have to travel further afield. Each village had its own infant and junior schools.

This school was much newer than either of my previous ones, bright and airy with big windows. However although a slightly newer style, the desks were still very similar to those at Bletchley. The desk tops were just not quite so bumpy and uneven.

My first teacher was a man who had just started there himself. I remember him as rather large man with a big moustache. As it turned out, he was quite a bully and sadist. When someone displeased him he would throw a chalk rubber at him or her. This was a block of wood with a pad attached, used as its name suggests to erase whatever had been written in chalk on the blackboard (chalkboard).

I had a horrible experience with that teacher. One morning, well into the lesson after playtime and before dinner, I really needed to go to the toilet. I put up my hand and asked permission. The teacher became angry and said I should have gone at playtime. He made me come out and sit on a chair at the front of the class. I felt dreadful and was desperate for the toilet. But he would not let me go. Before the class ended, I had wet myself. I felt so ashamed.

I was crying when I got home for dinner. Mum and Dad were horrified when I told them what had happened. Dad went down to the school to complain to the headmistress, Miss Stonton.

Perhaps other parents complained of the way he treated their children too. I only know that he was not quite so bad after that. Whatever transpired, he did not return for the next school year.

We joined the top class for some of our lessons, when Miss Stonton taught us. She was a really good teacher and head. I think she brought out the best in most of the children in her care.

The BBC presented singing lessons on the wireless - a programme called Singing Together, which taught us mainly traditional English songs. There was also another programme called Music and Movement, which was exercising. Then we did English Country Dancing once a week but I didn't really get the hang of that.

Occasionally a man turned up with a film projector and screen. The blinds were drawn shut at the classroom windows and we all sat and enjoyed a film show. As I recall, they were usually geography films. With no television we had never seen moving pictures of faraway places, with curious animals and what were to us strange people. I think we all really enjoyed those films.

We learned to write in cursive, having lessons allocated just to handwriting. We also started to use pen and ink. Our pens were steel nibs attached to handles like those of our paintbrushes. We dipped the nib in the inkwell and away we went or, I have to say, more often - not! Too much ink meant blotching and smearing. If you pressed too hard on the pen the nib would cross and you had double lines. Then the nib had to be changed. We were not allowed to use ballpoint pens, or even fountain pens, but just had to persevere.

The school nurse, after testing my eyes in the course of this year, said that I should see an optician. He found that I needed glasses for reading. I wore National Health glasses, which were free to children. They were round, with pink plastic frames and wires that hooked behind my ears. (I only started having to wear glasses all the time much later, when I was eighteen years old.)

A mobile clinic of the time

Now a mobile school dental clinic came round to us at Stewartby. It was a big van furnished as a normal dental surgery. Here I had my first extraction.

Mum came to the dentist with me, as I had to have the awful general anaesthetic. I hated it. I suppose that when the dentist put that mask over my mouth and nose, with the sickly sweet smell of ether, it reminded me of having my tonsils out. When I came round my mouth was very sore and my gum all torn and bleeding. I think that dentist was a bit of a butcher. Carole remembers him with the shudders too.

A few doors away from us in the square lived Paul, a boy who was a bit younger and smaller than me but bigger and older than Carole. He started to taunt and torment her on the way home from school, really upsetting her. He just would not stop, whatever I said to him. So one day I got really angry with him and hit him quite hard. Paul ran home crying. He told his mother that I had hit him but I'd lay odds that he did not tell her why.

That evening his mother came round and complained to Dad. She got short shrift from him! He more or less told her that if her son was going to behave like that then he should take the consequences and anyway not complain about being hit by a girl.

It was quite odd. Paul's mother worked at home as a hairdresser. Carole and I went to her to have our hair cut and she didn't turn us away after that or, as far as I recall, ever refer to it again.

Another boy, who lived down at the far end of the square, enjoyed bullying me rather than Carole. Dad did not fight my battles for me. He reminded me how to make a fist and swing a roundhouse punch. I think the boy was really shocked when I put that into practice. He was another who backed down when you stood up to him. But these two bullies were isolated cases.

I had some lower key teasing for a while. I put on weight and, until I had a growth spurt and became better proportioned again, suffered from puppy fat. During that time I was given the nickname of Bonzo Blane, which you won't be surprised to know I hated. I really did feel dreadfully self-conscious.

And I myself was sometimes very unkind to Carole. At nearly four and a half years younger than me she, like all little sisters, wanted to be with her big sister doing the things that big sister did. Sometimes that was OK. But often, like all *big* sisters, I did not want her hanging around. However nobody else was allowed to torment her if I knew about it.

'Bonzo': standing with Carole opposite the school. See the lime trees

Carole was a rather timid child and maybe her night-time behaviour was something to do with that. The head of her bed, with the chair beside it, filled the space in front of the curtain that shut off the short leg of her bedroom's L shape. For some time, Carole would often get behind the curtain in her sleep. I suppose it was like sleepwalking. She must have climbed over the head of her bed, as the chair at the side would be undisturbed. Even I remember waking sometimes to hear her crying. When Mum or Dad got to her she would be standing behind the curtain, half asleep still, confused and frightened. She didn't know why she was there or how she got there. It was really strange.

For a few weeks every summer Daddy Long Legs (Crane Flies) would swarm all over our 'stone' (actually concrete) front door step and door surround in the early evening. Carole was terrified of them. If she had been out playing, she would not come near the house until Dad had cleared them away. And if any got into the house, oh dear... We laugh about it now but it was not at all funny to poor Carole then.

Soon after we arrived in Stewartby Carole and I had to start going to Sunday School at the village church, Sir Halley Stewart's Scottish Free Church, on Sunday afternoons. But we did not enjoy it. Sadly we found it deathly dull. We were just taught, more or less by rote, with no games or singing, no competitions, no fun. We children were not actually involved at all. Looking back, I suppose it was a pretty Calvinistic attitude. We stuck it for a while but in the end Mum agreed that we need not keep going. So that was a real relief.

It was much nicer to go, as we often did, on a family bike ride. With so little traffic it really was pleasant to cycle around the area. We might go along to Ampthill Park, a favourite of ours.

Looking toward Stewartby from Ampthill Park

This was a lovely place for youngsters to roam. There were big areas of grass and trees. We children would roll down one particularly long, grassy slope, which was great fun. In the autumn we would go blackberrying there. We got a bit scratched and had purple fingers but collected a good haul of blackberries. Although we ate some while we were picking Mum still had plenty to bottle and make into jam, after baking pies and crumble.

There was a long, steep hill going up into Ampthill so we didn't quite cycle all the way, getting off our bikes to push them up that stretch of road. Over to the left, at the top of the hill, is an old ruined house called Houghton House. John Bunyan used both the hill and the house in his book Pilgrim's Progress. The hill was the inspiration for his Hill of Despair and Houghton House, which must have been lovely before falling into decay, for his House Beautiful. In Ampthill Park was a cross, marking the site of the house where Katherine of Aragon lived when Henry VIII sent her from Court prior to divorcing her.

Of course, as ever I was still reading a lot. Among those I read now were Just William and the other William books and the two Just Jane books. In one of the latter, Jane had tonsillitis. I had never seen the word written down before and asked Mum and Dad what ton-*sill*-it-is meant. That caused some amusement and I felt quite embarrassed and foolish at not having been able to work it out. I had a comic every week too, Girl and later Girl's

Crystal. They were mainly picture stories and really were designed and appropriate for young girls, not like some of the present day offerings. (Now I'm showing my age and prejudice!)

I also started collecting stamps. I had a proper album with a separate page for each country. I bought stamps in packets as well as being given them. However I got them, I would then spend time sorting out the stamps and sticking them in my album with little stamp hinges that I had to lick. Dad had collected stamps and apparently had made a large collection. His children being girls, he thought we would not be interested in stamps as a hobby and gave his collection to one of my cousins - who later sold it! My interest, to be fair, only lasted a couple of years.

Dad's work did not always end when he came home at 5 o'clock for his tea. Because he ran the club Dad was also down there on Monday evenings for the Tote, a kind of raffle where people had the same numbers every week. Then he was there at Sunday dinnertime for ordinary raffles as well, before coming home to eat. We would occasionally hear loud knocking on the front door at night too. If the village bobby found the club unsecured or the burglar alarm went off, Dad as key holder would be called out.

It didn't take long for the young lads of the village to get to know Dad. If any of them were hanging around the club, or underage youths trying to get in, he was soon there sorting them out. They grumbled about him but respected him.

When adult they all liked him and enjoyed remembering, and telling the stories of, his strictness because he was also always (or nearly always!) fair.

Our first autumn in Stewartby we discovered that we were to see very little of Dad each year in the few months before Christmas. He had a lot of extra work so would come home for tea and then be back again to his office at the club. First of all there were Christmas parties for pre-school and primary children, held in the village hall. The brick company paid for everything but Dad did all of the organising.

Any employee could put in a party application form with their child or children's name(s) and age(s). These parties were not just for Stewartby works but also for little brickworks either side of Stewartby and a number of other small brickworks around Peterborough. With so many children to cater for parties were held over several Saturday afternoons before Christmas. They all took place in Stewartby village hall, with transport laid on for those who had to travel.

Dad had to work out numbers and arrange for everything, including the catering and the entertainer, the transport and the volunteers who helped at each of the parties. He also had to buy a present for each and every child, as Father Christmas appeared to hand them out at all the parties in his traditional long, red, fur trimmed hooded robe.

Presents were bought by age and sex, so for example every five year old girl had the same present and so on. These presents were all wrapped, in a different paper for each age and sex. The children were even called by name to collect their presents. Dad and a colleague went to a toy wholesaler in Banbury in late summer every year to place the toy order.

Dad ordered the Christmas trees for the club and the village hall too. He would also order ours at the same time. Something I only found out years later is that, despite my parents having very little money, Dad bought a Christmas tree for an orphanage in Kempston every year until it closed - long after I had grown up.

New Year entertainment coach trips were organised for the older children. Dad would book seats for a pantomime or ice show in somewhere like Northampton and again arrange the transport. Each child on these trips had a packed lunch type meal in a folded cardboard box. Volunteer parents made the sandwiches and packed the meals at long tables in the club. Other parents accompanied the children on the coaches.

I went to parties and to the pantomimes and ice shows. We sat at long tables in the hall for the parties and I had never seen so many children in one room. I remember a magician coming to entertain us one year and the parties were always good fun. So later were the coach trips themselves, as well as the shows we went to see. We usually had a sing-song on the way home.

The company's pensioners and widows were not forgotten either. Again, it was Dad who did all the practical work. Each pensioner or widow household received a supply of coal and a chicken. The men also had a bottle of whisky and the women a box of chocolates. I suppose that was sexism and as such might not seem acceptable nowadays but nobody complained then. That's how things were and everyone seemed happy enough.

At the club there were whist drives and raffles, with all kinds of festive prizes. Again, Dad did the buying. One raffle, known as the Fur and Feather although it was now only poultry, was for fresh turkeys and chickens that were to be delivered just before Christmas. We didn't have any frozen birds. Uncle supplied the poultry at a good price. One year Dad was really teased at the club after the raffle. He and Uncle had the first two winning raffle tickets. I think there were cries of foul – or was it *fowl*?

Dad was present at all the events, ensuring the smooth running of them. He delivered the gifts to the pensioners and widows too (except for the coal!). He was generally offered a drink at various houses on his rounds. One man made his own wine. It was, "Try this one" and, "This one's good this year." Dad soon learned to be wary, as these seemingly innocuous wines were really potent.

There were additional benefits, too. Travelling reps came to the club from the various suppliers to take orders for the beer, spirits, soft drinks and snacks the club sold. At Christmas they would give presents to Dad. He always had malt whisky and vintage port, big boxes of chocolates, perhaps cigars. One year he was given a box of twelve really deluxe Christmas crackers and once just one huge cracker containing quite a number of lovely gifts.

That first Christmas in Stewartby I had gone to bed on Christmas Eve but could not get to sleep. At some point I heard my parents trying to stifle giggles as they carried the pillowcase of presents and my stocking into the bedroom. I lay very still with my eyes shut, pretending to be asleep. After they had left my room and closed the door, I waited impatiently. Then, when all seemed quiet, I excitedly felt at my stocking. I didn't dare put the light on! But it was not long before I was soon happily asleep, ready to be surprised when I woke on Christmas morning.

For a couple of years there was one thing that I really didn't like about winter. Mum made me wear a liberty bodice over my vest, to keep my chest warm. Liberty? It's true that they did supersede those full-length old-fashioned corsets, which were worn laced very tightly around the body. But I really hated the things.

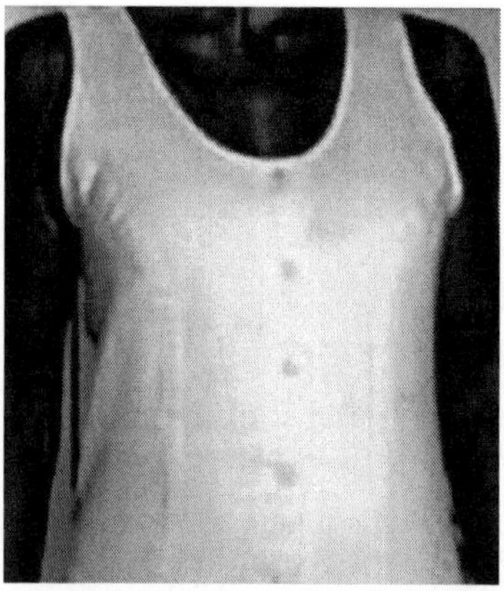

Liberty Bodice

They were sleeveless with a low, round neckline. Made out of some really stiff material stitched into panels, with a fuzzy lining and rubber buttons down the front, they were a struggle to get on and just felt confining. They were really warm but I was so glad when Easter came and I was allowed to leave them off.

I don't know if they still make liberty bodices. The one in this picture doesn't seem to fit the model nearly as tightly as the ones I had to wear fitted on me. They might have been a bit easier to get into if the buttons had served any useful purpose, although doing up such fiddly little buttons would have been no fun.

Mum still wore corsets, with suspenders (garters) to hold up her stockings. But these corsets, like a girdle, came just up to her waist. They were made of a satiny brocaded material in a pink, so-called flesh colour: not that I have ever seen any flesh that looked remotely like it. With a long row of small hooks and eyes up the side, those corsets must have been very fiddly to fasten.

I am sure Mum was really glad when the more modern girdles came in. I don't know if she was as glad as I was though, the winter I was twelve years old. That was the end of being forced into a liberty bodice, I think because by then I was wearing a bra.

Weekly swimming lessons with the school started after the Easter holidays each year. So I had my first one in 1955. We all walked down to the pool in the familiar crocodile formation, carrying our swimming costumes and towels. We girls also wore rubber bathing caps in the pool but the water always seeped up underneath them into our hair.

Foot and cycle path to pool, with lab in the background

There was a hatch in the wall to our right where, in opening hours when there was no school swimming, you paid for entrance. I think it was about 4d for children. Then you walked through a turnstile. A brick wall faced you, with a right hand turn into the pool area just before you reached it. On that wall was a blackboard on which was chalked the pool water temperature each day. I shall never forget seeing the temperature on that first day. It was 48ºF (just under 9ºC)! The water was really, really cold.

The boys' changing rooms were behind the entrance and the girls' opposite, both on the long sides of the pool. There were a number of individual changing rooms but if you couldn't get one of those there was also what we called the Cow Shed, a communal area. This was very spartan with just two long, slatted benches facing each other, duckboards to stand on and two rows of hooks on the walls.

We had five minutes to get undressed and into our swimming costumes. After the half hour lesson we had ten minutes to shower (just rinse off the chlorine water), dry and get dressed. There were only two showers in each changing area and the water was cold. The teacher was always hurrying us along, too. I remember dragging on clothes over my cold, damp, clammy body every time we went.

Nonetheless from the start I enjoyed it and swimming became one of my great loves, right until I left school and started work. Having a pool within walking distance of home was wonderful. In the summer holidays, when I was not away, I was at the pool nearly every afternoon. I would often go back after tea as well, until the pool closed at 8 o'clock. I did play and mess around with friends but the main thing for me was the swimming itself. It did make me hungry, though. I was always ravenous when I got home. I could have eaten an egg and chip supper then!

I made friends at school. My best friend in the village was Val. She was just about a year younger than me. Her family, who lived at the bottom end of the village, got a puppy named Spot that became a lively young dog.

Val with Bess and Spot

Our Bess could never be described as lively. The only time she ever ran was to chase a cat. If the cat stopped and defied her she would circle it growling - but if the defiance continued she would turn away with an air of disdain. When Dad once caught a mouse in the pantry he took it outside and held it in his hands in front of Bess, who was sniffing around very excitedly. He opened his hands. Bess jumped backwards and the mouse ran away. Who was the more frightened?

However across the square from us lived Mrs Raebone. She had a dog, crossbred but mainly Shetland Sheep Dog, called Flash. He was quite young and much livelier than Bess. I took him for walks instead. Val and I would go with the dogs to play in the old school sports field, at the far end of the lane that ran alongside the school. This was just a big grassy area surrounded by hedges and trees. There was a stand of elm trees at the far end that supported a very noisy rookery.

Just before this field was Gadstone's Pond. Beyond that was a little drainage ditch, where Carole later went to catch caddis fly larvae. The ditch led to another pond, at the near end of the sports field. I shudder to think of it now but Val and I used to cup our hands and drink from this, declaring it to be purer than the tap water at home. We often played games involving pretending to be on horseback, galloping around the field with the dogs chasing at our heels.

A group, or just pairs, of us would also go 'sticklebacking.' We would take jam jars, with string tied around the necks to make handles, down to the old works pond between the big knothole and the railway line.

There we would fish with our jars for sticklebacks and minnows in the clear shallow water. Although there were plenty of hiding places amongst the brickbats (broken bricks) littering the bottom of the pond, we did sometimes manage to catch one. Then we would take our catch proudly home to live in the jam jar and be fed on breadcrumbs. Guess what? They always died. And we were always upset. Very occasionally too, we found baby birds that we thought had been abandoned. We also brought those home and tried to raise them. But of course that never worked either, so it was more distress for us.

There was something better than sticklebacking though. Dad still entered fishing competition, winning more trophies. He also went fishing just for pleasure on Sunday mornings, mainly by himself now without Uncle to keep him company. He would quite often cycle down the track between the knothole and the railway, past the work's pond and on to Millbrook pit, just our side of that larger village. The pit was a worked out knothole, the size of a small lake. The area was very quiet and felt quite rural.

Carole and I at Millbrook pit

I sometimes went with Dad on my bike, as did Carole on hers when she was a bit older. I can't say I much liked the maggots that were used as bait but I very much enjoyed the fishing.

The fish were mostly quite small but it did feel like a real achievement to hook and land one. Any fish caught were placed in a keep net at the edge of the little lake until we left, when we released them back into the water.

After buying his maggots Dad kept them in a tin with a perforated lid in our brick shed, all under cover. This was fairly cool so few even became pupae and it was very seldom that any emerged as flies before use.

Mum used to prepare the bread for Dad's groundbait. She baked thick slices of stale bread in a slow oven until they had dried out and turned a pale golden colour, in effect becoming rusk.

When Dad wanted groundbait he would soak this rusk in water, making a thick paste of it. Then he threw a handful of the paste out over his fishing area. It would break up in the air and hit the water in a lot of little splashes. That then attracted the fish.

Dad weighs as Carole watches

In those first summers at Stewartby I remember lying on my stomach on the grass in front of the house, with my eyes close to the ground. I would just watch the ants scurrying back and forth in their own little world, feeling the sun warm on my back. Very occasionally I would hear the drone of a plane overhead. Then I turned over on to my back to watch the white vapour trails lengthening out across the sky.

I went up to Beighton again for a holiday in 1955 when Uncle Arthur, although he could not drive, had bought a car. Brenda was now going out with Keith, who was to become her husband, and he did the driving. We went to the seaside, Bridlington and Skegness, as well as round and about the local area. Sometimes we stopped at a pub. No children under fourteen years old were allowed inside pubs then. So I sat outside on a low wall with a bag of crisps and a bottle of pop, watching the world go by.

The rest of the time passed much as my previous visit the year before. And I was still fed up at having to go to bed when I could hear the local children playing and having a good time outside.

My second and final year at Stewartby School saw me with a new, very good friend. I was made Head Girl and Margaret, who lived at Cranfield a few miles away, was Deputy Head Girl. The chief advantage of this to us may seem strange. We washed the teachers' coffee cups and saucers after our morning playtime. That was when our class had times tables, chanting them by rote. We could spin out this washing up, in the girls' cloakroom, until things went quiet. I enjoyed that year in Miss Stonton's class.

I had already learned my tables (see appendix) well before then and they have stood me in good stead over the years. Nobody had a calculator during all the time I was at school. So we had to be able to work things out for ourselves.

The sinks in the girls' cloakroom were also used for soaking cane for basket weaving classes. I enjoyed that and the embroidery, which we did using brightly coloured wool on a quite open weave fabric. We learned all kinds of different stitches. Until their move into the care home Dad still had a bookmark I made using a variety of stitches, and Mum a square tablemat.

Something else I enjoyed were the plays we put on for our parents. One was based on The King's Breakfast, by A A Milne. I was the queen and there was a butter pat made of cardboard, with just a corner of real butter at one end, for using in the play. Another little play was The Queen of Hearts (based on the nursery rhyme) and Mum made jam tarts for that one, for the knave to steal. Each year in December the school also gave a concert where we acted out a Nativity play and sang Christmas carols.

I know that I did much better at school there than at Bletchley, because I was happy and also because Miss Stonton was a really good teacher.

Now I was enjoying reading Enid Blyton's Famous Five books and a series about Tamzin and Rissa, two girls with ponies who had adventures on Romney Marsh. At that time I couldn't imagine anything better than being like them.

Thinking of books reminds me of something that happened when I was ill in bed during that year. Mum had left me reading while she went into Bedford to do a bit of shopping. When she arrived home she came into my bedroom to see how I was feeling and said that she had bought me a book. I was quite excited, expecting that it would be another pony book and looking forward to reading it.

However Mum handed me a book with a plain blue cover, saying she thought I was ready to learn about this now. It was a book on human reproduction (with diagrams), written for my age group. I did read it and found it quite interesting - but at the same time I was very disappointed! But I suppose that Mum felt it was time that I knew about such things.

We didn't have sex education lessons at school. In fact they were unheard of. Mum never mentioned anything about the subject either. As younger children we picked up bits and pieces of information, or more often misinformation, from the older ones, so did need something to put us straight. At least this meant that I now had some real knowledge that I could pass on and we girls could talk about amongst ourselves.

There was one really sad event that school year though, in January. Grandad had been very ill with what was diagnosed as a form of leukaemia. I think it was actually myeloma, which two of his children also later died from. Grandad's strength failed and eventually he slept downstairs in the front room. One Saturday in January I couldn't find the time to visit Grandma and Grandad. I don't remember what I was doing that day but I know I told myself that I would go to see them the following weekend. However I was too late, as before then Grandad died.

I felt very upset and really bad about not having made the time to see him the previous weekend. This was partly from guilt but also because I really did love him. He was the first person close to me whose death I can recall. I always think of him even now, whenever I hear Handel's Largo. I'm not sure if it was a piece of music he liked or just that I was playing it a lot on the piano around the time of his death. It doesn't matter really because either way I shall always associate it with him.

Carole and I didn't go to Grandad's funeral, I don't know why. Nothing was said and it didn't occur to me to ask. It was just the way things were. What I do remember of that day, with Mum and Dad in Bletchley for most of it, is eating school dinner for the one and only time at Stewartby School.

My friend Margaret and I would sometimes stay with one another. Otherwise we did not meet outside of school, with living in different villages. She rode to and from her home in Cranfield on the school bus every day.

Margaret's family owned their own home and her dad had a car. Once when I stayed at her house he woke us at about 5.00am to go gathering mushrooms. Her mum loaned me a pair of her old shoes, as the dew was very heavy and I only had sandals with me.

Then Margaret's dad drove us out to the old aerodrome at Cranfield and we found lots of mushrooms growing there. We cut them and took them back to have fried with bacon for breakfast. I have never eaten fresher or better tasting mushrooms. Unfortunately the shoes I had borrowed were blue suede (really!) and all the dye came out in the dew, so I had blue feet for a few days after that.

I still played with Val sometimes and now I also had a new hobby. Dad gave me an old Box Brownie camera. The only place you could get film for it was a little shop on Aylesbury Street in Fenny Stratford but it worked perfectly well. There was no colour photography but I took black and white pictures - just outdoor ones as there was no flash either! I had great fun with it though. The pictures I took printed up very small but I was really pleased with them. I put my pictures into an album using 'photo corners.' You slotted each corner of a photograph into one of these, licked the gummed backs and stuck them into an album with the photograph in situ.

The cinema was still our main source of visual entertainment. The village hall at Stewartby had a film reel projector and showed films one evening a week, I think on a Tuesday. I went occasionally and especially remember going to see the black and white comedy Carry on Sergeant. About halfway through the film there was a power cut. We waited a while but then the showing was cancelled and everyone left the hall to walk home in the dark, the street lights all being out.

The brickworks used to sound a hooter for the beginning and ending of shifts. When the electricity was out they used an old wind-up air raid siren instead. We hadn't yet reached the top of the village that evening when the siren sounded. As Carole says, even without its wartime connotations it is a really spooky sound, the rise and fall of it. It's a good thing we had not been watching a horror film!

I had my second and final term of swimming lessons at Stewartby pool that summer and received a certificate for swimming a length of the pool. We had a little awards presentation there at the end of the summer term.

This picture shows Lady Stewart (in the hat) and Miss Stonton, presenting me with my certificate. What you can see behind is the works canteen with the wall here rather strangely forming one end of the swimming pool enclosure. So those eating in the canteen could watch the antics in and around the pool.

Before I go on to what happened next at school, I'll tell you about the three types of State (public) secondary schooling back then. Secondary Modern Schools were where most children completed their education. Then there were Technical Schools for those who showed practical abilities. The third and final type were the Grammar Schools, for pupils who proved themselves to have more of an intellectual ability by passing an exam known as the Eleven Plus. (We went on to secondary education at eleven years old.) The exam consisted of subjects such as spelling and English, mental arithmetic, written arithmetic and general knowledge.

That year I took the Eleven Plus exam myself. Although if we passed it we were supposed to go on to grammar school, Bedford did not have its own grammar school then. The Harpur Trust ran four private schools in Bedford. Two were boys' schools, Bedford School for Boys and Bedford Modern School for Boys. Two were girls' schools, Bedford High School for Girls and The Dame Alice Harpur School.

The local council paid the trust for a free place at one of these schools for any pupil who passed the Eleven Plus. The exam application had to state which of the schools was your first choice to attend, of the two boys' or girls' schools.

These schools were not just for those of secondary school age. They took in fee paying children from seven years old as private pupils.

As I recall, our family really knew very little about the schools in Bedford. Margaret said that if she passed she would go to Bedford High School, so my parents agreed to mark that as first choice on my application form. As it happened, I passed but Margaret didn't. Being the only girl from our school who did pass the exam in 1956, I was very much on my own.

What we did not know was that The Modern School and Dame Alice had a direct grant from the government and were required to take a certain number of state scholarship pupils each year.

Bedford School and Bedford High School were fully independent. If your Eleven Plus marks were high enough, they would offer you their own test to see if you met their entry criteria. If your Eleven Plus marks were not high enough, or if you failed their test, you went to one of the other Harpur Trust schools. So Mum took me on the appointed day to Bedford High School for the test.

# EXPANDING HORIZONS

Bedford town centre roughly comprised an area from the High Street on the east to partway down Midland Road on the west. The river was to the south and the High School, on Bromham Road, to the north side of the town centre. The school was a big, old, rather imposing building, surrounded by iron railings. The walls of Bedford Prison were on one side (across a side road to the right as you faced the school). An old disused church (which the school later took over) and graveyard were on the other, to the left. I remember the school as always rather dark and dingy inside.

Although a Harpur Trust boys' school had been founded several hundred years previously, Bedford High School itself opened in 1882. A single story annexe housing science laboratories and a domestic science kitchen, reached by a covered way, had been added in the 1920s but the big main building did date from the opening. That with its size probably helps to explain why it initially felt so daunting for me after Stewartby School.

Bedford High School for Girls

In fact both the school and the test were very daunting to me. The worst thing was that although I had learned simple fractions I had not learned anything about decimals at Stewartby School. Although these were in the test, I did somehow manage to pass.

Then came the summer holidays, with another stay in Beighton. I looked forward to that and really enjoyed it again. Uncle Fred bred and showed canaries. They were British Rollers, a breed judged not on their looks (although they were pretty, pale yellow with grey markings) but their singing and I loved them. That summer he told me I could have one if I saved up and bought a cage for it, so there was a target for me.

There was so much to be done before I started school. I had to have a complete school uniform. Although my parents may possibly have got some help with this, it was very expensive. The brickwork's manager Mr Forbes and his wife had a daughter Gayle, older than me, who was a private pupil at the school. They passed on some of her outgrown clothes for me, to help my parents out with the cost. All the uniform items had to be bought from one of two shops in Bedford, expensive ones naturally.

The basic colour of our uniforms was navy blue: knee length skirt, cardigan and outer garments. We wore these with white blouses, long sleeved in winter with a tie, and open neck short sleeved in summer after the first year, when we wore checked dresses.

Although we wore white vests (singlets) we had to wear navy blue knickers. These had elastic around the leg openings that left red marks when you took them off. Our games shorts were like an almost knee length, pleated divided skirt, culottes really.

Outer garments were a navy blazer, with the school badge on the pocket, a navy gabardine raincoat and a thick overcoat. Nobody ever wore the overcoat but every so often there was a uniform check and you had to bring it into school. Since all our clothes must have nametags sewn inside it would have been hard to borrow one! I had an overcoat from Gayle Forbes, never wore it and used it just for the checks throughout my High School life.

Our winter hats were navy blue round felt, 'pudding basin' shaped, with a brim. In the summer term we wore straw hats of the same shape, although the 6$^{th}$ form wore boaters. In my first year we wore knee length beige socks in winter and short white ones in summer. After that, all year round we wore stockings.

Initially these stockings were awful, made of thick lisle material with seams up the back. I could never keep my seams straight! And the suspender belts we had to wear to hold them up were a nightmare. They always pulled down to cut into my hips. Eventually as tights became more universal we were allowed to wear them instead of stockings, which was a real relief. We were still supposed to wear thick pairs but by buying a darker colour some of us got away with more sheer ones. We also had to wear black lace-up shoes all year round in the higher forms, after being allowed brown sandals for summer in my first year.

The contrast with the navy blue was our House colour. There were eight Houses in the school. Four were boarding Houses and four comprised daygirls. The boarding Houses were just that, four big old houses all within easy walking distance of the school site.

For the daygirls, Bedford itself was divided into three areas and the county area outside the town was the fourth, to make up the

Houses. Because I lived outside Bedford I was in Russell House. Our House colour was a very boring, disappointing brown. So my hatband was brown and white horizontal stripes and my tie was striped diagonally in brown, grey and white.

The hatband had the school badge on the front, as did our blazer: a spread eagle, similar to the Bedford town coat of arms. Our school magazine was called the Aquila, which is Latin for eagle.

There were all kinds of school rules to learn. In school we had to walk on the left hand side of the corridors and stairs, strictly no running. We could not chew gum or eat in the school building. We were not allowed to wear any jewellery, makeup, nail polish or to colour our hair. If hair was below shoulder length it had to be tied back or put up. And of course, no talking in class!

Outside school, we had yet more rules. We could not eat or drink in the street and must not remove our hats or any item of uniform between school and home. In term time we were not allowed in any hotel, restaurant, café, snack bar or milk bar without a parent or guardian. Also in term time, we could not go to any place of public entertainment with anybody at all without written permission.

Another petty rule was that girls at the school up to and including my first year were only allowed to wear watches if they were in Russell House and had to catch buses and trains. We were also the only girls allowed to carry money. But it had to be in a regulation (navy blue) zip purse on a cord, worn diagonally over a shoulder. So the rules were strict. Being basically a private school, you either accepted the rules or did not go.

Of course I did go. I had my cousin Brenda's old leather satchel in which to carry my schoolbooks and writing supplies. Now we had to buy my pens, pencils and so forth. At least we were allowed to use fountain pens at the High School, although still not ballpoints.

The private pupils also had to buy their schoolbooks but the council paid for mine. They were obtained from Hockliffe's, a big stationer come bookshop in Bedford. Most were second-hand books, as the shop would buy them back at the end of the school year to resell to the pupils coming up.

The council also paid for a season ticket on the bus for me. Because of course, now I had to catch the bus to and from school and there would be no more coming home for dinner. I left the house at about ten past eight in the morning and arrived home just before five in the afternoon, usually travelling on the buses that ran to the bottom end of the village.

The double-decker buses had open platforms without doors but you could not get off just when you wanted. They all had a conductor as well as a driver. The conductor came round the bus with a ticket machine and moneybag, worn on shoulder straps, and rang the bell to tell the driver when to stop and start. He, or she if a conductress, also kept order on the bus.

When all the seats were taken there was no congregating at the front of the bus by those standing. The conductor made sure everyone moved as far back as possible, so that there was room for those getting on the bus further along the route.

First thing every morning we had an assembly in the school hall. This hall was big enough to take the whole school population. It included a stage, where all the teachers sat for assembly, an organ and galleried seating as well as chairs in the main body of the hall. As long as we didn't try it too frequently, we could get out of assembly sometimes with," The bus was late."

Bedford High School Hall

During my first year I had school dinners. But I wasn't very keen. The only thing I remember really liking was the chocolate sponge pudding with chocolate sauce. It just wasn't worth the money.

As I think with all schools then, there was no choice of food. A set two-course meal was served and that was it. So after the first year I took sandwiches. What kind of sandwiches? I really loved tomato ones: just sliced, salted tomato on buttered bread that had gone quite soggy by the time I ate the sandwiches! Now it was for me that Mum plated up a dinner and steamed it over the saucepan when I got home.

I wasn't quite on my own as a schoolgirl on the bus going to school. The three Whiting girls, Judith, Honor and Janice, were private pupils at the school. They had all started going there at seven years of age. Judith was perhaps three years older than me, Honor about a year older and Janice a year younger. Their sister Venetia, who was only three or four, also went to a private school in Bedford. They were the daughters of Dr Whiting, the head of the laboratory. Their mother was a teacher at Stewartby Secondary Modern School and they lived on The Crescent.

But my first year at the school was miserable. I wasn't put in the top class of my year and there was just one other scholarship pupil with me, Deirdre nicknamed Dee. Her father was a police inspector. She was the only friend I really had that year and we remained friends throughout school and beyond. All the others had already been at the school for several years. One, Paula, was 'queen' of the class. She took a dislike to me from the first day and most of the others followed her lead. She really looked down on me, for example making fun of my hand knitted cardigans and my 'common' accent (common being used as a derogatory term).

The cut-off birth date for taking the Eleven Plus was the end of September. With my birthday being in October, I was always one of the oldest in my class. I was more physically developed than the other girls, wearing a bra from the start of my time at Bedford High. Nowadays I would probably be proud of that. Then, it was just another reason for those girls to torment me. As it transpired, I was also among the best in that class academically in most subjects. That did not go down well either. Nor did the fact that I was not sporty.

Sports - we had to play two sports in summer and two in winter. It was quite a walk from the school to and from the sports field on Beverley Crescent, along Bromham Road away from the town centre. At the school itself there was just too little ground.

I played hockey and netball in the winter. Netball was all right and I became quite good. I played hockey rather than the other choice, lacrosse, largely because I had been given Gayle Forbes' old hockey stick. Having never played before I really did not know what I was doing and I did not enjoy it. I didn't mind so much being in goal, which was where I ended up playing.

In that first summer I played tennis and went swimming. I had been given Brenda's old wooden tennis racket, together with a press to keep the rim straight. That determined my choice of sport, as the other was cricket and I didn't have a bat. But again, I had never played tennis and could not match the others so did not really enjoy that either. Swimming was fine but the pool was pretty disgusting. We used Bedford School's pool, another outdoor one. By the end of the season you could barely see the bottom. It must have been a real health hazard.

PE classes were pretty miserable for me. One reason was that I was not very athletic. But I think it might not have been too bad had I ever used the gym equipment before. This was something else that the other girls had been doing for several years and that I was just expected to get on with. Run at a vaulting horse? Climb a rope? These kinds of things were just outside my experience. Now give me a *tree* to climb and I would have been all right.

Needlework class, which was compulsory that year, was the one I hated most. Our first project was to make a full length underslip. We had to cut out the pieces from a pattern and sew them all together by hand. The stitching had to be pretty near perfect and then we had to oversew every seam in blanket stitch. Well, I didn't get mine finished until almost the end of the school year. Nearly everyone else had already finished making cookery aprons etc on the sewing machines by then. Dad said, "Our Jean, she can do owt (anything) with a needle bar (but) sew!"

During that year it was always a relief to get home, even with quite a lot of homework to do. French was compulsory and Mum still laughs as we recall my early attempts at speaking the simple sentences I had to learn.

For domestic science (just cookery really) lessons I had to take the ingredients and a container into school. I brought my efforts home for the family to eat. Some were successful and some less so. I once had to make a large jam tart. I was rolling my pastry out when the teacher came round. She told me it was too dry and made me put it back in the bowl to mix in more water. I already knew it wasn't right to treat pastry like that but had no choice. Sure enough, with all that handling that tart pastry was like leather when we came to eat it.

We did have one special occasion that first school year. 1957 was the school's 75$^{th}$ anniversary. The Duchess of Gloucester came to visit both us and Dame Alice Harpur School (which had begun as part of the High School) in the summer term. There were various celebrations that day but the only ones in which I was involved were a special assembly and a panoramic school photograph.

I had a pair of roller skates and nearly every evening in the winter before that anniversary would be out on them with John Ireland, who lived in the house nearest to the railway line. With a streetlight on the corner of Wavell Close the dark evenings didn't bother us. I remember things like the nuts on the soles loosening and the front of the skates shooting forward so that we'd have to stop and tighten them with a special little spanner. And it certainly wasn't smooth going on those pavements. On small wheeled roller skates we felt every little unevenness almost as though we were on cobblestones. But we had fun.

For several winters I suffered from chilblains on my toes. They were not such fun. Anyone who has had them knows how red and itchy they can get. The worst times were when I toasted my toes by the fire, or on a radiator at school, after coming in from the cold. Nothing seemed to help either. The chilblains just came and went.

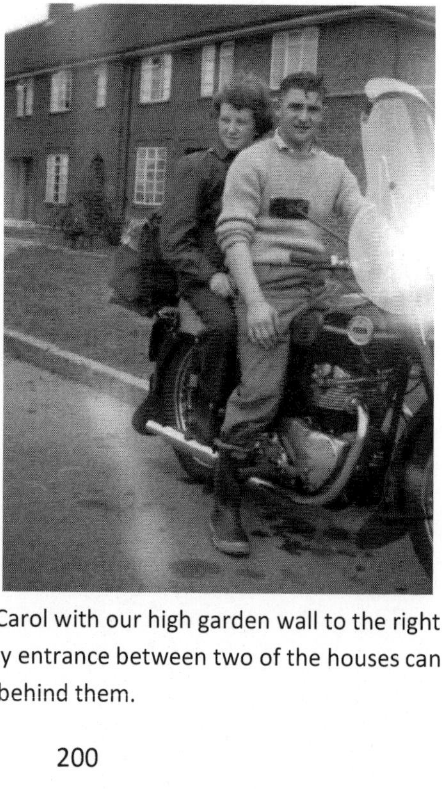

Charles and Carol with our high garden wall to the right. A passageway entrance between two of the houses can just be seen behind them.

That Easter we had a short visit from my Cousin Charles (Uncle Fred and Auntie Mary's older son), his wife Carol and another couple who were their friends. They rode down on motorbikes. We'd never had such a visit before. Sister Carole and I were suitably impressed.

Charles went into Kempston to buy fish and chips for our tea, taking me with him on the back of his motorcycle. That was very exciting and special, if not very safe in ordinary clothes and with no helmet. But as you know there was no law then requiring helmets and not a lot of traffic on the roads.

In the summer term and the holiday, as I have said, I spent most of my time at the swimming pool. Most days in the summer term I came home as usual and walked up the village for my tea. Then I headed off down to Stewartby pool, so much better than the school one, to get a couple of hours of swimming in before it closed at 8 o'clock. I did this for several years and came home from that very tired and very hungry; but then as you know I was always hungry after a couple of hours or more of swimming.

Reading remained a solace to me. Among the books I was reading now were Enid Blyton's 'Adventure' series: The Mountain of Adventure, The Sea of Adventure, and so on. I could escape into another world in my books and not notice anything going on around me. Anybody wanting to speak to me would have to raise their voice and repeat themselves to get my attention. I know it could be very irritating for others at times!

There was also always Cambridge Street at weekends. In term time I now travelled to Bletchley from St John's station, which was quite a walk from the High school, on Friday afternoons.

I had another camera now too. This was a bellows camera that Dad had brought back from Germany with him after the war. There was a hole in the bellows but we patched that over with sticking plaster that I painted black to match. Although it did not have flash, I could adjust the exposure. By trial and error I managed to take one or two pictures indoors.

When I finally did have a flash camera, sometime later, it was really basic. You had to change the flash bulb after every picture and each time a bulb flashed it gave off a very distinctive odour. A big advance was the flashcube. That rotated after each use so that you could take four pictures before changing it. The built in flash mechanism that came later was even more convenient, to be followed by automatic flash and then eventually digital imaging. It even seems that 3D photographs might become quite commonplace in the not too distant future.

I've always enjoyed taking pictures but now when I think of it I can still marvel at being able to review, download and edit my images myself rather than having to pay to get them developed and printed.

I did not see so much of Val now and gradually lost touch with Margaret. This picture must be from one of the last occasions that I went to stay with her. The rubber tyre reminds me of when hula hoops were all the rage!

But I did make friends with the Whiting girls, especially Honor. I would sometimes go to play at their house. A thing that sticks in my mind from one of those visits is the drink that Judith made us.

It was bright green and fizzy. What we found she had done was to mix orange squash with green food colouring and, for fizz, Andrews Liver Salts - which are a laxative! I don't remember what the results were, perhaps mercifully.

This picture of Honor was taken in the Whitings' back garden. It was a great place to pitch Venetia's tent and play in the summer.

Judith was often in hot water at school, mostly just bunking off. When she was a bit older though she got into real trouble. Milk bars were popular then. They basically sold milk shakes, which at that time in England were just made from milk that was flavoured with syrup and frothed up, to be drunk through a straw.

There was a milk bar near the old bus station. One day during school time Judith was spotted in the milk bar by a teacher. This particular elderly teacher would not go in but stood at the door and ordered Judith out. No chance! Judith didn't leave until long after the teacher had gone.

I'm not sure of Judith's punishment but know her parents were warned that she could face expulsion if she carried on like that. Still, she made it to the end of her school career and all the sisters did well in life. Now, after many years, we five are in touch again.

Mum bought me two new summer outfits that year, thinking I would really like them. They were cotton and each had a full white skirt with small coloured spots and a sleeveless, solid colour blouse that matched the spots on the skirt. One was red and one was blue. Each blouse had a little Peter Pan collar in the same material as the skirt.

When I first saw them I thought they were lovely. The trouble was, the skirts were much too long for me and I felt very self-conscious in them. Did I tell Mum? No, because I thought it would upset her if I did when she was so pleased with having bought them for me. It was really silly, for I know now that she would have been happy to shorten them for me had I told her.

That summer was a special one at Beighton. Brenda and Keith got married at the end of August. I was a bridesmaid and went up to stay before the wedding. We had to get my bridesmaid dress fitted and of course I was very happy to have the extra time there.

Originally Brenda was to have had four bridesmaids, two of them adults and two girls. One adult had to drop out. Brenda decided to have me as the other 'adult' one, paired with Sylvia who was engaged to her brother Brian. The other young bridesmaid, Andrea, was just ten years old. I naturally felt very pleased and quite grownup with this decision.

Looking at the photographs I think it was the right choice, as I was actually even just a little taller than Sylvia.

The rest of the family came up for the wedding, a day we all really enjoyed. There was a live band at the reception, which was held in the upstairs function room of a workingmen's club in Beighton High Street. Although we had a catered sit-down meal after the afternoon wedding, in the early evening we were back in Aunt Annie's kitchen making sandwiches to take down to the club for a late supper. I don't know what time I got to bed that night.

My second year at the High School was the start of a real improvement. I was moved away from my tormentors up into the top streaming. I felt much more at home there and although I was never right at the top of the class, I was always somewhere above the middle. I began to like the school better. I made friends with another Margaret and as time went by with other girls as well. My only sadness was that Dee was not moved up with me. I also wasn't enthralled that being in the top streaming meant I had to learn Latin in addition to French but I managed to cope. It was better than the needlework anyway!

Val had passed her Eleven Plus to go to Dame Alice and although not always coming home at the same time was on the morning bus every day, which kept us more in touch with one another.

We now had one black girl at the High School. She was the daughter of an African diplomat who had been posted to London. What I most remember is that, although none of the rest of us were allowed to wear any jewellery, she wore two little gold earrings. She was soon accepted into the school but I wonder now what *she* made of it all - and of us.

A big plus was that from now on I only had to do one sport at a time, so netball in winter and swimming in summer. I actually got into the House netball team and we didn't do too badly. But I still had to do the dreaded PE for another year.

At the start of one lesson that year's teacher said there was something that she thought we all ought to know now. She appeared very embarrassed so of course we all wondered what she was going to come out with. Eventually she managed to say that at our age it was time to start using underarm deodorant and perhaps shaving our armpits too. What an anticlimax!

Something that was very exciting that autumn however was the launch of the Russian Sputnik, the first unmanned artificial satellite. In fact it was the first man-made object ever to actually leave the earth's atmosphere. This happened in October, not long before my birthday. So now the dream of men in space was coming very close to reality.

I started to get toothache early on in this school year and we realised that I had not been to a dentist since leaving Stewartby Junior School. With Bedford High School being a private school, there was no school dentist. Mum and Dad still went to their old dentist in Bletchley. I spoke with my friend Margaret who lived in Bedford and she told me her dentist was Mr Ingrouille, who had an NHS practice in De Pary's Avenue. He took me on to his books so that was where I started to go too.

My teeth were in a terrible state. I was really upset and told Mr Ingrouille I truly did brush them twice every day and didn't eat a lot of sweet stuff. He said it was nothing to do with how I cared for my teeth, just the way they were.

Oh dear, I had about five months of regular treatment with a slow, old-fashioned drill. Then Mr Ingrouille said he might as well give me my next check up and found one more tooth that needed filling. After that I definitely went conscientiously for my six monthly checks and my teeth have never got into that state again.

What I did start to have now though were spots. I didn't have them nearly as badly as some teenagers but was still very conscious of them. Like most youngsters, I tried all kinds of remedies but sadly none of them worked! To this day I still get the odd one at times, on my chest and back as well as on my face.

I also started to suffer the normal teenage angst about my looks etc. But it didn't totally consume me, with other things going on.

One of these was the science fiction TV serial, Quatermass and the Pit. Mrs Raebone let me go across and watch it at her home. It was very scary and I can still vividly picture the monsters. I loved it but, with it being shown on winter evenings, I quickly ran home across the square in the dark when each episode was over. I also much enjoyed Journey into Space on the wireless. Carole however was really frightened by it.

Dad had made a wooden cased extension speaker to the wireless, which he mounted on the kitchen wall. It was for Mum to listen to as she worked. However when Journey into Space came on it wasn't Mum but me in the kitchen, with the wireless sound in the living room turned off. I could then listen without Carole being scared. I didn't mind, as long as I was able to hear it somewhere, and quite enjoyed sitting alone in the kitchen near the boiler.

We also listened to a lot of light comedy on the wireless. But one of the weirdest programmes must have been Educating Archie. Archie was a ventriloquist's dummy - on the radio?

I was also still, as I have remained, an omnivorous reader. At this time I was into old style horror stories. Often when I went to bed I would get right down under the covers with my book and torch (flashlight). I would then scare myself half to death and not want to stick my head up out of the covers to settle for the night.

Most of my reading at the time came from Bedford's two public libraries, now amalgamated into one. Bedford Town Library, in the centre, was free to people who lived within the town itself.

The County Library, which was then housed along The Embankment by the river, was free to all county inhabitants outside the town boundary. As a minor and at school in Bedford I didn't have to pay to use the Town Library. However the County was in any case the one I frequented the most. It was much larger and with a correspondingly greater selection of books.

The County Library is along here

We did get our own television set at around this time too. Looking like a box on legs it was not bought though but rented for a modest monthly sum. The screens were by now a larger size and, although remaining quite big, the cabinets were nonetheless much less bulky than previously. The picture was still just black and white and we also still only had two channels, BBC and the commercial station ATV.

The picture quality was often poor, as we were at the edge of the broadcasting range for our area. And we still had to manually adjust the picture. But we didn't mind too much. We just enjoyed having it.

Mum had a bad dose of flu that winter. It is the only time I remember her having to stay in bed. I was recovering from a sinus head cold, which had left me with a blocked up nose. I remember well one dinner I cooked when Mum simply could not do anything. I fried pork chops. Unfortunately the scent of the raw meat somehow just stuck in my nostrils and I couldn't smell anything else or believe the chops were cooked. By the time Dad and Carole got home for dinner those chops were so hard and tough they could probably have been used to sole our shoes!

With birthday and Christmas money, and saving from my pocket money, I had gathered together enough to buy a birdcage and stand. Uncle Fred sent a canary down for me in its own travelling box, which I collected from Midland Road station in Bedford. I was thrilled to bits. The bird had pretty markings and soon showed what a singer he was too. He seemed to try to outdo the wireless and television in volume, whenever either was on. Any noise and away he trilled. He always joined our conversations.

I didn't mind cleaning the canary's cage but the one thing I did not like was that his claws had to be cut every so often. I cut them with nail scissors but found it quite traumatic. First he had to be caught. Then I held him in my left hand, his little heart beating away. I had to be very careful as blood vessels ran a certain length into his claws, so I mustn't cut them too short. Once a claw did bleed and I felt dreadful.

It was when I was thirteen that I first went out with a boy. He was fifteen, lived in Bedford but had a Saturday job at the fish and chip shop in Bletchley. He travelled home on my train on a Saturday and he knew the guards too, so would also travel in the guard's van. That is how I met him.

I was so embarrassed. He went to Bedford Modern School, which was then in the centre of town near the market square, St Paul's Square. The school site is now a shopping centre. However, back then he would be waiting at the square on his bike when our bus arrived in the morning. Sometimes I did get off at the market but never if I saw him waiting. It was no good. He would then cycle after the bus to the old bus station and speak to me when I got off there. Eventually I agreed to go to the cinema with him.

He met me off the bus in Bedford that evening, reeking of aftershave. His pockets were filled with little paper bags of assorted sweets, which he kept offering to me all through the cinema programme. He was obviously very nervous. The trouble was, he hadn't cleaned his teeth and had black bits between them. I'm afraid that was something that I just couldn't stand! Looking back I feel sorry for him because I simply couldn't go out with him again after that. It was about two years before I went out with another boy.

A sad loss that year was Fritz. He had been suffering for quite some time with arthritis in his hind legs. Uncle had spent a small fortune on the new steroid treatment for him but Fritz had come to a point where he really did not want to move or do anything. He spent most of his time lying across the dining room doorway, where he growled unhappily when anyone but Uncle or I stepped over him. Uncle of course was his pack leader. As for me, I reckon he really must have looked on me as his puppy.

Then Dad had a phone call at the club one day to say that Fritz was in so much misery that Uncle had finally taken him to the vet to be put down. We were all very upset and I really grieved.

Uncle and Auntie never had another dog although Auntie did get one years later, after Uncle had died and Ken moved away for a while.

One more difficult thing that year was that Dad had to spend quite a long time in hospital. He slipped a disc in his spine and was put on traction for weeks. The tape they used on his ankles set off an allergic reaction that can still trouble him today. Even though he was off work in hospital colleagues would, when visiting, bring Dad their questions and problems about the club.

In those days Dad still smoked his roll-ups and believe it or not you were allowed to smoke in hospital. He also had a bottle of whisky there with him. Well he was not actually ill, was he?

After he came out of hospital it was still quite some time before Dad was well enough to go back to work. As he lay on the couch at home he taught me to play cribbage with him, which I enjoyed and which helped to relieve his boredom.

In swimming lessons that summer I worked toward my bronze life saving medal. One of the requirements for this was to duck dive in about six feet of water and retrieve a rubber brick from the bottom of the pool. The sides and bottom of the Bedford School pool were so green, and the water so murky, that you had to watch like a hawk where the brick splashed down as it was thrown in. Then you had to pretty much retrieve it by feel. I really felt I had achieved something when I gained that award.

There was still time for swimming in Stewartby pool. Over the next couple of years I sometimes, at weekends and in the summer holidays, worked in the little kiosk built into an end wall of the pool. It sold sweets, bars of chocolates, biscuits and soft drinks. I enjoyed doing that although at times it was very hot and stuffy.

I went up to Beighton as usual for a short holiday. Although she knew I was supposed to wear the laced shoes with built-up soles Auntie Annie, who spoiled me anyway, bought me my first pair of slip-on flat shoes, shiny black patent leather. I loved them.

I'd had a pair of slip-ons as a bridesmaid but I couldn't wear those ordinarily. These new ones though began the end of me wearing sensible shoes, apart from for school.

That summer of 1958 Mum, Dad, Carole and I had our first proper family holiday together. We all went to stay at the little town of Broadstairs on the Kent coast with Auntie and Ken.

I can't remember why Uncle didn't come with us. I know that he looked after our Bess though, while the rest of us were away enjoying ourselves at the seaside.

Dumpton Gap, Broadstairs

Our boarding house landlady, Mrs Mugford, owned a parrot. He stood on a large perch, shuffling up and down it and talking. He also picked up big seeds with a claw and cracked them open with his beak. He was fascinating to watch and listen to.

The boarding house was on the clifftop area of Broadstairs and we had to walk down long flights of steep steps to reach the little sandy bays that made up the shoreline. The nearest one, which we mostly went to, was called Dumpton Gap.

At the bottom of the steps there were kiosks. One hired out deck chairs and windbreaks. The other sold ice creams, sweets, biscuits and drinks. Fortunately there were also toilets down there. The main beach and town centre were in a flatter area of Broadstairs, a little further along the coast.

We played games, played in the sand and the sea, and swam. In the picture below I think Mum is writing postcards as Auntie sits knitting. Ken, with me next to him and Carole on the right, are busy in the sand. You can see the kiosks either side of the entrance to the bay and the cliffs in the background.

Busy Bees at Dumpton Gap

We laughed at Dad on the beach. His face, neck and lower arms were all quite brown from gardening and going fishing. But when he stripped off to his swimming trunks the rest of him stood out in stark contrast. I think you can see in the picture below of him on the beach with Ken why we called Dad the 'lily-white'!

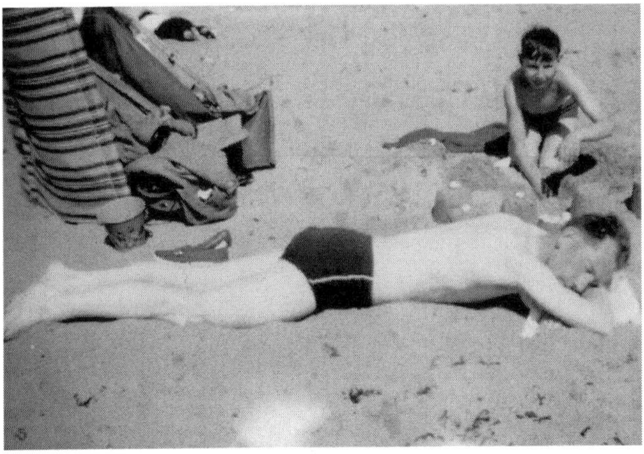

There were wide grassy areas on the cliff top where we played ball games and Jokari. We wandered around the sea front and the town and there was entertainment, too.

Here we are, ready to play: me with Mum, Ken and Carole

For us children, a little café was a magnet. It had a jukebox and we listened to, among others, the Everly Brothers - with the older teenagers there feeding in the money to play the records. As you can see, the weather was warm and sunny for us. We all had a lovely time. The week went by far too quickly.

The following school year the work got harder and homework took up more time. One good thing was that I finally got to grips with algebra. We had a teacher that year who had a frightening reputation as being very strict: Miss Addis, known as the adder. I discovered that whilst she was strict she was also very fair. If you were really trying, she would help you. It was her teaching that turned on the light bulb for me with algebra.

Thinking of maths, although we did not have calculators we did have little books of mathematical tables: logarithms, sine, cosine etc. We also learned to use a slide rule.

For Latin that year we had the deputy headmistress, Miss Batley, naturally known by us as 'Batty.' She was a little elderly woman with greyish white hair cut in a short bob. The edge of her fringe (bangs), where it hung down nearly to her eyes, was constantly stained a nicotine brown. Her classes always ended slap bang on time and never started early. Between every lesson she'd be in the staff room smoking. Nor was she a very good teacher. Half the time we did not really know what she was talking about.

I had my first job in that Easter holiday. It was on the sweet and hot nut counter in Bedford Woolworth's store. The counters were hollow rectangles. Each had an opening on one side with a flap in the counter top that you lifted to enter and exit. The staff stood inside and served customers as they came up. We also took the money, using an old-fashioned till. Goodness, we even had to work out the change ourselves! I really enjoyed working there.

The nuts were kept in deep metal pans with heating elements beneath them. We weighed both nuts and sweets out into small white paper bags. Extra supplies for topping up the pans were kept beneath the counter. Sometimes I would duck down and snatch a handful of cashew nuts, my favourites.

On the way home with my first week's wages I bought Mum a bunch of daffodils from the market. It was the first money I had ever earned myself and somehow that felt only right. As you know I did get pocket money, by now 7/6 a week. I have to confess that his was not dependent on any little jobs I might do for Mum as I had no chores, although I did keep my bedroom tidy!

Birthday and Christmas presents came out of my pocket money before I began working. At Christmas the shops did not start being festive until December, so there was no getting bored with things. We enjoyed all the decorations. I loved the toiletry scents too as I shopped for presents. No stores played any piped music, at any time of the year. Bliss! How I wish it was the same now.

Although I enjoyed swimming so much, I often managed to get out of lessons at that dirty Bedford School pool in both the summer term of this year and my remaining years at school. Nobody ever seemed to bother. My friend Margaret kept the excuses book and I'm not sure if anyone else even noticed.

As sport was always the last activity of the school day I then just took the bus home and went swimming in Stewartby pool instead. It was so very much pleasanter.

Mr Kitchener, the pool manager, even let me swim in the deeper water when the juniors had their lessons in the shallow end.

High Street from the river end with St Paul's (Market) Square on left.

Also in that summer term, Honor and I created real anxiety for our parents. I was fourteen years old and Honor just fifteen. To go home we both usually caught the 4.20pm bus (which went to the bottom of the village) at the bus station.

This day I had a seat but there were a number of people standing as the bus filled. I gave up my seat to an elderly woman, as I had been taught to do and as was in any case good manners and considerate.

By the time we reached the next stop, the market square, the conductress had been round and found there were too many people standing. She made me get off the bus. Was that unfair or what?

To add insult to injury, we knew that many of the passengers only travelled a short distance on that bus, using it because they could not be bothered to wait a few more minutes for the town buses. Honor got off with me to keep me company. We daren't wait at the market square where there was a big queue but ran back along the High Street toward the bus station. We were trying to catch the 4.40pm, which went along the Ampthill Road. When we reached the corner of St Peter's Street we saw that the bus had already left the bus station and was stopped at the traffic lights.

With the bus just having an open platform, we tried to climb on. Of course, the conductor was right there by the entrance and would not let us.

Crossroads at St Peter's with John Bunyan's statue

So there we were, and with an hour to wait for the next bus we decided to walk back home. We very unrealistically thought we could be there before the bus. I had no money but Honor had enough to buy some plums for refreshment on our walk.

Off we set, to walk along the Kempston Road to the main A421 and home. To say that we were over optimistic would be a real understatement. The walk was well over five miles long.

The day was still hot and we were soon getting tired but there was nothing to do but keep going. We could not even wait at a bus stop for the next bus that came along. Although I had my season ticket, Honor's return bus ticket had been cancelled on the first bus and she had spent her money on the plums.

With hindsight I think we would probably have been able to give her name and address to the conductor for the fare to be paid later, with perhaps an administration charge. However such a thought never entered our heads at the time. It's so often only after the event that realisation dawns.

A bus did pass us as we trudged on, getting more and more tired in the heat. This *was* the beginning of a very hot, dry, summer. As we got close to Stewartby we decided to take a short cut across a ploughed field. I think the farmer must have harvested his crop early and there was nothing growing that we could damage. That decision was a big mistake though. It was very hard work trudging through the thick, dry clay soil.

We separated when we finally reached Stewartby, each to our own home. Although I cannot now recall just what time it was when we got back, I think it must have been around 7o'clock. We were both afraid of being punished for being so late. Mum and Dad were extremely relieved to see me and, like parents anywhere and at any time, that relief did briefly translate into anger with me for causing so much anxiety.

My parents and the Whitings had realised that neither of us had arrived home and they had been worried sick. They'd contacted the school and then the bus company and the police, not knowing where to start looking. All they knew was that we hadn't come home on our usual bus or any of the later ones. When I had my own children I could understand what we put them through.

Anger swiftly turned back into concern. Mum got me a bowl of hot water to soak my feet and then I had something to eat and was so tired that I just went to bed. Dad spoke to Dr Whiting, who had a phone and let everyone know we were safe.

It really was a silly thing to do and we were both quite chastened by it. Our parents didn't need to punish us to stop us doing such a thing again. We'd already punished ourselves more than enough by the time we got home.

I haven't mentioned Dee for a while. Although she was not in my class at school any more, we continued to see each other at some break times and also spent some time together out of school.

Dee lived at Ampthill, where her father had a rented police house. I would sometimes go to stay with her and she sometimes came to us. We would also meet up in Bedford in the holidays, just looking around the shops and going into a café or milk bar. In the early days I thought that Dee was prettier and livelier than me and it was a while before I felt more equal. She was vivacious, outgoing and sometimes a bit of a tearaway. For the first few years of our friendship I gave her rather a lot of the initiative, although our decisions were really often more mutual. I won't tell you quite everything we got up to during our school days!

Once a year, for several years, Mum went to the club with Dad on an evening shortly before Christmas, to some function held there. With Carole in bed I would turn out the main living room light, put a cushion on the hearth and sit with my back resting against the fireplace. The Christmas tree to my right shone and glittered, as did the lights around the picture rail, whilst there was a warm orange glow from the fire to my left. I just sat for a while drinking in the way the room looked, transformed from the ordinary, and inhaling the warm, aromatic scent of the pine. Then I'd read whatever book I had on the go at by that soft light until it was time for bed. During those years that was one of my very favourite times in the run up to Christmas.

At other times from a quite young age I would sit, or lie sprawled with my head propped in my hands, on the hearth rug gazing into the fire. I could see shapes and images in the glowing coals that shifted and changed as the coals burned down. It was like looking into another world. I know that Carole felt the same. Bess just loved to get as close as she could to the fire and would only move when her belly was nearly scorched. She sometimes felt almost too hot to touch!

Toward the end of this school year we had to choose which subjects we would take for our General Certificate of Education (GCE) Ordinary ('O') level exams. These exams were quite tough, some being 2½ hours long (Art 3 hours), with two or more exams in most subjects. There was no continuous evaluation. None of the other work we had done over the years counted for anything. Everything rested on the exams themselves.

As an example, in English Literature we were examined on Shakespeare's Twelfth Night, Chaucer's Prologue to the Canterbury Tales (in Old English) and Trollope's The Warden. As you see, there were no modern works among them.

We had very little choice of subject. Being in the top streaming everyone in our class had to take Mathematics, English Language and English Literature, French and Latin. We were also required to take Chemistry unless we had already decided on a career in

medicine or nursing, when we could take Human Biology. I hadn't, so was stuck with the Chemistry.
We were expected to take the Scripture exam but after that I did have one choice. I could take either History or Geography. The Geography teacher and I did not get on, to put it mildly, so I opted for History. I also took Art even though I was not particularly good at it, as the year before I had chosen not to study Ancient Greek as a language and Art was the only other choice. I didn't care, as I quite enjoyed that. The two languages that I was studying were more than enough for me to cope with.

I did not know what I wanted to do when I left school. Only a small proportion of school leavers went on to university then, fewer than 10%. Many children who went to Secondary Modern Schools were not even given the opportunity to take O levels. Most children left school at fifteen years old, the minimum legal age to do so, with no formal qualifications. So even five passes at O level would get you a decent job.

I was encouraged at school to think of staying on into the 6$^{th}$ form to do my GCE Advanced ('A') level exams, with a view to possibly going on to university, but I shelved any decision for the time being. There was no culture of university in the family and at fourteen years old I just did not know what to do.

It seemed easy to put off making the decision as I reckoned that there was no rush with, in any case, two more years in which to make up my mind.

There were not that many universities and they were all quite elite. The other type of higher education establishments, Polytechnic Colleges or 'polys' as they were more commonly known, have all since been upgraded to university status. Together with the newly built universities, this means that there are very many more than in my own school days. Yet now, with higher fees and fewer students seemingly applying for university, who knows? Perhaps things will change back to some degree.

The few good friends I had made at school all did seem to be planning on going to university. It may appear strange, but although I liked them very much and was well accepted by both them and their families, I always felt a little bit awkward when I visited their homes. I think it was probably both a class and a money thing. It wasn't that I thought they were better than me, just that somehow in some ways we inhabited different worlds. The exception to this, as you may have gathered already, was the Whiting family in Stewartby. I never felt awkward there.

Nonetheless perhaps that slight general awkwardness was partly why I remained so friendly with Dee, the only one I really knew in my year at school who seemed to come from the same world as me. And of course we had bonded in that first year, the only two scholarship girls.

# GROWING UP

The summer of 1959 was a real scorcher. Drought warnings had been issued all across the country and the reservoirs were running low. But I really enjoyed that long, hot summer.

I went on holiday with Dee, her parents and grandparents. Dee's father drove us all in his big saloon car. I think it must have had a bench front seat but I know it was still a bit of a squeeze. We went all the way down to Charmouth, a village in Dorset on the southwest coast of England. Although he was a terrible driver and full of road rage before the term was invented, nonetheless Dee's father did somehow get us there safely.

Main beach, with 'our' cliffs beyond

The river Char had cut through cliffs to the sea and the village rambled up over these same cliffs. The big old house we stayed in was on top of the cliffs, on the seaward side of the village, a few hundred yards from the cliff edge itself. Dee's parents and grandparents had an upstairs flat (apartment). Dee and I had a room that had been built on to the back of the house, facing toward the cliffs, and that was completely separate.

Posing on the cliff top

We had taken Dee's record player and a stack of 45rpm singles with us (a real advance on the big old 78s). The Everly brothers were still a big favourite that year. We had real freedom in the late evening, to stay up and play our music for as long as we wanted. Nobody came and checked up on us after we'd gone off to our room.

In the house garden

From the top of the cliff, not far from the house, a precipitous path led to a little bay and the beach. We used this path but the adults went down by road to a larger bay where the river emptied into the sea. That area was quite busy but ours was fairly quiet. We did join up with Dee's family some of the time and ate our meals with them. For the rest, we had a good few hours to ourselves every day of the holiday.

There was a Boy Scout camp that week, set up at a little distance from the house. We saw boys from the camp quite frequently and one pair in particular. We hatched a plan together.

One very moonlit night, when everyone else was in bed, we left our room and met these two boys. We had to be a bit careful as there was some low electric fencing across one area on our way.

The daft thing is, we didn't really do anything other than talking and a bit of kissing and cuddling - no sex, no drugs, no drink, no cigarettes. The excitement for all of us lay in what was just the really quite slight risk of being caught. We arrived safely back at our room after a couple of hours and the Scouts went home the next day. We left a few days later and the long journey home was as much of a nightmare as the journey there. But that could not spoil our holiday memories.

I also holidayed at Beighton again that year. Brenda and Keith now lived in their own home on Cairns Road, just a few streets away from Manvers Road, so initially I had Brenda's big back bedroom to sleep in. Soon after I arrived Uncle Arthur bought another car that was larger and more comfortable than his old one. We went to Clumber Park and Sherwood Forest and to Ladybower Reservoir to see the villages, drowned to create the reservoir there, showing again above the water. There were other, shorter rides out as well and we also went back to the seaside several times.

Picnicking at Clumber Park

Brian was away on holiday with friends when I got to Beighton. One afternoon soon after my arrival, on returning from a drive we heard loud music coming from the house. We could barely get into the living room. Brian was on a drum kit, other young men playing guitars, all singing pop songs. Uncle Arthur went barmy at them and everything quietened down.

One of these young men was really tall, the lead singer of the group. His name was Dave Grundy, changed for stage purposes to Dave Berry. (He greatly admired Chuck Berry.) For some reason his nickname was Sugar. He and the rest of the group were doing the rounds of the local workingmen's clubs and hoping they could break into professional work. Meanwhile they kept their pit jobs.

Dave did break on to the professional scene and is still working now. Brian though gave up his drumming soon after this, as Sylvia his fiancée didn't like it and didn't much care for Dave either.

Brian and Dave at the front door of 164 Manvers Road

The music that year! There were still singers such as Pat Boone and Perry Como. Then there was skiffle with Lonnie Donnegan. But by now it was the era of Elvis Presley, of Tommy Steele, Cliff Richard, Buddy Holly... The music forms a backdrop to all my memories of that summer.

I was accepted into the group that included Brian, Dave and Stan, who is seen here with Uncle Arthur at the front of the house. The shop entrance is out of view to the right of this picture.

I spent quite a lot of time with the group, even sitting in on some of the band practice, thoroughly enjoying it all. Perhaps in fact I appreciated it the more because I didn't even know of any group like this at home, never mind being part of one.

In the evenings we would often go to the Cumberland's Head pub (otherwise known as the Butcher, the Duke of Cumberland's nickname). We all sat outside in the heat, in what cannot really be dignified with the name of beer garden. It was a courtyard with some wooden tables and benches.

The landlord would come out and shout, "Nobody under eighteen, is there?" and we would all call back, "No!" (Not much changes, does it?)

Cumberland's Head

The bay windows came later but you can see how the pub is situated toward what is literally the top end of the High Street

My drink was a half (10 fluid ounces) of lager and lime (a splash of lime cordial), not exactly strong stuff especially given the lager of the day. I can't stand it now but back then I thought it was really quite something. The drink may not have been heady but the experience certainly was.

Part way through the holiday I had to give my bedroom back to Brenda and move again into Brian's. He went to stay with Dave, who lived round the corner on Robin Lane.

Brenda was expecting her first child. This was August and she was over seven months pregnant. Her legs and ankles in particular puffed up dreadfully. At first she thought it was just the heat but when she had her next check up her blood pressure was found to be sky high.

The GP wanted her to go into hospital, fearing pre-eclampsia. But Brenda was determined not to go in and to have her baby at home. So Aunt Annie (who had been a St John's Ambulance Brigade volunteer) said that she would look after her if Brenda moved back in to Manvers Road. Keith spent his nights there too.

So that was the one fly in the ointment that summer. Poor Brenda had to stay in bed from then on, only allowed up to go to the bathroom. I was concerned but being young and optimistic was not really worried, as I now realise the adults were. But we had no more trips out and my holiday was cut a bit short. However I'll let you know that Tim was eventually duly born in October and all was well with both him and Brenda.

When I got back to real life, schoolwork was hard over those last two years. We had to work toward taking mock O levels in the summer term of 1960, with a great deal of homework and revision. Latin and Chemistry were the hardest for me. I really had to struggle and spend a lot of time over those.

The other subjects were not so bad and I loved English, especially English Language.

That December I had a very short story in print in our school magazine, the Aquila. It is in the appendix so see what you think but please be gentle. Remember, I was after all only a really young writer!

Over the next few years I occasionally had quite bad pain in my lower right abdomen. This was eventually diagnosed as a grumbling appendix and sometimes meant I couldn't go to school. When the pain came on while I was at school I would have to lie down in the sickroom. If you didn't feel ill before, you would after spending any time in there! I lay on what passed as a bed but was more like a hard examination couch. It did have a pillow and a blanket, the pillow hard and the blanket scratchy.

The walls of the room were painted in a dark, depressing shade of green. By the bed there were areas where the paint had been picked away to the plaster, I suppose by bored pupils. Or perhaps it was abortive efforts to strip that dreadful paint.

Out of school Dee and I began to rather flout authority. Some afternoons after school we went into a little café, rather like the one in this picture, which was situated in an alleyway opposite the market square.

We felt pretty safe from teachers there. It always had a small crowd of youths in it and we all played the jukebox. We took our hats off too - and ties in the winter. We only stayed for about half an hour before catching the bus home. I think what we most enjoyed was the knowledge that we should not have been there.

One weekend when I stayed with Dee we went to a riding school at the edge of Ampthill town. Dee helped out here and also rode. She had booked horses for both of us although I had never ridden before. Off we went and I was fine for a while. I grew more confident and when we reached open ground was happy for the horse to break into a canter. It felt wonderful for a time, even though I didn't really know what I was doing.

I think the horse did know that a real novice was on board. He decided on a flat out gallop and there was nothing I could do about it. I hung on for dear life but then lost a stirrup. Fortunately, as I was coming off I managed to slip the other stirrup and fell with a thud. I was winded and bruised but not really hurt. I was lucky, as we were not wearing hard hats.

Dee rode up and eventually my horse returned to me. I did remount but we went slowly back and were rather late. I was somewhat stiff and sore for a few days. That was the beginning and end of my horse riding.

This was the era of full, flared skirts, stiffened out with layers of net petticoats. For my birthday that year Mum and Dad bought me a blue, layered net petticoat. I loved it, especially under my favourite dress. This was of blue and white gingham, with the flared skirt of course. I wore this dress with a wide, white belt and thought I was the bee's knees.

For some young men this was still the Teddy Boy era of long, velvet collared fitted jackets, string ties and often very tight fitting 'drainpipe' trousers.

Their footwear was crepe-soled shoes (known as brothel creepers). These youths wore their hair quiffed up, with a D A at the back. What was a D A? Just think of the rear end of a duck!

Really full, pencil pleated skirts also became very popular somewhere around this time. It was a fashion made possible for the mass market by the advent of permanent press fabrics. I had a lovely white skirt that swung around me beautifully when I moved but I cannot imagine what it would have been like to have to press in all the pleats every time it was washed.

I had a little battery-powered transistor radio (a 'tranny'), on which I would listen to all the pop music on the only commercial station, Radio Luxemburg. I enjoyed The Goon Show humour on the Light Programme too. Now, as well as reading, I'd also listen to the radio programmes in bed at night.

Meanwhile the platforms at Stewartby Halt, along with the other halts along the Bletchley to Bedford railway line, were being rebuilt in record time to raise them into proper station platforms. Admittedly these were still made from wood but nonetheless the work was done. This was because in November 1959 the first diesel train on that line came into service. It just wasn't possible for a diesel to let down steps in the way that a steam train could.

Although it was some time before all the steam trains were replaced, I'm afraid that this was the beginning of the end of the age of steam for us.

Dee's father had been relocated to Bedford. They now lived in a little side street off Goldington Road, quite a way from the town centre.

In the holidays Dee and I occasionally went to the cinema and to dances in Bedford. I felt pretty much like Cinderella though. The last bus home to Stewartby left at about 10.30pm so there was no staying out *really* late for me. The cinemas ran their programmes on a constant loop. There was a B film, a newsreel and trailers for forthcoming releases, then the main feature.

If we went to the cinema in the evening I either had to go early enough to see the end of the film before seeing the rest, or just miss the ending! So we would often go to the afternoon showing. I quite envied Dee living in Bedford and often wished that we lived there too. Sadly, I couldn't afford to take a taxi to get home.

There was a dance at the Conservative Club on St Peter's Street, near the Granada cinema, on a weekday evening and one at the Corn Exchange on the market square on a Saturday. It was all live music, of varying quality admittedly, but we weren't fussy. It was pop, it was loud, and we were enjoying ourselves. We didn't go to all that many dances but when we went we had great fun. We perfected our own version of the jive and enjoyed performing it at every opportunity. We didn't bother about dancing with the boys although we'd do a bit of light flirting.

I started smoking just occasionally when I was out in the evenings. The advertisements made smoking look so glamorous and it was still not seen as a health hazard at that time. I didn't have a lot of money but when I did smoke I would buy Sobranie cigarettes. They came in a beautiful flat, shiny black box with gold lettering.

The cigarette papers came in several, what I can only describe as bright pastel, colours. The filter tips were gold. I thought smoking these was so sophisticated! Now of course I know better.

A few times when Dee and I went to dances we got up to some mischief. I would pretend to be French, visiting Dee and knowing no English. When a boy seemed interested, Dee would act as 'translator.'

It was a bit wicked really but so funny to listen to those boys. Sometimes it was very hard to keep a straight face as they talked with Dee, thinking that I could not understand them!

This may sound as though we were always out. But don't forget, it was only in the holidays and then no more than once or twice a week. In term time I hardly went out at all in the evenings. For one thing, I had two hours or more of homework every night.

I also still read a lot and for a while was very interested in books on caving, on big game hunting in Africa and then for some time I read everything I could find on Egyptology. That really fascinated me. I was still reading fiction as well.

Two of my favourite authors then were H Rider Haggard, author of King Solomon's Mines, and Jules Verne, especially his Twenty Thousand Leagues Under the Sea. And of course I still went to Bletchley on a Friday. So I had plenty to keep me busy.

There were four cinemas in Bedford at that time, when the town had a population of around 60,000. There were the Granada on St Peter's and the Empire on Midland Road, not far from the railway station. The other two stood on opposite banks of the river, diagonally across from one another.

The Plaza was near the County Library. The Picturedrome, on the south bank near the bridge, was known as the Fleapit, with it being the shabbiest and least salubrious. A large hotel stands on the site now.

The Granada, by far the nicest cinema of the four, also put on live stage shows. We never went to one of those but saw that Billy Fury, a big UK pop star at that time, was to appear there one night in term time.

St Peter's Street: the Granada is along on the right.

We knew where the star dressing room window was, down a little passageway at the side of the cinema. So we left school (unauthorised, naturally) at dinnertime and dropped our autograph books through an open window that was about five feet above the ground, even though we knew we were taking a chance on never seeing them again.

That was a chance we were prepared to take!

After school we went back and called at the window. We were thrilled when we had a reply and the books were handed through to us with Billy Fury's autograph. That was the closest we came to a star. I'm afraid though that I lost the book and its autographs, including that very special one, somewhere along the way.

That Easter Aunt Annie, Uncle Arthur, Brenda and Keith, with Tim, started the custom of coming down from Beighton to us for the day on Easter Monday.

They would arrive midmorning and stay until after tea. Mum had made her usual big batch of Hot Cross Buns on Maundy Thursday. Auntie and Ken came over for that and perhaps we youngsters were a bit more help by now. We'd have buns warm from the oven and Auntie took some back to Bletchley, so that they too could also still eat fresh homemade ones on Good Friday.

There were always enough left for us all to enjoy warmed up when the Beighton contingent arrived on the Monday. I liked it when they came but I found out later that Mum got fed up with not being able to make any other plans for that day. For several years she spent a good part of the holiday in the kitchen; cooking, making drinks, clearing dishes and washing up between meals.

By the end of the school year I had decided not to continue into the 6$^{th}$ form. I was getting fed up with school and wanted to be free, getting out to work, earning money. I just did not realise the benefits of higher qualifications. As I have said, even A levels then were very uncommon.

Another reason for not going on seems silly now. But the only subject I was interested in taking was English and I thought that all I could do with that qualification was to teach, which I didn't want to do. In truth, at the time a decent university degree in any subject, as they were all academic then, would have led to a really good job in many fields. Yet although asked to stay on to the 6$^{th}$ form, I wasn't given any real advice as to the benefit.

I am not sure if Mum and Dad fully realised the opportunities offered by 6$^{th}$ form or university either. I did know that it would have been harder for them if I had stayed on. I would have needed new uniforms and they would still have had to keep me. Carole had passed the Eleven Plus too, so that was more expense. Not that Mum and Dad ever suggested any of this to me. They said they would support me in whatever I chose to do

Who knows how my life would have been if I had not made the choice to leave school? I can't regret it. Although there have been difficulties along the way there have also been very good times - and in any case I wouldn't have the wonderful children and grandchildren that I do. Loving them all so dearly, I couldn't want things any other way. It's never too late to learn either and I did take training opportunities when older.

I had my last holiday at Beighton this year, a lovely stay as always. Something that I really enjoyed was when Aunt Annie and Uncle Arthur would occasionally let me run the paper shop. One day I was there with nobody else in the house at all. I think Uncle Arthur must have been either working at the pit or collecting paper money and I can't remember where Aunt Annie had gone. However it came about, I was on my own for a couple of hours.

I had spent so much time in Beighton that I thought I could understand anyone who spoke to me, no matter how strong their local accent. But I was stumped that day. A little boy came into the shop and asked me for something. I really struggled to try to find out what he wanted. In the end I told him to go home and ask his mother to write it down for him. He never came back and so to this day I do not know what that was about. Aunt Annie laughed when I told her but I did feel foolish.

We had a trip out to the Blue John cavern in Derbyshire. Blue John is a type of crystalline stone mined there and I bought one or two little ornamental pieces made from it, both as gifts and as a memento for myself.

Now baby Tim accompanied us on our outings. One really nice one that we all enjoyed was when we went for the day to Skegness.

Brenda and Tim on Skegness beach

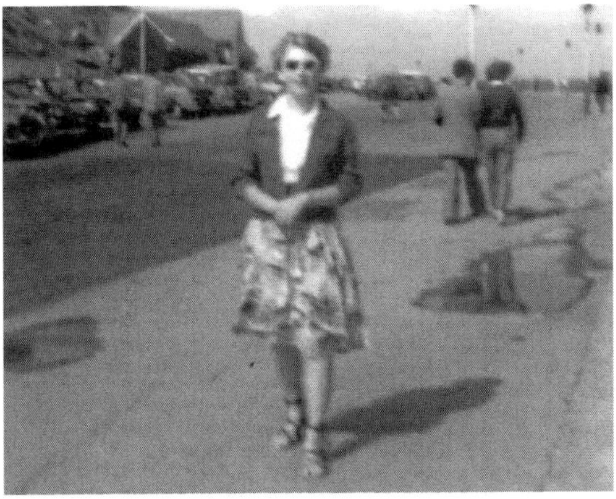

On Skegness sea front

I went to the cinema several times while I was at Beighton that year too. The films changed twice a week and the big bonus was that I could walk back to the house without having to worry, as I did at home, about catching my bus.

There was very often a big queue for the cinema, with it being such a popular form of entertainment. The films changed twice a week so there was plenty of variety.

For some reason, I don't know why, they painted the exterior walls of the cinema white. The façade always looked grey and grubby from the effect of all the coal dust in the atmosphere there.

I often imagined Auntie Nellie here in the cinema, playing the piano for the silent films as she had done when a young woman. Without pausing she would have kept glancing up at the screen to see the mood of the moment and then suited her playing to match it.

# CHILDHOOD'S ENDING

With my music case on Bletchley Road, October 1960

There was a new bus station in Bedford. It was built in the area between Midland Road and Bromham Road, not far from the High School. It was more spacious than the old one but now we no longer had any excuse to get off at the market square and wend our way slowly to school in the mornings.

Although Carole like me had passed her Eleven Plus, she was disappointed. She had hoped to come to the High School where big sister was. However the place she was offered was at Dame Alice. We did ride on the bus to Bedford together, Carole having to almost run to keep up with me as we went to catch it in the morning. That's because I would wait until the very last minute to set out! Although she wouldn't have seen much of me anyway, Carole was still very nervous about going into a new school for the first time on her own. She soon made friends there though.

School for me was really serious now, with the countdown to our O levels and a lot of practice papers. There was also even more homework and revision. Nonetheless Dee and I still saw each other and did things together occasionally. And of course I was still reading for pleasure. By now I had started reading crime stories, as I continue to do, and was enjoying Ngaio Marsh and some Agatha Christie, although annoyed at the way Christie never gives you all the clues to solve the mystery. As I collected the books I bought kits for turning paperbacks into hardbacks, with the lettering in gold leaf. Eventually I had a matching set.

I also started going out with a boy named Frank I met at one of the dances. He was about a year older than me and lived in a flat in Bedford with his dad. His mum had died a couple of years earlier. I went round to the flat a few times and got on really well with his father, a kind and likeable man.

My birthday present from Mum and Dad that year was about the best thing they could have given me. It was a second-hand bookcase, around three feet high and five or six feet long. The wood was stained almost black and a band of scalloped leather ran along the top edge of each of its two shelves. I loved it.

Frank and a few friends came to my 16th birthday party. But I am afraid that was really the end for us. That evening Frank told me that his father had said we could get engaged on my 17th birthday. Engaged? I liked Frank very much but marriage to him had never entered my head. I got cold feet and although I was sorry to upset him, the next time I saw Frank I told him I wasn't going out with him any longer.

One evening we had to go back into school for a careers talk. A teacher saw Dee and me without our hats as we were on the way to the school. That was trouble and we both got detention for it. Goodness knows what would have happened had we been seen after the talk.

We had our 'civvy' clothes with us, got changed in a toilet and went off for an hour to Condelli's coffee bar on Foster Hill Road, opposite the old bus station, before I had to catch the bus home.

Then one evening in November Dee and I were in Condelli's again when we started talking to two American airmen who were based at Chicksands. We arranged to meet up as a foursome but after that first date Dee and the other airman didn't see each other again.

I however did start going out with Ralph, who was in the Air Police, for almost eighteen months until he went back to the USA, beyond the ending of this story. He had an old Ford Popular, with running boards and indicators that flicked out from the body of the car. I drove it too, on one of the rural back roads. It's a good thing that I didn't have an accident, being unlicensed and uninsured. I don't recommend it, with it not only being illegal but there now also being much so more traffic on the roads.

I was really happy most of the time to be going out with Ralph. But occasionally he didn't turn up to see me when I was expecting him. He couldn't let me know if he had to work because we still had no telephone at the house. So then I would be plunged into despair, imagining he did not want to see me anymore. Young love can be so excruciating! However we did keep seeing one another. We went to the cinema and to tenpin bowling on the base. We visited friends and also went to a pub on the outskirts of Bedford, on Goldington Road. Well, the school rules didn't mention pubs, did they?

I know that Ralph missed his home and was really pleased to spend some of Christmas, that year and the next, with us. My parents liked him and he them. He bought Christmas presents for all of us, including Carole. Ralph's birthday was in December too and he turned twenty the month after we met.

In those Christmas holidays I had a job as fulltime child minder, five days a week, to a four year old girl. The job was advertised in the local paper. To satisfy his mind Dad met and spoke with the little girl's father, whom he found to be a middle-aged, very kindly, professional man.

The little girl was called Jane and her mother had died fairly recently. She had started school and I think, poor little mite, was going to be a boarder at the Convent School in Bedford in the New Year. Her father needed someone to care for her in the holidays while he was at work. I took the bus into Bedford in the morning and then had quite a long walk to the street where they lived in the Putnoe (northeast) area of the town. I didn't mind that at all, even though it was dark by the time I went home.

I played with Jane, took her for walks, read to her and made her lunch. Of course part of the deal was that I ate lunch there too. And sometimes Jane had a friend round to play, so then I would be looking after two.

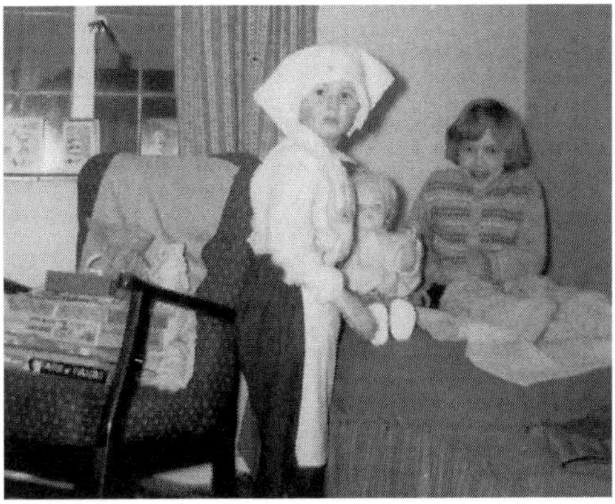

'Nurse' Jane and friend

I became very fond of Jane over those few weeks. When the holidays were over we were both sad that I had to leave. We exchanged Christmas cards for a while but then lost touch. Sometimes I think of her and her father and find myself wondering what has become of them.

Beehive hairstyles were all the fashion and I started to grow my hair longer. By the time I left school it was just long enough to put up at the back in a French pleat. Although I never went to real extremes, I did backcomb (tease) the hair on top until it was a tangled mess, to raise it up, then smoothed over the very top layer.

To hold our hair in place we had hair lacquer which came in a pump spray (no aerosols back then). Lacquer? It left a coarse grey coating unless you washed your hair with a special lacquer removing shampoo. It can't have done our hair any good at all. At least it was better than using white lead based cosmetics, as was once very fashionable. It's all for the sake of vanity really, yet what is all the rage today is old hat tomorrow.

Pencil slim skirts were in fashion now, as were stiletto heeled winkle picker shoes. Winkles are a shellfish that you use sharp pointed pins to dig (winkle) out of their shells. The shoes were so called because of their sharply pointed toe shape. That was a fashion I've cause to regret in later life, as my poor feet now suffer the consequences!

By 1961 the Twist was becoming the dance rage and I can tell you it wasn't the easiest thing to do in those skirts and shoes. But when Dee and I went to the occasional dance now, we twisted with the best of them and if I say so myself, I was pretty good.

I was still going to Bletchley most weekends that winter. Mum had broken the big bowl she used for mixing the Christmas puddings and Hot Cross Bun dough. So I wanted to find another for her birthday. I went on to the market at Bletchley one Saturday to look around. On a secondhand stall I found a pretty washbasin set. It was complete with large jug and bowl, soap dish and toothbrush holder. I thought that Mum could use the jug for flowers as well as the bowl for her mixing. It cost the princely sum of sixpence! Goodness knows what it would be worth nowadays, when such things are sought after as collectables.

Getting the set home would have been a bit of a job. It was bad enough carrying it back to Cambridge Street. But Uncle brought it over to Stewartby for me on one of his Bedford trips. Mum was really pleased and the jug was ideal for the chrysanthemums Dad now gave her on their wedding anniversaries.

Piano practice began to feel really irksome and I no longer wanted to be in Bletchley every Friday night and Saturday. So I gave up my piano lessons. It was a shame, because I was close to taking my final exam. But with school and social life filling my time, and wanting to be able to look around the Bedford shops on a Saturday, it simply wasn't a priority for me then. In that respect I suppose I was just a typical teenager.

However one of my last regular trips to Bletchley coincided with Grand National day. We were all watching the buildup to the race. There was a grey horse running, most unusually. His name was Nicolaus Silver. I said that I bet he would win, just because I liked his colour. Uncle took me up on that, saying that he would bet me £5 to 1/- that Nicolaus Silver lost. £5 was an awful lot of money. But to me, my 1/- was a lot of money too. So I wouldn't take the gamble and of course the horse did win - only the second grey ever to do so! Uncle didn't let me forget my faint heart very quickly.

A really exciting event this April was the launch of the first man into space. He was the Russian, Yuri Gagarin, who orbited the earth and came back safely, to everyone's relief. Unsurprisingly he was fêted as a real hero - even though there was some chagrin in the West that Russia had won that particular race.

I had been using makeup for a while, including the fashionable thick black eyeliner. Now at the weekends I would also paint my fingernails bright red for when I was going out. Along with not being allowed to wear makeup to school I had of course to remove that nail varnish before going in on Monday mornings. However it did stain my nails.

One of the teachers noticed this colour and told me to take off the nail varnish. When I explained what the colour was, she had such a pained look on her face. "How disgusting!" she remarked but couldn't do anything about it. This was unlike one poor girl, who went to school after colouring her hair. She was made to go in the cloakroom and keep on rinsing it to get the colour out. When that didn't work she was sent home.

On another occasion, as Dee and I walked across the playground at the end of the school day, a teacher rode by on her old-fashioned bicycle. Now this was in our final term and we were wearing our straw hats, which by this time were really too small for us. Dee had her hair backcombed and her hat perched on the back of her head. The teacher got off her bike and cried, "Where's your hat, girl?" Dee showed her; whereupon the teacher walked up to Dee, lifted her hat and plonked it back down squarely on the top of her head, causing her hair to splay straight out all round.

When it came time to take our O levels we only had to go into school for the actual exams. There were a lot of these as we had more than one paper in most subjects, plus French oral and Chemistry practical.

Ah, the Chemistry practical! I was convinced that it was in the afternoon. So there I was, still in bed of course at 9.30 in the morning (I *was* a teenager). Dad rode up on his bike from work to tell me that the exam had started at just that time. When the teacher realised I wasn't there, the school secretary had rung Dad at the club. What a rush I had then. I was up, washed and dressed in record time. Mr Forbes the works manager gave me a lift to school. I got into the science lab about halfway through the exam, quite flustered, and could not be given any extra time. So I did not feel very confident about that one at all, especially as I rather struggled with the theory too.

During these exam weeks I went for a job interview at Texas Instruments, which had recently located its UK headquarters in Bedford. They made semiconductors for electrical equipment there. The buildings were new and spacious, on the northeast edge of the town. I was offered a job for when I left school at a starting salary of £10 per week, a good wage then for a school leaver, which I accepted. I planned to take my bike on the train from Stewartby to St John's station and then cycle up to work from there. So that aspect of my immediate future was sorted.

One Saturday I took a complete break from exams and revision. I went on a day trip to Clacton, a seaside resort on the east coast. This trip was by train and I am not sure how they got us cross-country but they did, although it was a long journey. A group of us youngsters set off from Stewartby station early in the morning. Naturally, I couldn't dress sensibly and comfortably, could I? Oh no, I had to be dressed up to the nines.

The day was quite hot and I wore a very nice sleeveless, glazed cotton two-piece outfit with a pencil skirt. I could barely fit into it. I had bought the outfit at a cheap fashion shop in Bedford and it was really a size too small. As I had fallen in love with the outfit on seeing it in the shop, when they did not have my size I tried on the smaller one. I did somehow get into it and then did not dare try to peel it off. I left the shop wearing my new clothes, with the ones I'd taken off in a bag. I wore 3 inch high stiletto heeled shoes for the excursion to complete my smart new outfit.

I thoroughly enjoyed the whole day but my calves were extremely sore by the time I had walked home from the station at about 2.00am, what with hobbling in the skirt and teetering on my shoes. I couldn't bear the pain so ran a hot bath and soaked for about half an hour before getting into bed.

We didn't have much to do at school after the exams were over. But we did have to go in as usual regardless and the teachers managed to find us work. The maths teacher even decided to start us on Calculus over those last couple of weeks.

It was quite frustrating, knowing that the serious business of school was over and yet having to keep going through the motions every day. The last two or three weeks really seemed to drag on.

Then finally it was our last day. We finished at dinnertime. A group of us who were leaving the school for good headed to the main town bridge over the river, near the market square.

We all followed the established tradition of throwing our straw hats into the river, with much excitement and noise. There were no further celebrations or ceremonies. We simply then said our goodbyes and made our various ways home.

Bridge over the River Ouse
St Paul's Church spire to the left

We had no proms, no formal ceremonies of graduation and no formal leave takings. As I turned away now I felt anticipation, apprehension, some sadness and a faint sense of anti-climax. Was that it? Was that really the end of school, forever?

Although I haven't spoken a lot about my emotions, at one time or another I felt the whole range - as children do, and sometimes very strongly. From all that I have actually said in this story of my childhood you could be forgiven for thinking that one of the things I never did suffer from throughout these years was boredom. But that's just it: this is the story of the things I *did.*

Like all children everywhere, there were times throughout my childhood when I felt just as bored as anyone reading this has ever done. I particularly remember quite a few wet, miserable, Sunday afternoons. But since all those boring times were really simply that, boring, there is nothing more to say about them!

Before I close this narrative though, I will just tell you that when the results came out in August I learned that I had passed eight of the nine O levels I sat. Passes were graded into levels 1 - 6, the equivalent of A - C passes in today's GCSEs.

The one exam I failed was Scripture. I know that for one thing I did not put in the work, thinking it a less important subject. But after having a really good teacher who had made the subject live we then had a teacher, those last two years for O level, who could make absolutely anything seem as dull as ditchwater.

Still, miraculous to relate, somehow I *did* pass Chemistry! It and History were my only two lower grades.
Now for me, with the ending of my childhood it was off into the world of work and the real beginning of young adulthood.

Memories are very individual and I am sure that those of others will not agree with all of mine. Family members and friends have jogged and augmented my recollections and helped with some of the factual information. This narrative however is my own personal memoir of my childhood.

I hope that I have given you a flavour of what my world was like, a baby born toward the end of WWII and growing up in a very different era to that of today.

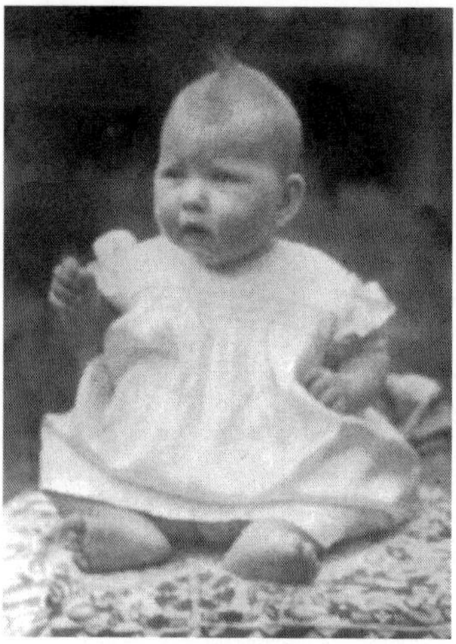

Bletchley, March 1945

Ampthill Park, summer 1961

Finally, I leave you with a picture from an even earlier era: that of the wedding of my father's parents in 1904.

# APPENDIX

## Pre-Decimal Currency

In England after 1066 the Normans used their own French coins, each impressed with a small star. Norman French for little star was *esterlin*. The pound sterling was a pound weight of *esterlin*, roughly 240 coins. So *esterlin* became Anglicised to sterling, which became the name for the whole currency. The coin itself was called a penny, its pre-Conquest name. Pennies are believed to be named after King Penda of Mercia. Shilling comes from the old English 'to divide,' from when coins were often cut to make smaller denominations.

Pre-decimal currency was sometimes called LSD, written £ s d. The pound symbol is an ornate L, from the Latin libra - a pound. The penny symbol was d for denarius, a Roman coin. The s is also from a Roman coin, the solidus.

This is how prices were written and spoken. Two shillings and sixpence (a half crown) would be 2/6, and could be said as 'two and six' or 'half a crown.' You would not normally say 'shillings' and 'pence' if the amount was a pound or larger. But you would say the 'pounds.' So one pound seven shillings and sixpence would be written £3/7/6, and would be spoken as 'three pounds, seven and six.' If there were no pennies, then you wrote a dash and did say 'shillings.' So for example: 4/-, spoken as 'four shillings.' The Mad Hatter in Alice in Wonderland has a price tag on his hat saying "In This Style 10/6." So this hat would cost ten shillings and sixpence (said as 'ten and six'), just over half of a pound. It might be paid for with four half crowns or a 10 shilling note, plus a sixpence - or any other combination of currency.

There were notes for 10/- and for £1, £5 on upwards, all much larger than today's bank notes. Silver coloured coins were half crowns, florins (worth 2 shillings), shillings and sixpenny pieces (sixpences). Copper coins were thr'penny bits worth, as their name suggests, three pence (thr'pence); pennies; half pennies, commonly called ha'pennies (pronounced with a long a) and farthings, quarters of a penny. A crown, worth 5/-, was no longer in common usage when I was growing up and nor was the sovereign coin, worth £1.

Some prices were still written in guineas, although the guinea coin itself was also obsolete. A guinea was worth £1/1/-. There were slang terms, some still in use such as 'quid' for pound, and some now redundant, such as 'bob' for shilling, 'tanner' for sixpence or 'half a dollar' for half a crown.

Confused? It's easy really!

This system, more sophisticated than the decimal, allowed for much finer gradations of the amounts of money

| ***Money tables*** | |
|---|---|
| | |
| 12d = 1/- | 84d = 7/- |
| 18d = 1/6 | 96d = 8/- |
| 24d = 2/- | 108d = 9/- |
| 30d = 2/6 | 120d = 10/- |
| 36d = 3/- | 240d = £1 |
| 42d = 3/6 | 20s = £1 |
| 48d = 4/- | 100d = 8/4 |
| 60d = 5/- | Third of £1 = 6/8 |
| 72d = 6/- | Two thirds of £1 = 13/4 |
| | |

## Pre-decimal Coins Sterling

All reverse side.  Monarch's head on obverse

Farthing Ha'penny Penny Thr'pence

Sixpence Shilling Florin (two shillings)

Half a crown Golden Guinea

## Pre-Metric Weights and Measures

Weights went from ounces, through pounds, stones and hundredweight, to tons. You will know some of these, especially those still in official use in the US and common use in the UK. This weight system is specifically known as 'avoirdupois,' pronounced as the French, from Middle English words meaning goods sold by weight.

The measurement system for weight, length and area was known as Imperial and temperature was measured on the Fahrenheit scale. The main length and area measurements, such as inches, feet, yards and miles, are still used for many purposes. Others are archaic but some of them, such as a 'chain' length for a wicket on a cricket pitch, are still in specialised use.

Here are tables of the measures we had to learn:

| Length | | Area | |
|---|---|---|---|
| 12 inches | = 1 foot | 144 sq. inches | = 1 foot$^2$ |
| 3 feet | = 1 yard | 9 sq. feet | = 1 yard$^2$ |
| 5.5 yards | = 1 rod, pole or perch | 4840 sq. yards | = 1 acre |
| 22 yards (4 pole) | = 1 chain | 640 acres | = 1 mile$^2$ |
| 10 chains | = 1 furlong | | |
| 8 furlongs | = 1 mile | | |
| 5280 feet | = 1 mile | | |
| 1760 yards | = 1 mile | | |

As you know a pole is, rather confusingly, also a measure of area. So one rod, pole or perch also equals 30.25 yards$^2$, which is actually the length measure squared. Yet this was never specified: presumably taken for granted that you would know by the context whether length or area.

| Mass | | Capacity | |
|---|---|---|---|
| 16 ounces (oz) | = 1 pound (lb) | 20 fluid ounces | = 1 pint |
| 14 pounds | = 1 stone | 4 gills | = 1 pint |
| 8 stones (112 lb) | = 1 hundredweight [cwt] | 2 pints | = 1 quart |
| | | 4 quarts | = 1 gallon |
| 20 cwt | = 1 ton (2240 lb) | | |

Volume

| | |
|---|---|
| 1728 cu. inches | = 1 cubic foot |
| 27 cu. feet | = 1 cubic yard |

It was partly to cope with all these different measures, including the currency, that we learned our 2 through 12, 14 and 16 times tables by rote in junior school. You know what I mean: 1 times 2 is 2, 2 times 2 is 4 etc, chanted in singsong voices. We learned by heart, too, how many feet and yards in a mile, a quarter of a mile and half a mile, as well as many of the other measurements.

The difference between the UK and US systems seems strange. For so long, our monetary system in the UK was alien to the US. Now we have a decimal system for currency but have also changed, or are changing, all our other measures too. So now people in the US will be finding these other measures alien instead. This includes temperature measurements. I still think in Fahrenheit, which of course we also learned, even though I can convert fairly readily to Celsius, the official system in the UK now. That is another measure where the old one was more sophisticated, allowing for finer gradation, with 180 degrees Fahrenheit between freezing and boiling, rather than the 'mere' 100 degrees in Centigrade or its slightly more exact version, Celsius.

Whichever measure you use, this is cold!

## English Roads

There were no motorways (freeways) in England during most of my childhood. The main trunk roads remained mostly single carriageway, with only a few dual carriageways. Although there were some straight stretches in between, nearly all the main roads still wound through every town on their route.

For example the A5 still followed the route of the old Roman Watling Street, as the A1 followed that of the Great North Road. Indeed, it was the same with the other old roads in England. So when travelling any distance you were continually having to slow as you made your way through one town after the other. And these were the best roads.

As for the more minor roads, you would think the line from a poem which runs: "...the rolling English drunkard made the rolling English road" very apt. Many of these roads, but by no means all, have had the worst bends straightened out since those days.

However in November 1959 the first motorway in England, the M1, opened. It ran close to Bletchley and Uncle took us for a ride along it when it was still very new. With three carriageways going in each direction it looked amazingly big to me - and so straight. It also looked very empty, with few cars travelling along it.

There was no proper central reservation and there was also initially no speed limit on that road at the time. Uncle got the car up to over 80mph, faster than I had ever been in my life. It almost felt to me as though we were flying.

Given how primitive cars were then, compared to the modern day, it was indeed real speed.

# The M1 Motorway Opens

You can see here how few cars there were travelling on the motorway when the first section opened in 1959

(Acknowledgements to The Guardian newspaper for this picture)

# Maps

## My Home Area

This is an old map I managed to find of the area of my childhood. You can see the roads as they were then, and the railway line between Bletchley and Bedford, quite clearly. I don't know just how old the map is but as you can see Bletchley is shown as the old village, before the town grew to be bigger than Fenny Stratford. So I think it must be at least pre WWII.

I have marked Bow Brickhill Halt and Stewartby. The last Halt shown on the railway line just before Kempston, known as Cow Bridge, had been closed by the time I can remember. My father used to travel there from Bletchley as a child, to visit an aunt and uncle who lived in nearby Elstow.

I think everything else is about the same as I recall.

The large figures show the road distance in miles between the junctions.

## Bletchley and Fenny Stratford

## Bletchley and Fenny Stratford Key

1 Bletchley Railway Station

2 Co-op Department Store

3 Co-op Butcher's Shop

4 Cattle Market

5 New Found Out

6 14 Brooklands Road

7 12 Cambridge Street

8 Central Gardens

9 Waste ground and small gravel pit

10 Approximate location 106 Western Road

11 Studio Cinema

12 School Clinic

13 Bletchley Road School

14 Co-op on Victoria Road

15 Fenny Stratford Railway Station

16 County Cinema

17 Spurgeon Memorial Baptist Church

18 Recreation Ground ('Rec')

Far Bletchley

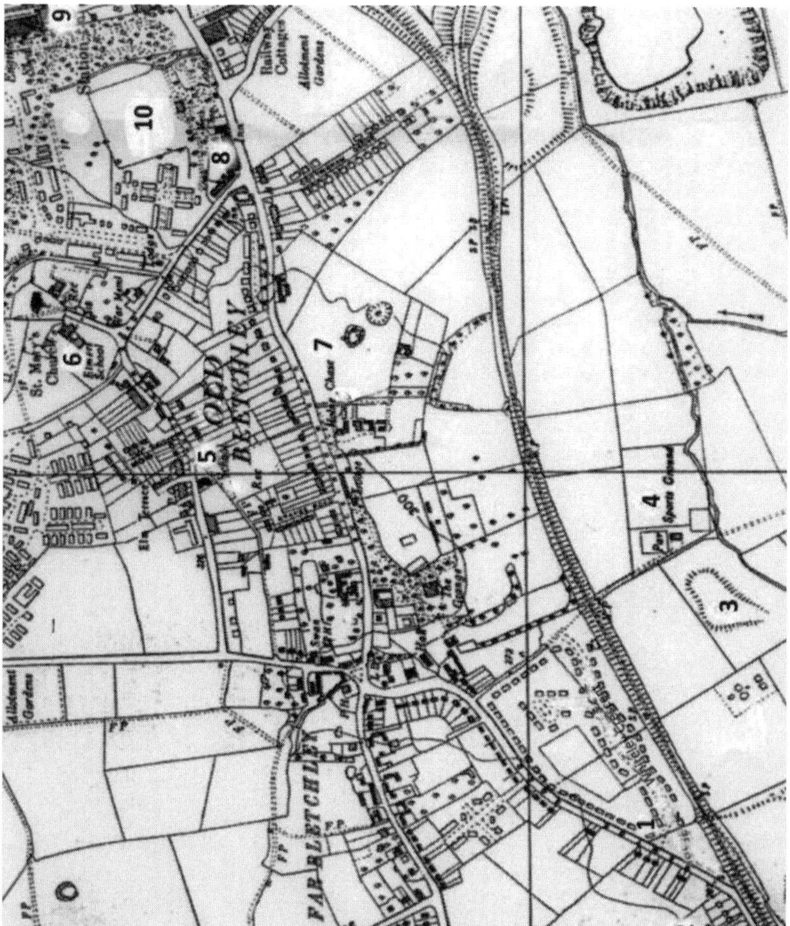

## Far Bletchley Key

1 1 Whiteley Crescent

2 New Housing Estate with Shops

3 Knothole

4 Brick Company Sports Ground

5 Church Green Road Church of England School

6 St Mary's Church

7 Holne Chase Spinney

8 Eight Bells Pub

9 Bletchley Railway Station

10 Bletchley Park

Stewartby

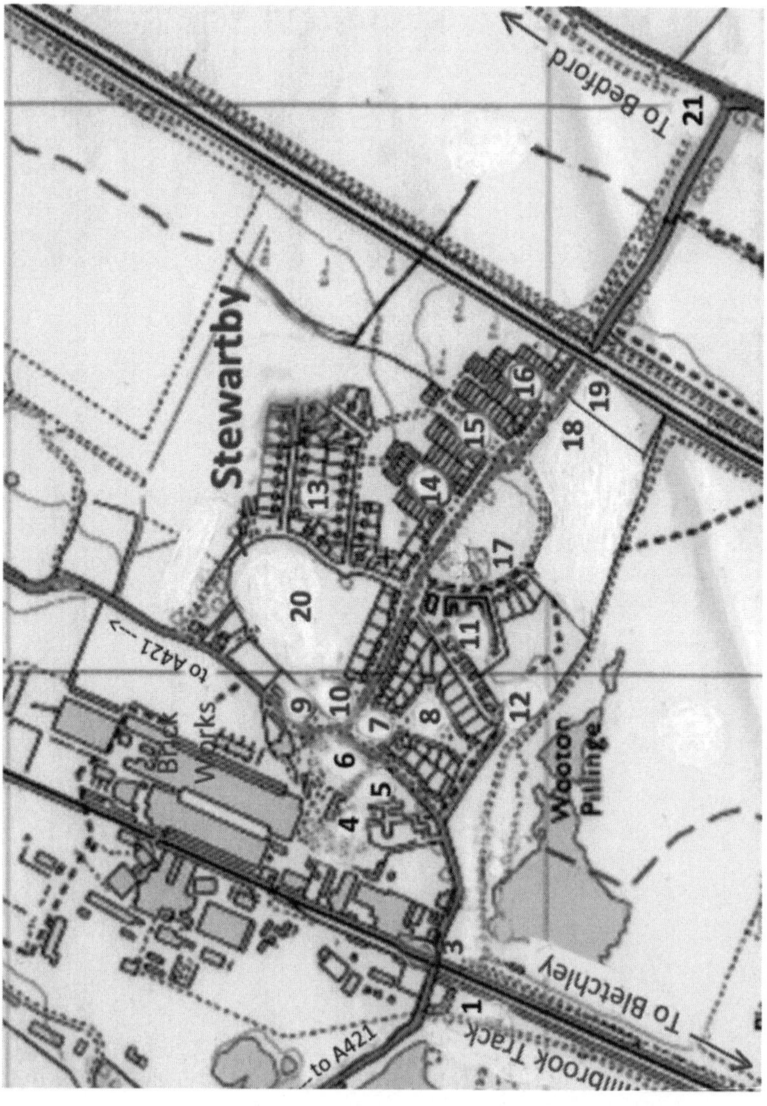
Stewartby
To Bedford
to A421
to A421
To Bletchley
Works
1
3
4
5
6
7
8
9
10
11
12
13
14
15
16
17
18
19
20
21

Stewartby Key

1 Knothole
2 Old Works Pond
3 Stewartby Halt
4 Swimming Pool
5 Laboratory
6 Bus Stop
7 Village Hall
8 Churchill Close
9 Stewartby Club
10 Co-op/Post Office
11 Schools
12 Old School Sports Field
13 'New Houses'
14 Alexander Close
15 Montgomery Close
16 Wavell Close
17 The Crescent
18 Carter's Farm
19 Allotments
20 Playing Field
21 Stewartby Turn

Bedford

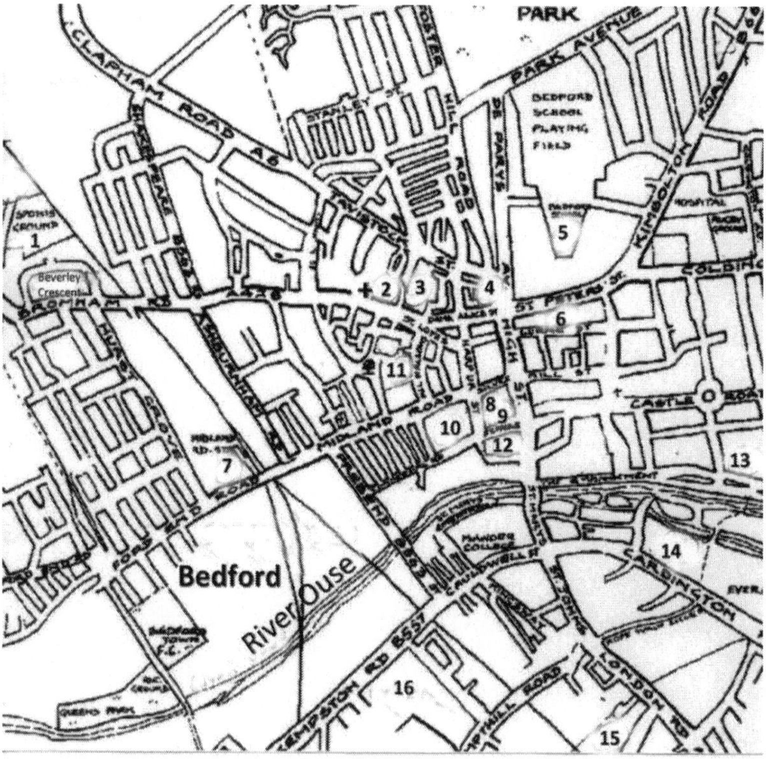
PARK
PARK AVENUE
CLAPHAM ROAD A6
STANLEY ST.
BEDFORD SCHOOL PLAYING FIELD
KIMBOLTON ROAD
SPORTS GROUND
1
Beverley Crescent
BROMHAM RD
A428
2
3
4
5
ST PETERS ST.
6
HIGH ST.
11
MIDLAND ROAD
CASTLE ROAD
8
9
10
12
13
7
14
Bedford
River Ouse
CAULDWELL ST
CARDINGTON
16
15
KEMPSTON RD
LONDON RD

## Bedford Key

1 Far left: Bedford High School Sports Ground, off Beverley Crescent)
2 Bedford High School
3 Bedford Prison
4 The Old Bus Station
5 Bedford School
6 Granada Cinema
7 Midland Road Railway Station
8 Bedford Town Library
9 The Corn Exchange
10 Bedford Modern School
11 The New Bus Station
12 St Paul's (Market) Square
13 Bedford County Library
14 Dame Alice Harpur School
15 St John's Railway Station
16 Bedford Hospital South Wing

# Songs

## Abdul Abulbul Amir

The sons of the prophet were hardy and bold,
And quite unaccustomed to fear,
But the bravest of these was a man, I am told
Named Abdul Abulbul Amir.

This son of the desert, in battle aroused,
Could spit twenty men on his spear.
A terrible creature, both sober and soused
Was Abdul Abulbul Amir.

When they needed a man to encourage the van,
Or to harass the foe from the rear,
Or to storm a redoubt, they had only to shout
For Abdul Abulbul Amir.

There are heroes aplenty and men known to fame
In the troops that were led by the Czar;
But the bravest of these was a man by the name
Of Ivan Skavinsky Skivar.

He could imitate Irving, play euchre and pool
And perform on the Spanish Guitar.
In fact, quite the cream of the Muscovite team
Was Ivan Skavinsky Skivar.

The ladies all loved him, his rivals were few;
He could drink them all under the bar.
As gallant or tank, there was no one to rank
With Ivan Skavinsky Skivar.

Bucks, Beds and Bricks

One day this bold Russian had shouldered his gun
And donned his most truculent sneer
Downtown he did go, where he trod on the toe
Of Abdul Abulbul Amir

'Young man,' quoth Bulbul, 'has life grown so dull,
That you're anxious to end your career?
Vile infidel! Know, you have trod on the toe
Of Abdul Abulbul Amir.'

'So take your last look at the sunshine and brook
And send your regrets to the Czar;
By this I imply you are going to die,
Mr Ivan Skavinsky Skivar.'

Quoth Ivan, 'My friend, your remarks, in the end,
Will avail you but little, I fear,
For you ne'er will survive to repeat them alive,
Mr. Abdul Abulbul Amir!'

Then this bold Mameluke drew his trusty chibouque
With a cry of 'Allah Akbar!'
And with murderous intent, he ferociously went
For Ivan Skavinsky Skivar.

They parried and thrust and they sidestepped and cussed
'Til their blood would have filled a great pot.
The philologist blokes, who seldom crack jokes,
Say that hash was first made on that spot.

They fought all that night, 'neath the pale yellow moon;
The din, it was heard from afar;
And great multitudes came, so great was the fame
Of Abdul and Ivan Skivar.

Bucks, Beds and Bricks

As Abdul's long knife was extracting the life -
In fact, he was shouting 'Huzzah!' -
He felt himself struck by that wily Kalmuck,
Count Ivan Skavinsky Skivar.

The sultan drove by in his red-breasted fly,
Expecting the victor to cheer;
But he only drew nigh to hear the last sigh
Of Abdul Abulbul Amir.

Czar Petrovich, too, in his spectacles blue
Rode up in his new crested car.
He arrived just in time to exchange a last line
With Ivan Skavinsky Skivar.

A loud-sounding splash from the Danube was heard
Resounding o'er meadows afar;
It came from the sack fitting close to the back
Of Ivan Skavinsky Skivar.

There's a tomb rises up where the blue Danube flows;
Engraved there in characters clear;
'Ah stranger, when passing, please pray for the soul
Of Abdul Abulbul Amir.'

A Muscovite maiden her lone vigil keeps,
'Neath the light of the pale polar star;
And the name that she murmurs as oft as she weeps
Is Ivan Skavinsky Skivar.

*(Yes, it's long and yes it's true: we didn't always sing it all the way through!)*

## O'Rafferty's Pig

O'Rafferty's pig was a wonderful animal
Built like a battleship, sturdy and stout.
His ignorance would have disgraced any cannibal,
Impudence written all over his snout.

The day he broke loose there was such a commotion;
The women were screaming, the men turning pale.
There was running and jumping,
Colliding and bumping
And everyone making a grab at his tail.

The Widow McMahon fell through a shop window,
In herring and cheeses and pickles she lay.
She had eggs and 'termarters'
*(I know, I **know** but it has to rhyme!)*
All over her garters,
The day that O'Rafferty's pig ran away.

## Mary Ellen

Mary Ellen at the church turned up,
Her ma turned up,
Her papa turned up.
Her Auntie Gert,
Her rich Uncle Bert,
The parson in his little white shirt turned up.

But no bridegroom with the ring turned up,
Then a telegraph boy with his nose turned up
Brought a telegram that said
He didn't want to wed,
And they found him in the river
With his toes turned up!

## She Sat on Her Lilo

She sat on her lilo and played her guitar,
Played her guitar,
Played her guitar.
She sat on her lilo and played her guitar,
Played her guit-ar-har-har-har.

He sat down beside her and smoked a cigar,
Smoked a cigar,
Smoked a cigar.
He sat down beside her and smoked a cigar,
Smoked a cig-ar-har-har-har.

He said that he loved her, but oh, how he lied,
Oh, how he lied.
Oh, how he lied.
He said that he loved her but oh, how he lied,
Oh, how he lie-hie-hie-hied.

*(I think you have the idea! So I'll just write the first lines from here on.)*

Next day they were married but somehow she died,

He went to her funeral just for the ride,

He sat on her tombstone and laughed 'til he cried,

The tombstone fell on him and squish squash he died,
(Sung with gusto)

She went to heaven and flip, flap, she flied,

He went to t'other place and frizzled and fried,

The moral of this story is don't tell a lie.

We loved this next one when we were young, thinking it very rude!

## There is a Happy Land

There is a happy land, far, far away,
Where little piggies run, three times a day.
Oh, you should see them run
When they see the butcher come.
Three slices off their bum,
Three times a day!

I am not going to write out 'On Ilkely Moor Bah't At' (On Ilkely Moor Without a Hat), another long one that we enjoyed, as it is all in Yorkshire dialect. I shall let you find that one for yourselves if you wish. Suffice to say, as children we relished the story that one who had been so foolish as to go courting his girl friend on Ilkely Moor without wearing a hat would die of cold and be buried. And that eventually, via worms eating him and ducks eating the worms, our eating the ducks would mean that we should all really end up having eaten him!

I taught this song to a group of 3rd Grade children riding on a field trip bus in Crete, in the early 1970s. They seemed to enjoy it and sang it with relish. I wonder how many still remember the words and tune?

These are the songs I remember most clearly though there were certainly more. Earlier of course there were all the nursery rhymes.

## Story in the Aquila, December 1960

### The Twilight Hour

Soft-footed, stealthily, they crept into the little copse. When they were all assembled they convened in groups of two and three until the red orb of the sun, just visible as it sank lower on the western horizon, stretched forth its rays to penetrate the clouds resting on top of the mountains behind them.

Then with no word spoken, they all, as if puppets on invisible strings, turned to face the mountain, the small groups of people dissolving into one large crescent.

As the last rays of the dying sun struck the topmost, snowy peak of the mount, turning it blood-red, the assembly fell - again as if motivated by some unseen power - to their knees, dropping their heads to the ground, that they might not witness this great tragedy. The moment passed, the blood-red dissolving into deepening shades of grey. The people, themselves like pale, shadowy ghosts, moved hither and thither preparing, in this twilight hour, for the long dark night ahead, a night which might never end.

For the earth had ceased, oh so slowly, to turn on its axis and for those on this side of the world, should it never turn again, life would be perpetual night and all would be darkness.

They faced it calmly, courageously, knowing that they could not divert it and, these last few, that neither could they desert their homeland.

So as night, a night one might think, black with despair, crept on, these people watched, waited and, in their long vigil, kept faith - faith that in some future time, however far hence it might be, a new day would dawn.

# Bedford High School

BEDFORD HIGH SCHOOL

## Rules

*for the keeping of which the co-operation of parents is necessary*

## ATTENDANCE

No pupil may be absent, except through illness, without leave previously obtained from the Head Mistress on a written request from a Parent or Guardian ; if she is absent without leave, through illness or any other unforeseen cause, an explanatory note should be sent to the Head Mistress immediately. Telephone calls explaining absence should only be made for urgent reasons, e.g., infectious disease, and should be followed by a note. All such correspondence should be addressed to the Head Mistress and not to the Form Mistress.

Regular attendance is expected at Music, Elocution and Dancing lessons, at Games and the Clinic, if any of these have been undertaken at the beginning of the term. Leave of absence, except when a girl is absent from School, should be requested from the Mistress concerned.

## DRESS

Girls must wear School uniform when they attend School, the Field or the Swimming Pool, and when they represent the School in Bedford or elsewhere.

Watches may be worn only by the ~~VIth Form~~ IVA Forms → upwards and members of Russell House.

Money should only be brought to School when absolutely necessary and should be kept on a girl's own person (in a small purse with a strap, or a safe pocket) or handed to her Form Mistress.

Everything brought into School or taken to the Field or the Swimming Pool must be clearly marked with the owner's name and initials.

## OUT OF BOUNDS

No girl may visit a hotel, restaurant, café or milk bar during term-time except in the company of a Parent or Guardian. All places of public entertainment, *whether in Bedford or elsewhere*, are out of bounds in term-time unless a notice of the event is posted in the Hall or general permission is given. No girl may assist in outside entertainments, bazaars, fêtes, etc., during term-time; exceptions can only be made on very special occasions, on written application to the Head Mistress.

School Prefects are allowed some discretion with regard to exemption from some of these rules.

## DAY GIRLS AND BOARDERS

No day-girl may take a letter or do any shopping for a boarder.

## BEHAVIOUR OUTSIDE SCHOOL

In the street not more than three girls may walk abreast, and then only when there is sufficient room ; courtesy and consideration for other pedestrians must be observed. A girl may not cycle alongside a person who is walking ; no girl may ride in the playground or through the gates or stand about near the gates ; loitering and eating in the streets are forbidden.

Every girl is expected to know and conform to the rules of the Highway Code.

Girls are expected at all times, whether the School is in session or not, whether they are in uniform or not, to behave with common sense and good manners, and to see that their appearance is neat and in good taste.

## Leaving Certificate

B.H.S

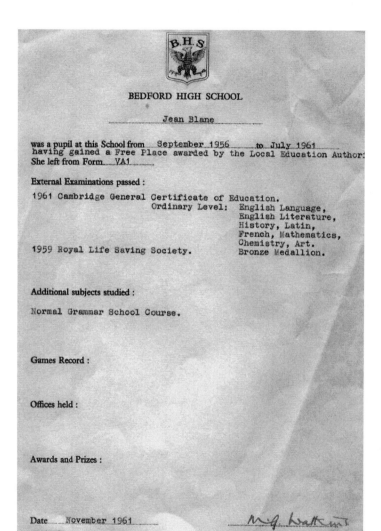

**BEDFORD HIGH SCHOOL**

Jean Blane

was a pupil at this School from September 1956 to July 1961
having gained a Free Place awarded by the Local Education Author
She left from Form VA1

**External Examinations passed :**

1961 Cambridge General Certificate of Education.
Ordinary Level: English Language, English Literature, History, Latin, French, Mathematics, Chemistry, Art.

1959 Royal Life Saving Society. Bronze Medallion.

**Additional subjects studied :**

Normal Grammar School Course.

**Games Record :**

**Offices held :**

**Awards and Prizes :**

Date November 1961

*Head Mistress.*

# General Certificate of Education Ordinary Level
# Sample Questions

## University of Cambridge Local Examinations Syndicate

These are samples all taken from my 1961 exam papers.

Some of the actual papers are in the Addendum at the end of this book.

## Mathematics

Remember: no calculator! Only a ruler, compasses, set square and protractor could be taken into the exam room.

Mathematical tables, squared paper and drawing paper were provided.

In order to be marked, our completed papers had to show how we worked out our answers.

1. i) Simplify: $(2\ 7/10 - 1\ 7/8) \div (1\ 5/8 \times 2\ 1/4)$

   Express 6.6in as a fraction of 1¼ miles, giving your answer in its simplest form.

   ii) A sum of money is divided into two parts in the ratio 5:3. If the smaller part is £384, find the original sum of money.

2. In a particular year 24 inches of rain falls on area of land which covers 31½ square inches on a map whose scale is 1:20,000. Only 32% of this water collects in a reservoir which serves a town with a population of 25,000.

3. Calculate

   i) The total volume of water collected, in cubic feet.

   ii) The number of gallons available for each person for the year. (Take 1 cubic foot to be 6¼ gallons.)

In the next year the amount of water collected decreases by 9% and the population increases by 12%. Calculate the percentage change in the amount available for each person.

4. The pilot of a helicopter, which flies at 110mph in still air, leaves a place A at noon. The wind is blowing at 45mph. In order to fly to B, which is due north of A, the pilot finds that he must set a course N 18º E. Find, by calculation or by drawing (using a scale of 1in to represent 20mph) the two possible directions of the wind.

   If the distance from A to B is 200 miles, find the time of arrival at B, in each case.

   (Each line in a velocity diagram must be clearly marked with a direction arrow.)

Using ruler and compasses only, construct

   iii) The circle, which passes through P and Q and has QR as the tangent at Q. Measure the radius of this circle.

I had to answer a total of nine questions in 2½ hours for each paper, so 18 questions and 5 hours in total.

Bucks, Beds and Bricks

Chemistry

Theoretical paper

1. State the law of multiple proportions and describe experiments you could do to test it.

Two oxides of a metal contain respectively 22.2% and 30% of oxygen. Show that these figures support the above law.

2.

a) Name two forms of carbon and give two uses for each. Describe two ways in which they differ.

b) Draw a diagram to show the preparation and collection of some gas jars of sulphur dioxide. Name the chemicals used and state the reaction conditions.

c) What maximum weight of barium sulphate could be precipitated by a solution containing 7.1mg of sodium sulphate?

3. Describe carefully the action of water on each of the following substances and name the products:

i) Sodium
ii) Quicklime
iii) Gaseous nitrogen dioxide

How would you prove whether or not a liquid was pure water? Outline the commercial preparation of hydrogen from steam.

There were eight questions in this paper altogether, of which I had to answer five in 2½ hours.

The practical exam was 2 hours long.

## English Language

Answer both a) and b).

a) Study the following sentence and then select from it the word or groups of words described by the following grammatical terms:

As we neared the station we heard the distant rattle of an approaching train and saw, some way off, the faint puffs of smoke which told us its position on the open plain.

- i) The finite verb in a co-ordinate main clause
- ii) A subordinating conjunction introducing an adverbial clause
- iii) An indirect object (dative case)
- iv) An adjectival clause
- v) A non-finite part of a verb, used as an adjective
- vi) A possessive adjective

b) Use each of the following adjectives in a separate sentence so as to bring out its full meaning. Use only one sentence for each adjective.

- i) fertile
- ii) mercenary
- iii) impartial
- iv) amicable
- v) contemporary
- vi) salutary

In addition to this question, we had to précis a passage of 318 words into not more than 120, taking care to give a continuous connection of ideas. Exceeding the 120 word limit was penalised. We also had to read a passage and answer questions on comprehension.

We had 1½ hours for this paper and another 1½ hours for the second English Language paper. For that, we had to choose one title from a list of nine and use it as the subject for a written essay.

Bucks, Beds and Bricks

English Literature

There were eight questions on Chaucer: The Prologue to the Canterbury Tales

Choose two of the passages a) to c) and answer the questions which follow:

a) This ilke worthy knight hadde been also
*Somtyme* with the lord of Palatye
Agayn another hethen in Turkye;
And evermore he hadde a *sovereyn prys*.
And though he were *worthy*, he was wys,
And of his port as meeke as is a mayde.
He nevere yet no *vileynye* ne sayde
In al his lyf unto no *maner wight*.

i) Rewrite this passage in fluent modern prose, paying careful attention to the italicised words.

ii) Describe and give Chaucer's comments on the Knight's dress.

iii) How, and by whom, had the Knight been honoured before all others?

b) And *over-al, ther* as profit sholde aryse,
Curteys he was *and lowly of servyse*;
Ther nas no man nowher so *vertuous*.
He was the beste beggere in his *hous*,
For thogh a widwe hadde noght a sho,
So plesaunt was his In Pricipio,
Yet wolde he have a farthing we he wente:
His *purchas* was wel better than his *rente*.

i) Rewrite this passage in fluent modern prose, paying careful attention to the italicized words.

ii) State two details from the information Chaucer gives us about this Friar's attitude to poor and sick people.

iii) Mention with brief details two accomplishments, not directly associated with hearing confession or begging, possessed by this Friar.

c) Whoso shal telle a tale after a man,
He moot reherce, as ny as ever he can,
*Everich* a word, if it be in his *charge*,
Al speke he never so *rudeliche* and *large*,
Or elles he moot telle his tale untrewe,
Or *feyne thing*, or fynde wordes newe.
He may nat spare, althogh he were his brother,
He moot as wel seye o word as another.

i) Rewrite this passage in fluent modern prose, paying careful attention to the italicised words.

ii) Give two examples that Chaucer uses to support his argument in this passage.

iii) Against what possible complaint is Chaucer defending himself? What error does he ask to be forgiven?

There were four questions on Shakespeare: Twelfth Night.

Did Malvolio, in your opinion, get what he deserved, or do you think that the treatment of him by Maria and the others was cruel or unfair? Give reasons for your opinion and make clear in your answer exactly what did happen to him.

(This is one of the simplest!)

There were three questions on Trollope: The Warden.

What were John Bold's motives for interfering in the affairs of Hiram's Hospital, and what did he hope to achieve? Say briefly what were, in fact, the results of his interference.

I had to answer five out of eight possible questions, split between the three different works I had studied. I answered two each on the Shakespeare and the Chaucer, one on the Trollope.

The time allowed for this paper was 2½ hours.

Bucks, Beds and Bricks

British and European History (1865 - 1939)

1. Describe Disraeli's handling of foreign and imperial affairs during his ministry of 1874 - 80.

3. Describe the growth and fortunes of the Labour Party from 1900 to 1931.

4. Give an account of the development of Anglo-Irish relations between 1914 and 1939.

5. Give an account of the movement for the social and political emancipation of women during this period.

6. Explain the various dangers which threatened the French Republic, at home and abroad, from its proclamation in 1870, to 1890.

7. What were the main causes of friction between Great Britain and Germany between 1890 and 1914?

8. Describe in outline the organisation of the League of Nations. What proved to be its main weaknesses?

9. In the history of Italy between the two world wars what was the importance of the following:

    the 'march on Rome' (1922);
    the Corporative State;
    the Lateran Treaty (1929);
    the Berlin-Rome Axis (1936)?

10. Why were the Bolsheviks able to seize power in Russia in 1917? What had they achieved by 1939?

This was a 2½ hour paper.

## Scripture

The Life and Teaching of Christ as Contained in the Gospels of St Mark and St Matthew chapters 5 - 7

1. Choose four of the passages a) to f) and answer the questions which follow:

a) And he answereth them, and saith, Who is my mother and my brethren? (Mark 3. 33)

How did it come about that Jesus asked this question? What reply did he give to it himself? Comment on the meaning of the reply.

b) This is my beloved Son: hear ye him. (Mark 9. 7)
Indicate the occasion of this statement and command. Mention another occasion when similar words were said and comment on the difference in the wording used.

The question of which the above is a sample was compulsory. Three other questions out of six had to be answered.

2. Describe how Jesus began his ministry in Capernaum. What important truths about his work and teaching does this story indicate?

3. Relate the parable of the wicked husbandmen, and give its meaning, with special reference to Jesus' own comment upon it.

4. Write a careful account of the crucifixion of Jesus, and briefly comment on the actions and words of those who were present.

The Acts of the Apostles

1. Choose four of the passages a) to f) and answer the questions which follow:

   a) Ye shall be my witnesses both in Jerusalem, and in all Judaea and Samaria and unto the uttermost part of the earth.

   Who said this and to whom? Who was the first 'witness' to Samaria and how did it come about that he went there?

   b) But an angel of the Lord by night opened the prison doors and brought them out.

   Who are referred to here? By whom were they imprisoned and why? What did the angel tell them to do?

Again, this was a compulsory question, with three more out of seven to be answered.

2. Give an account of two miracles worked by St Peter. What effect did they have on those who saw or heard about them?

3. What are we told in this book about St Barnabas?

4. Illustrate by reference to three examples the attitude of Roman officials to St Paul.

The time allowed for each of these papers was 1½ hours, so 3 hours in total.

# Languages

## French

For one French paper I had to translate a long passage of French prose into English. A second long passage was for reading, not for translation. Questions on it, written in French and that I also had to answer in French, followed.

That paper had 1¾ hours allowed for its completion.

For a second French paper I had to listen to a story read to me and retell it in French in 150-200 words. Marks were awarded for comprehension and for the quality of the language used in the answer. We did have a summary to refer to, as follows:

'The Doctor's Fruitless Journey'

Le jeune médecin - le coup de telephone - le médecin part en voiture - pas de lanterne - il rentre - deuxième coup de telephone - excuses - response de paysan.

So that was our help.

I also had to translate a passage of prose from English into French. 1¼ hours was the time allowed for this one too, so 3 hours in total for both.

Then there was an oral exam. I'm not sure how long that lasted but it seemed ages to me.

## Latin

In the first paper I had to translate some sections of Caesar, Gallic War Book 1 and Virgil, The Story of Camilla, from Latin into English. I also had to answer questions on Latin extracts from each work as well as more general questions on the works themselves.

These two were the works that we had studied for our O levels.

In a second paper I had to translate a previously unseen section of Latin prose into English, then an unseen section of English prose into Latin.

The time allowed for each of these papers was 2 hours, a 4 hour total.

## Art

In the first exam I drew and painted a still life picture of a basket with fruit and a picture of plant life: a dandelion with its root. These were both compulsory.

For the second exam we had a choice of four questions and I answered the following:

Design, in two colours, an all-over pattern (which need not necessarily be made up of repeating units) suitable for use as end-papers in one of the following books:

Mediaeval Stained Glass

Varieties of Sailing Craft

Constellations and Galaxies

Shell Fish

The design was to be a pattern rather than an illustration but with the motifs chosen suggested by the title. It was to be worked to a double-page size of 13inches x 7inches.

I chose Constellations and Galaxies, with stylized figures in pale yellow on a deep blue background.

The time allowed for each of these exams was 3 hours, a 6 hour total.

## About the Author

The author spent a number of her adult years living overseas on three of the five continents, before returning to England for good in 1974. Her career path took several unexpected and surprising, but ultimately fulfilling, twists and turns. Happily settled with John in Lincoln she is now retired.

Various activities and interests keep the author as busy as she has ever been. For leisure, reading still remains a great love.

The author conceived the idea for this account of her childhood at a time of serious illness and major surgery, when she began the gathering of memories and pictures. She remembered her regret that her own grandparents had died before she had discovered very much about their early lives. This concentrated her mind on the possibility that, whatever the outcome of her illness, she might not be around to satisfy her own grandchildren's curiosity in later years.

The author has three children, each born in a different country and on a different continent, and six grandchildren. With all of them living overseas, in the USA and New Zealand, she has gratefully embraced the technology that enables instant communication around the world.

The author can be contacted at j.flannery@hotmail.co.uk

1940

2004

# Resources

To find out more about where Dad went and what he did in the war, see the BBC website, WW2 The People's War and search for Jack Blane's War.

That is the account that Dad eventually wrote out for his family. As I note at the end, what he doesn't mention are the horrors of war that he encountered. Mum says he had nightmares for years afterwards and there are still things he will not speak of and programmes he will not watch or listen to.

You can also hear the spoken account in Jack Blane's Wartime Memoir on YouTube. There you can view a slide show of wartime pictures and I've added a bit more knowledge, for example that Dad's D-Day landing was with 30 Corps on Gold Beach.

www.mkweb.co.uk takes you to a website where there is information on the history of the area around Bletchley and Fenny Stratford, as well as the present day new city of Milton Keynes.

A book entitled Bletchley Voices, by Robert Cook, is an oral history with people telling their own memories of the town. Dad, His brothers Donald and Martin, and Martin's wife Gwen, are all contributors.

If you are interested in railway history and anecdotes you might like A Railway Man's Tales of Old Bletchley by A E Grigg.

Typing Marston Vale Brickies into your search engine should bring up a site with all kinds of information on Stewartby and the brickworks. It even shows a panorama of the village to scroll around.

Bedford, Milton Keynes and Sheffield libraries are rich sources of information. It is some years since I was sourcing material for this book but staff at all three were very helpful to me.

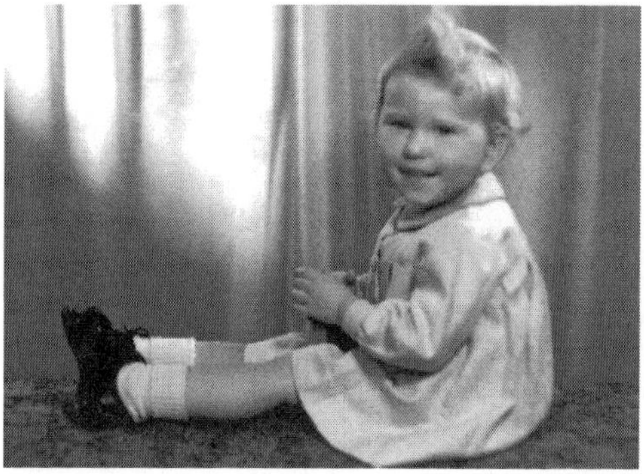

1947

2011

**Then and Now**

When I hear talk of the good old days I find it somewhat sad
That those who feel so nostalgic now can see nothing of the bad.

Diseases that now hold no fear, those days were just not curable.
And some I love would then have died: a thought night unendurable.

Houses cold and housework hard, between then and now what a gap:
With heating that we take for granted and all modern gadgets on tap.

We had more feel for community: less traffic and less noise and crime.
The pace of life was much slower; there was more of a sense of time.

Yet don't believe all in the tabloids: a climate of fear they have made.
You'd be too scared to go out on the streets, huddled behind barricade.

I do think education was better and that's not the word of a toff.
But I'm sure that this generation can't really be just written off.

We'd not heard of E numbers in food and not many additives you see.
But then on the other side of the coin - we sprayed crops with DDT.

There wasn't the factory farming, no GM foods being grown;
More foods were fresh and local though with less variety, I own.

The EU to be a nation of which Britain would be just one small part?
That thought and the rules to control us, bring me heaviness of heart.

But oh, the delights of technology, with the instant contact it brings.
With my children all flung far and wide, it's in this that my heart sings.

I have email and social networks and Skype.  It isn't like my younger day
When all that we had were air letters to connect us when so far away.

Things were much better in bygone times. No, things are better today!
Each is true in one way or another - but now is where I'm glad to stay.

# ADDENDUM

## UNIVERSITY OF CAMBRIDGE
## LOCAL EXAMINATIONS SYNDICATE

## GENERAL CERTIFICATE OF EDUCATION

## ORDINARY LEVEL

## 1961

Selected Papers and Questions



The original papers are pale blue in colour. Though faded to various degrees now, some creased and stained, they are all still legible.

412/1

412/1
ORD. LEVEL
MATH. (ALT. B)
PAPER I

*Wednesday*
**28 JUNE 1961**
*2½ hours*
Morning

UNIVERSITY OF CAMBRIDGE
LOCAL EXAMINATIONS SYNDICATE
GENERAL CERTIFICATE OF EDUCATION

**MATHEMATICS**

ORDINARY LEVEL, ALTERNATIVE B

PAPER I

(*Two hours and a half*)

*Answer* **all** *the questions in Section I and any* **four** *in Section II.*

**All working must be clearly shown; it should be done on the same sheet as the rest of the answer.**

*Mathematical tables, squared paper, and drawing paper are provided.*

SECTION I. [52 marks]

1. **Mathematical tables must not be used in this question.**

(i) Find the value of $\frac{(0{\cdot}02)^2 \times 0{\cdot}72}{0{\cdot}048}$.

(ii) By selling a chair for £10. 7*s*., a shopkeeper makes a profit of 15%. Find the cost price of the chair.

(iii) A man builds a fence, 63 ft. long, using 8 posts at 10*s*. each and 228 planks costing 8*s*. 6*d*. per dozen. Calculate, in shillings and pence, the average cost per foot of the fence.

2. (i) Solve the equation $(2x-3)(x+1) = 18$.

(ii) Factorise $27-3a^2$.

(iii) A man travels $p$ miles at $x$ miles per hour and then for $k$ minutes at $y$ miles per hour. Write down expressions for

(*a*) the total time taken, in minutes;

(*b*) the total distance travelled, in miles.

I've omitted page 2, which is copied into the appendix.

3

8. Prove that angles in the same segment of a circle are equal.

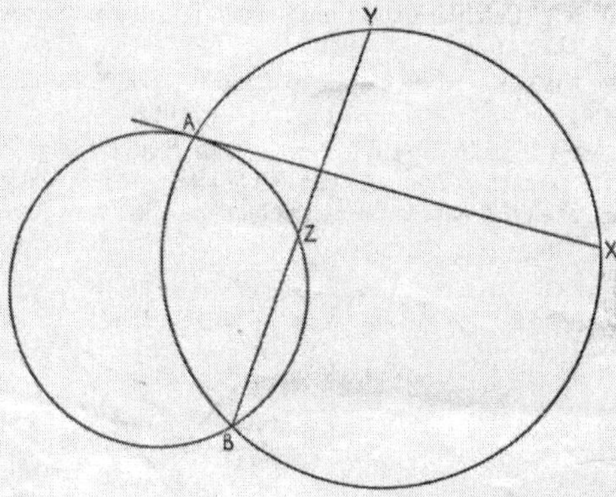


Two circles intersect at $A$ and $B$. The tangent at $A$ to the first circle cuts the second circle at $X$. A line through $B$ cuts the first circle at $Z$ and the second circle at $Y$. Prove that $AZ$ is parallel to $YX$.

9.

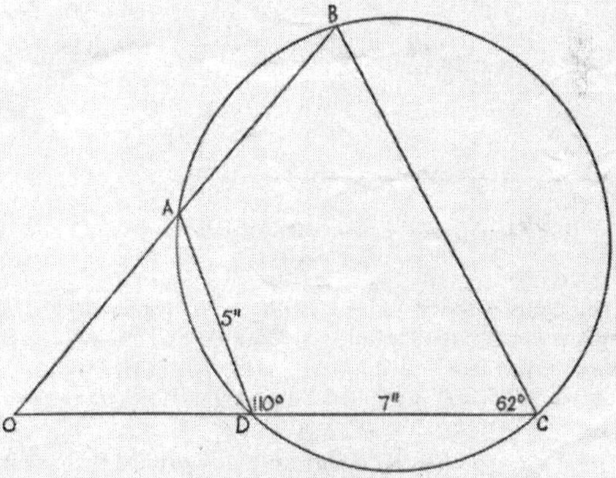


In the figure $AD = 5$ in., $DC = 7$ in., the angle $ADC = 110°$, and the angle $BCD = 62°$.

Calculate (i) the length of $AC$; (ii) the length of $OD$.

[TURN OVER

10. An aircraft flies eastwards along the equator from $P$ (long. 70° E.) to $Q$ (long. 105° E.). It then flies due north to $R$ (lat. 10° N.). Calculate the time for the journey if the average speed is 275 m.p.h.

[Take the earth to be a sphere of radius 3960 miles and $\pi$ to be 3·142.]

A second aircraft flies due north from $P$ to $T$ (long. 70° E., lat. 10° N.) and then along the parallel of latitude to $R$. Calculate, in miles, the difference between the lengths of the two journeys.

11.

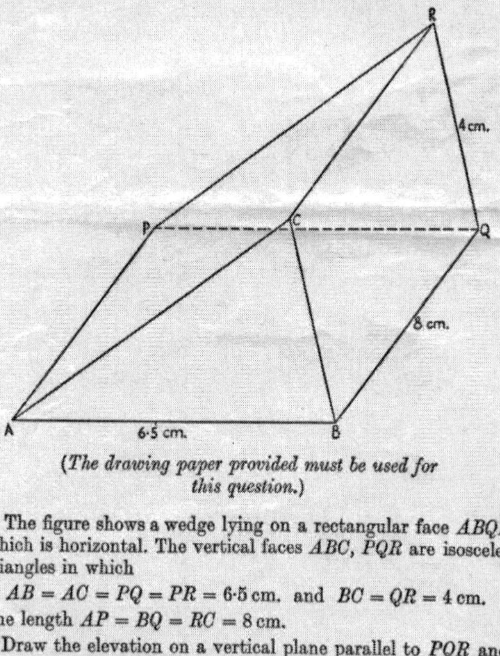


(*The drawing paper provided must be used for this question.*)

The figure shows a wedge lying on a rectangular face $ABQP$ which is horizontal. The vertical faces $ABC$, $PQR$ are isosceles triangles in which

$AB = AC = PQ = PR = 6{\cdot}5$ cm. and $BC = QR = 4$ cm.

The length $AP = BQ = RC = 8$ cm.

Draw the elevation on a vertical plane parallel to $PQR$ and hence draw the plan of the solid. Use these drawings to find, by further construction, the angle between the diagonal $AR$ and the horizontal face $ABQP$.

540/1

540/1
ORD. LEVEL
THEORETICAL
CHEMISTRY

*Wednesday*
**5 JULY 1961**
$2\frac{1}{2}$ *hours*
Afternoon

UNIVERSITY OF CAMBRIDGE
LOCAL EXAMINATIONS SYNDICATE
GENERAL CERTIFICATE OF EDUCATION

## CHEMISTRY

ORDINARY LEVEL

THEORETICAL PAPER

(*Two hours and a half*)

*Answer the whole of Part I and any* **four** *questions in Part II.*

*Candidates are advised to spend not more than 50 minutes in answering Part I.*

### PART I

*Answer this part on the sheet attached and hand it in with the rest of your answers.*

*Essential working must be shown.*

[H = 1; C = 12; N = 14; O = 16; Na = 23; S = 32;
Cl = 35·5; Ca = 40; Fe = 56; Pb = 207.

One gram molecular weight of a gas occupies 22·4 litres at N.T.P.]

## Part II

*Answer* **four** *questions from this part.*

*Unless otherwise stated, diagrams and equations must be given wherever possible. When fully labelled diagrams are given, descriptions of apparatus are not required.*

*Mathematical tables are provided.*

[O = 16; Na = 23; S = 32; Ba = 137.]

1. How would you prepare and collect some gas jars of oxygen? Describe experiments to show the combustion of sulphur, magnesium and iron in oxygen. In each case state carefully what you would observe.

Give **two** different uses for oxygen.

2. Describe carefully the action of water on each of the following substances and name the products: (i) sodium, (ii) quicklime, (iii) gaseous nitrogen dioxide.

How would you prove whether or not a liquid was pure water?

Outline the commercial preparation of hydrogen from steam.

3. (*a*) Describe the working of a simple fire-extinguisher. [A diagram is not required].

(*b*) Draw and label a diagram to show how quicklime is manufactured. State **two** important uses for quicklime and/or slaked lime.

(*c*) By means of a simple diagram show the essential parts of a bunsen burner.

Explain why a bunsen burner will sometimes strike back.

4. State the law of multiple proportions, and describe experiments you could do to test it.

Two oxides of a metal contain respectively 22·2 % and 30 % of oxygen. Show that these figures support the above law.

5. (*a*) Draw a labelled diagram of the apparatus you would use to prepare fairly concentrated hydrochloric acid from sodium chloride. [Your labelling should indicate necessary reaction conditions and precautions.]

(*b*) Describe carefully how you would obtain crystals of ammonium chloride from concentrated hydrochloric acid.

(*c*) What precautions are necessary when diluting concentrated sulphuric acid?

6. (*a*) Name **two** forms of carbon and give **two** uses for each. Describe **two** ways in which they differ.

(*b*) Draw a diagram to show the preparation and collection of some gas jars of sulphur dioxide. Name the chemicals used and state the reaction conditions.

(*c*) What maximum weight of barium sulphate could be precipitated by a solution containing 7·1 gm. of sodium sulphate?

7. How is sodium carbonate manufactured by the Solvay process? [Diagrams and technical details are not required, but the essential chemical reactions must be given.]

How does sodium carbonate solution react with (i) carbon dioxide, (ii) copper sulphate solution, (iii) nitric acid?

Give **two** uses for sodium carbonate.

540/2

540/2
ORD. LEVEL
CHEMISTRY
PRACT.
*Friday*
**7 JULY 1961**
2 *hours*
Morning

UNIVERSITY OF CAMBRIDGE
LOCAL EXAMINATIONS SYNDICATE
GENERAL CERTIFICATE OF EDUCATION

**CHEMISTRY**

ORDINARY LEVEL

PRACTICAL TEST

(*Two hours*)

*Answer* all *the questions.*

**Read the questions carefully and follow the instructions.**

N.B. *In Question* 1 *all burette readings and the capacity of the pipette must be recorded,* **but no account of experimental procedure is required. All calculations** *must be done on the paper actually given in; if a slide rule is used, a statement to this effect must be made.*

*Mathematical tables are provided.*

*In Questions* 2 *and* 3, *credit will be given for good observations precisely recorded, and for well-drawn inferences.*

[H = 1; O = 16; S = 32.]

1. **B 1** is a solution containing 8·60 gm. of sodium bicarbonate $NaHCO_3$ per litre.

**B 2** is a solution containing sulphuric acid.

Put the acid into the burette, and titrate portions of the alkali. Name the indicator used.

Calculate: (*a*) the normality of the acid **B 2**, (*b*) the concentration of the solution **B 2** in grams per litre.

[TURN OVER

2. Carry out the following experiments with the substance **B 3**, record carefully all that you observe, and identify the gas evolved in reactions (*a*) and (*b*):

(*a*) Put a portion of **B 3** into a test-tube and cover it with water. Now add 2 c.c. of solution **B 4** and gently warm the tube and its contents.

(*b*) Put a second portion of **B 3** into a test-tube and just cover with dilute sulphuric acid.

(*c*) Put a third portion of **B 3** into a test-tube, cover well with water, and add 1 gm. of ammonium sulphate. Warm gently.

3. The mixture **B 5** contains one metallic and two acidic radicals. Identify all three radicals. State carefully how your solutions are obtained.

110/1

110/1
ORD. LEVEL
ENGLISH
LANGUAGE
PAPER I
*Monday*
**26 JUNE 1961**
1½ *hours*
Morning

UNIVERSITY OF CAMBRIDGE
LOCAL EXAMINATIONS SYNDICATE
GENERAL CERTIFICATE OF EDUCATION

**ENGLISH LANGUAGE**

ORDINARY LEVEL

(*One hour and a half*)

There are **TWO** alternative papers, PAPER IA on page 3, PAPER IB on pages 5 and 6.

Choose the paper for which you have been prepared. **You must not attempt both papers.**

Write *Paper* IA or *Paper* IB at the head of your answer.

3

**PAPER IA**

One subject only to be chosen.

*At the head of your composition write the number of the subject you have chosen.*

Write a composition on **one** of the following subjects:

1. Motorways.

2. Fishing as a sport and as an industry.

3. Is it sensible to give girls the same type of education as that given to boys?

4. 'Advertising is becoming a menace.'

5. Beauty treatment.

6. From your own acquaintance with science fiction, try to account for its popularity.

7. Discuss the advantages and disadvantages of linking England and France by bridge or tunnel. You may consider, among other things, the following points: problems of cost and of revenue; trade; speed of communication; the comfort of travellers; Customs.

8. Give an account of the circumstances which led you to miss the last train (or bus) home.

9. 'These I have loved:
White plates and cups, clean gleaming,
Ringed with blue lines; and feathery, faery dust;
Wet roofs, beneath the lamp-light; the strong crust
Of friendly bread.'
What ordinary things in life do you love?

If choosing Paper 1B you would have had to write two shorter essays, one subject from each of two more lists.

110/2

110/2
ORD. LEVEL
ENGLISH
LANGUAGE
(PAPER II)

*Monday*
**26 JUNE 1961**
1½ *hours*
Morning

UNIVERSITY OF CAMBRIDGE
LOCAL EXAMINATIONS SYNDICATE
GENERAL CERTIFICATE OF EDUCATION

**ENGLISH LANGUAGE**

ORDINARY LEVEL

PAPER II

(*One hour and a half*)

*Answer Question* **1** and *Question* **2**,
*and* **one** *of Questions* **3** *and* **4.**

Read the following passage carefully, and then answer Question 1.

It is almost impossible to escape from advertisements. Hoardings stare down at us from the sides of the roads; crude neon signs wink above shops; jingles and slogans assault our ears; in magazines, pictures of washing machines and custard powders take up more room than the letter-press. All these are twentieth-century developments which have grown side by side with the spread of education and technical advances in radio and television.

Advertising assaults not only our eyes and ears but also our pockets. Its critics point out that in this country 1·6 per cent of national income is spent on advertising and that this advertising actually raises the cost of products. When a housewife buys a pound of flour, 5 per cent of what she pays goes to some advertiser or other, even if she has not bothered to ask the shopkeeper for a particular brand. If she buys a named brand of aspirin, up to 29 per cent of what she pays may represent the cost of advertising the name.

These amounts seem a great deal to pay for the questionable benefits of advertising, but there are a few things to be said in its favour. Although some things cost more because of advertising, other things cost less. Newspapers, magazines, commercial radio and television all carry advertisements, and the money received from the advertisers helps to lower the cost of production. In this way we get information and entertainment at lower prices than would otherwise have to be charged, and so what we lose on the swings we gain on the roundabouts. Apart from this very important consideration, advertising to some extent ensures that a product will maintain its quality. It also gives rise to competition among manufacturers, which benefits the customer by offering him a wider choice. Competition may even succeed, in some cases, in reversing the influence of advertising and causing a reduction in price.

**Question 1**

Make a summary of the whole passage, which contains 318 words, **in not more than 120 words.** Take care to give a continuous connexion of ideas. Failure to keep within the limit of 120 words will be penalised.

4

**Question 2**

Read the following passage carefully, and then answer (*a*), (*b*) and (*c*).

An amenity for which many people are pleading today is quiet. Road traffic, aeroplanes and loud forms of entertainment have caused a surge of disturbing noise for which thoughtlessness and selfishness are largely to blame. As a result, our capacity to tolerate noise without injury to our health has almost reached its limit.

Noise has a detrimental effect upon our nerves, and it is a fallacy to argue that they are resilient, and can adapt themselves to any amount of it. Noise imperceptibly wears down the nervous system, with serious effect on our bodily health, and, what is more grave, thwarts the spirit, which is what distinguishes man from the beast. Creative work becomes difficult, or even impossible, whether man is merely thinking or translating his thought into action.

The conclusion is inescapable: more stringent legislation is urgently needed to suppress all uncontrolled and unnecessary noise.

(*a*) For each of the following words, which are taken from the above passage, give a word or short phrase which could be used to replace it in the passage without change of meaning:

(i) capacity (l. 4); (ii) tolerate (l. 5); (iii) detrimental (l. 7); (iv) imperceptibly (l. 9); (v) distinguishes (l. 11).

(*b*) What do you understand by:

(i) translating his thought into action (ll. 13–14);

(ii) more stringent legislation (l. 15)?

(*c*) State briefly:

(i) a reason suggested by the writer for thinking that noise could be reduced without legislation;

(ii) the most harmful effect which the writer thinks noise has upon the individual;

(iii) what the writer suggests has been put forward to prove that noise is not a matter for serious concern.

*Answer* **one** *of Questions* **3** *and* **4.**

**Question 3**

*Answer* **both** *(a) and (b).*

(*a*) Study the following sentence and then select from it the words or groups of words described by the following grammatical terms:

As we neared the station we heard the distant rattle of an approaching train and saw, some way off, the faint puffs of smoke which told us its position on the open plain.

(i) The finite verb in a co-ordinate main clause.

(ii) A subordinating conjunction introducing an adverbial clause.

(iii) An indirect object (dative case).

(iv) An adjectival clause.

(v) A non-finite part of a verb, used as an adjective.

(vi) A possessive adjective.

(*b*) Use each of the following adjectives in a separate sentence so as to bring out its full meaning. Use only **one** sentence for each adjective.

(i) fertile;

(ii) mercenary;

(iii) impartial;

(iv) amicable;

(v) contemporary;

(vi) salutary.

[TURN OVER

210/1 | 210/1
ORD. LEVEL
ENGLISH
LITERATURE
*Monday*
**3 JULY 1961**
$2\frac{1}{2}$ *hours*
Morning

UNIVERSITY OF CAMBRIDGE
LOCAL EXAMINATIONS SYNDICATE
GENERAL CERTIFICATE OF EDUCATION

**ENGLISH LITERATURE**

ORDINARY LEVEL

(*Two hours and a half*)

*There is an allowance of ten minutes extra for you to study the questions before you begin to write your answers.*

*Answer* **five** *questions in all, of which at least* **three** *should be taken from Section* A, *and at least* **one** *from Section* B.

**SECTION A**

*Answer at least* **three** *questions (but not more than* **four**) *from this Section, selecting your questions from at least* **two** *books (but not more than* **three**).

**N.B.** *You* **must** *answer* **one** *context question; you may, if you wish, answer* **two** *but not more than* **two** *context questions.*

SHAKESPEARE: *Twelfth Night*

✓ 1. Choose **three** of the passages (*a*) to (*d*) and answer *briefly* the questions which follow:

(*a*) *Malvolio.* I marvel your ladyship takes delight in such a barren rascal; I saw him put down the other day with an ordinary fool that has no more brain than a stone. Look you now, he's out of his guard already; unless you laugh and minister occasion to him, he is gagg'd.

(i) What exchange of wit between Olivia and Feste has just taken place, provoking Malvolio to call the clown 'a barren rascal'?

(ii) Express in your own words the meaning of the last sentence ('Look you now...gagg'd').

(iii) Who echoes these words of Malvolio later in the play, and on what occasion?

2

(*b*) *Malvolio.* Seven of my people, with an obedient start, make out for him. I frown the while, and perchance wind up my watch, or play with my—some rich jewel. Toby approaches; curtesies there to me—

(i) Complete Malvolio's account of this imagined interview.

(ii) Suggest an explanation for his hesitation after the words 'play with my—'.

(iii) Briefly say what in fact does happen when Malvolio and Sir Toby next meet.

(*c*) *Olivia.* O, what a deal of scorn looks beautiful
In the contempt and anger of his lip!
A murd'rous guilt shows not itself more soon
Than love that would seem hid: love's night is noon.

(i) To whom is Olivia referring in the first two lines of the passage? What had provoked the 'contempt and anger' to which she refers?

(ii) What is the meaning of the third and fourth lines ('A murd'rous...is noon')?

(iii) What has been said by Orsino, earlier in the play, about the same person's lip and voice?

(*d*) *A.* For the fair kindness you have show'd me here,
And part being prompted by your present trouble,
Out of my lean and low ability
I'll lend you something. My having is not much;
I'll make division of my present with you;
Hold, there's half my coffer.

*B.* Will you deny me now?
Is't possible that my deserts to you
Can lack persuasion? Do not tempt my misery,
Lest that it make me so unsound a man
As to upbraid you with those kindnesses
That I have done for you.

(i) Name *A* and *B*. What 'fair kindness' has *B* just shown to *A*, and what is *B*'s 'present trouble'?

(ii) What is it that *B* accuses *A* of now denying him?

(iii) What does *B* mean when he refers to 'those kindnesses that I have done for you', and why does *A* not understand what is meant?

✓ 2. Did Malvolio, in your view, get what he deserved, or do you think that the treatment of him by Maria and the others was cruel or unfair? Give reasons for your opinion, and make clear in your answer exactly what did happen to him.

3. **Either** (*a*) What makes Sir Andrew Aguecheek such an entertaining character in the play? Illustrate your answer by close reference to **at least two** episodes in which he is involved.

**Or** (*b*) Suppose that a member of the audience at a performance of *Twelfth Night* has had to leave the theatre at the end of Act IV. Write for him an account of the last act of the play (a single scene at Olivia's house) in such a way as to make clear how all the loose ends of the plot are brought together and neatly tied.

4. Develop the contrast suggested by a consideration of any **one** of the following pairs:

(i) Viola and Olivia as young women in love;

(ii) Sir Toby and Feste as clowns;

(iii) Maria and Malvolio as servants to Olivia.

13

20. 'Chesterton is continually surprising us by what he says and how he says it.' Illustrate this quality of surprise in Chesterton's work by reference to several essays.

**SECTION B**

*Answer at least* **one** *question (but not more than* **two)** *from this Section.*

BRIDIE: *Tobias and the Angel*

21. **Either** (*a*) Illustrating your answer from the play, say what you learn of Anna as a wife and as a mother.

**Or** (*b*) Show by close reference and some quotation how Bridie gives to the play an oriental atmosphere of strangeness and colour.

22. Illustrate, by close reference to the play, what Bridie means when he says that his Raphael is a thorough Modern, with

You've seen questions on the Chaucer.
We studied the Trollope, not the Bridie.

TROLLOPE: *The Warden*

24. Describe the part taken in the action of the novel by the Bishop of Barchester in such a way that you bring out his character and account for the affection that existed between him and Mr Harding.

25. 'Trollope keeps his female characters very much in the background in this novel.' Show how far you believe this to be true by writing on Mary Bold, Eleanor Harding and Mrs Grantly.

26. What were John Bold's motives for interfering in the affairs of Hiram's Hospital, and what did he hope to achieve? Say briefly what were, in fact, the results of his interference.

[TURN OVER

231/1

231/1
ORD. LEVEL
BRITISH AND EUROPEAN HISTORY
(1865–1939)
*Wednesday*
**5 JULY 1961**
2½ *hours*
Morning

UNIVERSITY OF CAMBRIDGE
LOCAL EXAMINATIONS SYNDICATE
GENERAL CERTIFICATE OF EDUCATION

**BRITISH AND EUROPEAN HISTORY (1865–1939)**

ORDINARY LEVEL

(*Two hours and a half*)

*Answer* **five** *questions.*

SECTION I

1. Describe Disraeli's handling of foreign and imperial affairs during his ministry of 1874–80.

2. What measures were introduced by the Liberal ministries between 1906 and 1914 to reform (*a*) the Trade Unions, (*b*) the Army, (*c*) the House of Lords?

3. Describe the growth and fortunes of the Labour Party from 1900 to 1931.

4. Give an account of the movement for the social and political emancipation of women during this period.

5. Describe the career and importance of **two** of the following: Cecil Rhodes; Lord Kitchener; Lawrence of Arabia; Mahatma Gandhi.

6. Give an account of the development of Anglo-Irish relations between 1914 and 1939.

7. What were the chief electrical inventions during this period, and what have been their most important applications in every-day life?

[TURN OVER

2

## Section II

8. Explain the various dangers which threatened the Third French Republic, at home and abroad, from its proclamation in 1870, to 1890.

9. What were the main causes of friction between Great Britain and Germany between 1890 and 1914?

10. Describe the policies of the European Powers in the Far East during this period, down to 1914.

11. Explain and illustrate the importance of sea power during the war of 1914–18.

12. Why were the Bolsheviks able to seize power in Russia in 1917? What had they achieved by 1939?

13. Describe in outline the organisation of the League of Nations. What proved to be its main weaknesses?

14. In the history of Italy between the two world wars what was the importance of the following: the 'march on Rome' (1922); the Corporative State; the Lateran Treaty (1929); the 'Berlin-Rome Axis' (1936)?

## Section III

15. Write shortly on **three** of the following: (*a*) Parliamentary Reform Act (1867); (*b*) Forster's Education Act (1870); (*c*) 'Parnellism and Crime'; (*d*) the South Africa Act (1909); (*e*) the Ottawa Agreements (1932–33); (*f*) the Reinsurance Treaty (1887); (*g*) the Young Turk Revolution (1908); (*h*) Italia Irredenta; (*i*) the Washington Conference (1921); (*j*) the Reichstag fire (1933).

303/1

303/1
ORD. LEVEL
FRENCH I
*Wednesday*
28 JUNE 1961
$1\frac{3}{4}$ *hours*
Afternoon

UNIVERSITY OF CAMBRIDGE
LOCAL EXAMINATIONS SYNDICATE
GENERAL CERTIFICATE OF EDUCATION

## FRENCH

ORDINARY LEVEL

PAPER O. I

(*One hour and three-quarters*)

*In Questions* 1 *and* 2 *leave a line between the paragraphs, as in the French.*

1. Translate into ENGLISH:

La porte d'entrée donnait directement sur un couloir sombre où un garçon de bureau montait la garde. D'une voix timide je lui dis:

— Une de mes amies, Mlle Ménochet, qui travaille ici, m'a dit de me présenter pour une place de secrétaire. Je dois voir M. Patin.

Il m'emmena alors dans un petit bureau de trois mètres sur deux mètres, où une jeune personne tapait sur une machine à écrire comme si elle voulait la détruire.

Je prononçai à nouveau mon petit discours. La jeune fille inscrivit mon nom et le motif de ma visite sur un petit papier et le tendit au garçon de bureau, puis lui répéta mes explications.

— J'ai compris, dit-il avec fierté, et il disparut.

La jeune fille me pria de m'asseoir sur une chaise sale placée contre le mur derrière la porte. Puis elle se remit à taper avec une telle énergie que les meubles vibraient.

Un quart d'heure plus tard le garçon revint et grogna quelque chose que je n'entendis pas très bien.

— M. Patin vous attend, dit la dactylo sans lever les yeux. Dans le couloir, troisième porte à droite.

Après avoir frappé à la porte j'entrai et trouvai en face de moi, assis dans un fauteuil, et tournant le dos à une étroite fenêtre, un petit monsieur absolument chauve qui portait de grosses lunettes.

2

2. Translate into English:

Nicolas et Sophie descendirent de la voiture au coin de la rue Jacob. Le quartier semblait calme. Marchant côte à côte, ils arrivèrent à la librairie Vavasseur. Des volets de bois couvraient la devanture et à la porte se tenait un gendarme.

— Il va nous empêcher d'entrer ! souffla Nicolas.

— Je ne le pense pas, dit Sophie. Pour l'instant, la police ne s'intéresse qu'à Monsieur Vavasseur. C'est seulement s'il révèle le nom de ses amis que les recherches iront plus loin.

— Mais. . . mais il se peut qu'il ait déjà parlé ! balbutia Nicolas.

— Evidemment !

— Alors?

Elle haussa lentement les épaules:

— Que voulez-vous? C'est un risque à courir !

Nicolas regarda le gendarme, qui était robuste, mais qui avait l'air un peu bête. S'ils hésitaient ils éveilleraient les soupçons de cet homme.

— Allons-y ! reprit Sophie.

Ils s'avancèrent délibérément vers la porte. Le gendarme les laissa passer sans rien dire. Ils traversèrent le vestibule et montèrent l'escalier.

L'appartement de M. Vavasseur se trouvait au deuxième étage. Sophie tira une clef de son sac, ouvrit la porte et se glissa dans une pièce obscure. Elle ouvrit une armoire très haute et très large, pleine de linge, et grimpa sur une chaise pour essayer d'atteindre le dernier rayon.

— Vous allez vous rompre le cou ! dit Nicolas. Que voulez-vous faire exactement?

— Sortir tous les papiers qui sont cachés là-dedans ! dit-elle en lui cédant sa place sur la chaise.

3. Read carefully the following passage, which is **not** to be translated:

Son travail à la boulangerie ennuyait Julien et un matin il annonça à ses parents qu'il avait décidé de partir voir le monde. Son père leva les bras au ciel.

3

— Ah non, alors! n'avons-nous pas assez d'ennuis? Maintenant tu vas dépenser tes maigres économies.

— Je ne dépenserai pas grand-chose, dit Julien. Où que j'aille, je travaillerai.

Et c'est ainsi que Julien partit pour le Havre.

Arrivé dans cette ville il chercha du travail mais ne trouva rien. Il dut vivre avec parcimonie et, avant la fin d'un mois, ayant épuisé ses dernières ressources, il accepta des besognes de mendiant, gagnant quelques francs à laver des automobiles et à balayer les trottoirs.

Souvent il se promenait le long des quais, attiré irrésistiblement par les grands bateaux. Un jour, comme il passait le long d'une petite rue, quelqu'un lui mit la main sur l'épaule. C'était un jeune homme d'une vingtaine d'années comme lui au visage maigre.

— Tu m'intéresses, déclara celui-ci. Je m'appelle Daniel, et je cherche comme toi à m'embarquer sur un paquebot. J'ai déjà navigué, et je possède assez d'expérience. Je veux t'aider parce que tu es un révolté comme moi. Dans une semaine il y a de fortes chances pour que nous nous embarquions ensemble.

Julien ne voulait pas se fier à cet espoir. Mais le jeune homme montra sa bonne foi en lui donnant un peu d'argent et, avant de le quitter, il renouvela encore ses assurances. Une semaine passa. Le samedi, comme Julien, l'estomac creux, regardait les bateaux dans le port, le nommé Daniel l'aborda de nouveau.

— Ça y est, j'ai trouvé, dit-il, c'est un bateau de croisière, qui fait le tour du monde pour un prix dérisoire. Il y a une majorité de vieilles dames et quelques personnages d'âge moyen en quête d'aventures ou qui ont un petit héritage à dissiper. Mais la Compagnie veut faire des économies. Elle nous engage au mépris de tous les règlements. Nous allons nous occuper des cabines et servir dans la salle à manger.

Answer the following questions in FRENCH. Your answers should be **concise** but should make complete sentences, the form and tense of which should suit those of the questions:

(i) Quelle sorte de travail Julien faisait-il avant de quitter la maison paternelle?

[TURN OVER

More questions did follow!

303/2

303/2
ORD. LEVEL
FRENCH II

*Thursday*
**29 JUNE 1961**
1¼ *hours*
Afternoon

UNIVERSITY OF CAMBRIDGE
LOCAL EXAMINATIONS SYNDICATE
GENERAL CERTIFICATE OF EDUCATION

## FRENCH

ORDINARY LEVEL

PAPER O. II

(*One hour and a quarter*)

*The time allowed for answering this paper is 1¼ hours, of which you should devote about 30 minutes to your answer to Question 1.*

**Hand in your answer to Question 1 together with that to Question 2.** (*Any notes which you may take for Question 1 are to be given* **separately** *to the Supervisor.*)

1. *You are allowed two minutes in which to study the following instructions and summary before the passage is read. Additional instructions will have been given to you by the person who is to read the passage.*

Re-tell in FRENCH in 150–200 words the story which will be read to you and of which a summary is printed below. You are not expected to try to reproduce the story word for word, but you should give the principal points of it, and you should not introduce into your answer material which is not in the story read to you. The story contains about 200 words.

Marks will be awarded both for comprehension of the story and for the quality of the language used in your answer.

SUMMARY OF THE STORY

*The summary is given in the present tense, but your narrative should be written in the past tense. Where direct speech occurs in the passage you may render it as either direct or indirect speech.*

*The Doctor's Fruitless Journey*

Le jeune médecin — le coup de téléphone — le médecin part en voiture — pas de lanterne — il rentre — deuxième coup de téléphone — excuses — réponse du paysan.

[TURN OVER

2. Write on every line and keep the paragraphs **quite separate**, as in the English.

Translate into FRENCH:

There was once a merchant who lived in a far country. One day he lost a very precious jewel.

He searched everywhere without finding it. At last he decided that it had been stolen by a servant, for nobody had entered the house.

He called the servants and questioned them, but in vain. He was about to send for a policeman when his wife declared that she could find the thief.

'I am going to give to each of you a piece of wood of equal length,' she told the servants. 'Put it under your pillow. You will give it back to me tomorrow morning.

'When you wake up the thief's stick will be longer than the others by four centimetres.' The next day, when they showed her the sticks, that of the guilty man was four centimetres shorter.

301/1

301/1
ORD. LEVEL
LATIN I
*Tuesday*
27 JUNE 1961
2 *hours*
Afternoon

UNIVERSITY OF CAMBRIDGE
LOCAL EXAMINATIONS SYNDICATE
GENERAL CERTIFICATE OF EDUCATION

## LATIN

ORDINARY LEVEL

PAPER O. I

(*Two hours*)

**Candidates must satisfy the Examiners in this paper as a whole.**

1. Translate into ENGLISH:

*Cato, in despair because the troops are not keen to defend Utica, commits suicide*

complures interim ex fuga Uticam perveniunt. quos omnes convocatos Cato hortatus est ut servos liberarent oppidumque defenderent. quorum cum partem assentire[1], partem animum mentemque perterritam habere intellexisset, plus de ea re agere destitit. naves eis attribuit, ut in quas partes vellent proficiscerentur. ipse omnibus rebus diligentissime constitutis, liberis suis L. Caesari, qui tum ei legatus erat, commendatis, sine suspicione, vultu atque sermone quo superiore tempore usus erat, in cubiculum ivit. eo gladium clam tulit atque ita se traiecit. eum medicus amicique ruentes in cubiculum ex suspicione vulnus obligare[2] coepissent, ipse suis manibus crudelissime id divellit atque celeriter se necavit. eum Uticenses propter eius singularem integritatem maxima cum laude sepeliverunt.

[1] assentire = to agree. [2] *obligare* = to bandage.

[TURN OVER

2

2. Translate into Latin:

(*a*) Let us all go to Athens this summer.

(*b*) I asked him whether he was happy.

(*c*) If Caesar had come, the soldiers would now be fighting bravely.

(*d*) You are allowed to see your friends, aren't you?

(*e*) We persuaded him to give us the money.

3. Translate into Latin Prose:

On his defeat, Hannibal fled to Asia before he could be captured by the Romans. Within a few days he arrived at the palace of the king, who promised not to betray him. If the king had kept his word[1], Hannibal would have been safe. But a few months later a number of Roman soldiers arrived, asking his whereabouts. On being informed by the king, they went to Hannibal's house so quickly that he could not escape. Being ashamed to surrender, he killed himself.

[1] *fidem praestare* = to keep one's word.

301/2

301/2
ORD. LEVEL
LATIN II
*Friday*
30 JUNE 1961
2 *hours*
Afternoon

UNIVERSITY OF CAMBRIDGE
LOCAL EXAMINATIONS SYNDICATE
GENERAL CERTIFICATE OF EDUCATION

**LATIN**

ORDINARY LEVEL

PAPER O. II

(*Two hours*)

*All candidates must take* **either** (*a*) *this paper as a whole, viz. one prose book, and one verse book*; **or** (*b*) LATIN III (*Unprepared Translation*) *as a whole*; **or** (*c*) *one prose book from this paper and the verse unseen from* LATIN III; **or** (*d*) *one verse book from this paper and the prose unseen from* LATIN III.

**N.B. Candidates offering part of this paper with part of Latin III must write** LATIN II, ***part only*, at the head of the first page of their answers to this paper.**

**Answers to questions from Latin II MUST be given up separately from those to questions from Latin III.**

CAESAR, *Gallic War* I, 1–12, 38–54

1. Translate any **three** of the following passages:

(*a*) is sibi legationem ad civitates suscepit. in eo itinere persuadet Castico, cuius pater regnum in Sequanis multos annos obtinuerat et a senatu populi Romani amicus appellatus erat, ut regnum in civitate sua occuparet, quod pater ante habuerat; itemque Dumnorigi Aeduo, fratri Divitiaci, qui eo tempore principatum in civitate obtinebat ac maxime plebi acceptus erat, ut idem conaretur persuadet, eique filiam suam in matrimonium dat. perfacile factu esse illis probat conata perficere.

2

(*b*) eo opere perfecto, praesidia disponit, castella communit, quo facilius, si se invito transire conarentur, prohibere possit. negat se more et exemplo populi Romani posse iter ulli per provinciam dare et, si vim facere conentur, prohibiturum ostendit. Helvetii, ea spe deiecti, navibus iunctis ratibusque compluribus factis, alii vadis Rhodani, qua minima altitudo fluminis erat, non numquam interdiu, saepius noctu, si perrumpere possent conati, operis munitione et militum concursu et telis repulsi, hoc conatu destiterunt.

(*c*) tantus subito timor omnem exercitum occupavit, ut non mediocriter omnium mentes animosque perturbaret. hic primum ortus est a tribunis militum, praefectis reliquisque, qui ex urbe amicitiae causa Caesarem secuti non magnum in re militari usum habebant: quorum alius alia causa illata, quam sibi ad proficiscendum necessariam esse diceret, petebat, ut eius voluntate discedere liceret: non nulli pudore adducti remanebant. hi neque vultum fingere neque interdum lacrimas tenere poterant.

(*d*) biduo post Ariovistus ad Caesarem legatos mittit: velle se de eis rebus, quae inter eos agi coeptae neque perfectae essent, agere cum eo: uti aut iterum colloquio diem constitueret aut, si id minus vellet, e suis legatis aliquem ad se mitteret. colloquendi Caesari causa visa non est, et eo magis quod pridie eius diei Germani retineri non poterant quin in nostros tela conicerent. legatum e suis sese magno cum periculo ad eum missurum et hominibus feris obiecturum existimabat.

2. Choose **two** of the following passages and, without writing out a translation, answer *briefly* the questions set on them:

(*a*) Caesar, quod memoria tenebat L. Cassium consulem occisum exercitumque eius ab Helvetiis pulsum et sub iugum missum, concedendum non putabat.

(i) To what previous occasion does this passage refer?

(ii) *sub iugum missum.* Explain.

(iii) *concedendum non putabat.* What request had been made?

(iv) To what modern country did the territory of the Helvetii roughly correspond?

3

(*b*) quod cum fieret, non irridicule quidam ex militibus decimae legionis dixit, plus, quam pollicitus esset, Caesarem ei facere.

(i) What unfamiliar employment had Caesar just ordered for the Tenth?

(ii) *pollicitus esset.* What special honour had Caesar paid the Tenth in a recent speech?

(iii) Give the name and nationality of the leader whom Caesar was to meet.

(iv) How did the parley end?

(*c*) C. Valerius Procillus, cum a custodibus in fuga trinis catenis vinctus traheretur, in ipsum Caesarem hostes equitatu persequentem incidit.

(i) *Procillus.* What are we told about him earlier?

(ii) *vinctus.* How had he become a prisoner?

(iii) How did Procillus say he had escaped death during the flight?

(iv) Name his companion and say what happened to him.

*Eighteen Roman Letters* (ed. Horn)

3. Translate any **three** of the following passages:

(*a*) rem dicam ex qua mores aestimes nostros; vix quemquam invenies qui possit aperto ostio vivere. ianitores conscientia nostra, non superbia, opposuit; sic vivimus ut deprehendi sit subito aspici. quid autem prodest recondere se et oculos hominum auresque vitare? bona conscientia turbam advocat, mala etiam in solitudine anxia atque sollicita est. si honesta sunt quae facis, omnes sciant, si turpia, quid refert

We also studied and answered questions on Camilla, not the Roman Letters.

221/4

221/4
ORD. LEVEL
ACTS

*Thursday*
**13 JULY 1961**
$1\frac{1}{2}$ *hours*
Afternoon

UNIVERSITY OF CAMBRIDGE
LOCAL EXAMINATIONS SYNDICATE
GENERAL CERTIFICATE OF EDUCATION

## THE ACTS OF THE APOSTLES

ORDINARY LEVEL

*(One hour and a half)*

*Answer Question* 1 *and any* **three** *other questions.*

*Candidates are advised to spend not more than* 30 *minutes on Question* 1.

*For Knox Version of Q.* 1 *see p.* 2.

*Questions* 2–8 *for all candidates are on p.* 3.

1. Choose **four** of the passages (*a*) to (*f*) and answer the questions which follow:

**REVISED VERSION**

(*a*) Ye shall be my witnesses both in Jerusalem, and in all Judaea and Samaria, and unto the uttermost part of the earth. (1. 8.)

Who said this, to whom and when? Who was the first 'witness' to Samaria, and how did it come about that he went there?

(*b*) But an angel of the Lord by night opened the prison doors, and brought them out. (5. 19.)

Who are referred to here? By whom were they imprisoned and why? What did the angel tell them to do?

(*c*) And when they had appointed for them elders in every church, and had prayed with fasting, they commended them to the Lord. (14. 23.)

Who appointed these elders and when? What other references are there in this book to Christian elders?

610/5

610/5
ORD. LEVEL
ART:
PAPER O. V.
CRAFTS 'A'
*Monday*
**10 JULY 1961**
3 *hours*
Morning

UNIVERSITY OF CAMBRIDGE
LOCAL EXAMINATIONS SYNDICATE
GENERAL CERTIFICATE OF EDUCATION

STILL LIFE: BASKET, FRUIT.
PLANT LIFE: DANDELION + ROOT

ART: PAPER O. V.

**CRAFTS 'A'**

ORDINARY LEVEL

(*Three hours*)

*Instruments and tracing paper are allowed, but you are advised to restrict your use of them as far as possible.*

*Answer* **one** *question, stating its number.*

*Write your name, centre number, and index-number in the top right-hand corner.*

1. Make, in pen-lettering, a decorative title-page for the following work:

*An Anthology of Modern Verse*, selected and edited by John Penn, published by the Belfry Press, 1961.

You must also incorporate in your design the following quotation:

He sat in the meadow and plucked with glad heart the spoil of the flowers, gathering them one by one.

EURIPIDES: A Fragment, quoted on the title-page of Palgrave's *Golden Treasury*.

The page size of the book is 13 in. × 9 in. but the size, arrangement and decoration of this lettering is left to your own judgment.

Work in black ink and one other colour, and use a good foundational or Italic script.

[TURN OVER

2215554R00190

Printed in Great Britain
by Amazon.co.uk, Ltd.,
Marston Gate.